W9-BYV-851

66 ·

You ask how I have lasted—particularly given all my flaws, my limitations both artistically and as a person, my phobia, my idiosyncrasies, and my artistic pretensions and absolute creative demands in a venal cutthroat industry—operating with only a minor gift?

Here's the answer: As a kid I loved magic and might have become a magician if I hadn't been sidetracked. And so, using all my sleight-of-hand skill, my misdirection, my subtle subterfuges and showmanship—that is, everything I've learned from poring over my magic books as a kid— I've been able to pull off a brilliant illusion that has lasted now over fifty years and includes scores of movies. Houdini, Blackstone, Thurston, all the prestidigitators of my youth would have been proud.

I wish I was kidding.

—Woody Allen, 2000

· 99

THE ULTIMATE

Woody

Allen

FILM

COMPANION

Jason Bailey

Voyageur
Press

For Lucille,
Who Tops My "Manhattan" List

First published in 2014 by Voyageur Press, an imprint of Quarto Publishing Group USA Inc., 400 First Avenue North, Suite 400, Minneapolis, MN 55401 USA

© 2014 Quarto Publishing Group USA Inc.

Text © Jason Bailey

All rights reserved. With the exception of quoting brief passages for the purposes of review, no part of this publication may be reproduced without prior written permission from the Publisher. The information in this book is true and complete to the best of our knowledge. All recommendations are made without any guarantee on the part of the author or Publisher, who also disclaims any liability incurred in connection with the use of this data or specific details. This publication has not been prepared, approved, or licensed by Woody Allen or any studio or production company. We recognize, further, that some words, model names, and designations mentioned herein are the property of the trademark holder. We use them for identification purposes only. This is not an official publication.

Voyageur Press titles are also available at discounts in bulk quantity for industrial or sales-promotional use. For details write to Special Sales Manager at Quarto Publishing Group USA Inc., 400 First Avenue North, Suite 400, Minneapolis, MN 55401 USA.

To find out more about our books, visit us online at www.voyageurpress.com.

ISBN-13: 978-0-7603-4623-5

Library of Congress Cataloging-in-Publication Data

Bailey, Jason, 1975-
   The ultimate Woody Allen film companion / Jason Bailey.
      pages cm
   Includes bibliographical references.
   ISBN 978-0-7603-4623-5 (hardback)
   1. Allen, Woody--Criticism and interpretation. 2. Allen, Woody--Film catalogs. I. Title.
   PN1998.3.A45B33 2014
   791.43'092--dc23
                              2014011492

Editor: Josh Leventhal
Design Managers: James Kegley, Brad Springer
Cover designed by Brad Norr Design
Designer: Brad Norr Design

Background patterns on pages 24, 47, 53, 72, 76, 80, 98, 108, 110, 117, 142, 144, 156, 174, 176, and 178: Shutterstock.com

Printed in China

Contents

Prologue 6
The "Reasonably Happy" Early Life and Career
    of Allan Stewart Konigsberg 8

What's Up, Tiger Lily? (1966) 12
Take the Money and Run (1969) 14
Bananas (1971) 16
*Everything You Always Wanted to Know
    About Sex* (*But Were Afraid to Ask)*
    (1972) 20
Play It Again, Sam (1972) 22
Sleeper (1973) 26
Love and Death (1975) 28
Annie Hall (1977) 30
GUEST ESSAY: *"Jew Eat?": Jews and Judaism
    in Allen's Films*, by Ezra Glinter 35
Interiors (1978) 38
Manhattan (1979) 42
Stardust Memories (1980) 50
A Midsummer Night's Sex Comedy (1982) . . 54
Zelig (1983) 56
Broadway Danny Rose (1984) 60
The Purple Rose of Cairo (1985) 62
Hannah and Her Sisters (1986) 66
Radio Days (1987) 70
September (1987) 74
Another Woman (1988) 78
New York Stories: Oedipus Wrecks (1989) . . 82
Crimes and Misdemeanors (1989) 83
GUEST ESSAY: *Woody the Philosopher:
    The Bad Luck Philosophy of Woody Allen*,
    by David Detmer 86
Alice (1990) 90
Shadows and Fog (1991) 92

Husbands and Wives (1992) 94
Manhattan Murder Mystery (1993) 100
Bullets Over Broadway (1994) 102
Don't Drink the Water (1994) 106
Mighty Aphrodite (1995) 112
Everyone Says I Love You (1996) 114
Deconstructing Harry (1997) 118
Celebrity (1998) 126
Sweet and Lowdown (1999) 128
GUEST ESSAY: *Wild Man Blues: Woody's Great
    American Songbook*, by Jason Gubbels . . . 130
Small Time Crooks (2000) 134
The Curse of the Jade Scorpion (2001) 136
Hollywood Ending (2002) 138
Anything Else (2003) 140
Melinda and Melinda (2004) 146
Match Point (2005) 148
Scoop (2006) 152
Cassandra's Dream (2007) 154
Vicky Cristina Barcelona (2008) 158
GUEST ESSAY: *Woody the Tourist: Allen's
    European Phase*, by Ashley Clark 160
Whatever Works (2009) 164
You Will Meet a Tall Dark Stranger
    (2010) 166
Midnight in Paris (2011) 168
To Rome with Love (2012) 172
Blue Jasmine (2013) 180

Closing: The Escape Artist 182
Bibliography 186
Index 188
Acknowledgments 192
About the Author 192

Prologue

Woody Allen's mother took him to buy the Olympia typewriter when he was sixteen years old. It cost $40, a hefty sum for a comedy writer just starting out in the business, but it was a smart buy. "It's heavy and solid," he recalled decades later, "not like these plastic typewriters they have today. I remember when my mother took me to buy it, the salesman told me, 'This typewriter will last longer than you will.' It looks like he might have been right."

Every year, Woody sits down at that Olympia typewriter and writes whatever movie he's in the mood to do next. Sometimes it's a comedy and sometimes it's a drama; he's written musicals and mysteries and farces and chamber pieces. When he's done writing the script, he goes off and makes the film. He is involved in every step of the process: casting (often using the hottest and most talented actors, who will gladly take considerable pay cuts for the street cred of making an Allen film), scouting, shooting, and editing. Once he has approved the final cut, he goes to work on his next script, usually without a single day off. That script will occupy him for the next year. He does not write to please critics, whom he does not read, or win awards, which he does not accept. He does not bend to the will of the box office, where his record is spotty at best, nor of studio executives, from whom he has complete independence. He just goes off and makes a film, and then he makes another. He's been doing it this way for nearly half a century.

"Who the hell is good for *twenty* years?" asks Chris Rock, not unreasonably. "This guy is good for *forty* years. He's kind of peerless." And he is. *New York Times* critic Vincent Canby, one of Allen's first champions, called him "America's most authentic, most serious, most consistent film auteur," and that's as good a description as any. Allen, of course, would disagree. He holds himself to the highest standards, to that of his heroes Bergman and Bunuel and Kurosawa and Welles, and by that barometer, he says, "I haven't even come close. I think I've made some decent movies and a large number of okay movies, but I've never made a great movie."

This book begs to differ. Woody Allen has made many great movies, perhaps more than any filmmaker of his time. Granted, some have also been merely decent or just okay (and a couple less than that), but all are worth considering within his body of work, which is unparalleled in modern American film. The director will allow at least that: "I would think even the ones that were not popular when they came out will have supportive interest to the more

Woody Allen on location at Coney Island during shooting for one of his best-loved films, *Annie Hall. Brian Hamill/ Getty Images*

popular ones, because I think at the minimum, there are things in all of these pictures that are worth seeing."

This volume will consider all of his movies—well, as close to all of them as possible, since in the window between the completion of its writing and its arrival on shelves, a new Allen film will appear. In between the film-by-film exploration of his body of work, we'll examine Woody's working methods, look at the evolution of his distinctive style, dig deep into issues of persona and autobiography, and explore the common threads in his filmography—what Allen calls "certain issues and questions that repeat themselves in the movies over and over again." Charles Champlin wrote of Allen by recalling Jean Renoir, who once said he had made "not twenty-eight films but one film in twenty-eight versions or chapters." The comparison is apt. Allen's filmography lends itself to this kind of bulk consideration because he has spent so much of his life and art returning to the subjects that interest him, but from surprising new angles and in vastly contrasting tones, building out from previous observation.

What this volume will not do is tackle, at any great length, the scandals and accusations that have circled Mr. Allen for the past two decades and sprang back into the headlines shortly before going to press on this book. This is in no way meant to dismiss the importance of these allegations, but simply to acknowledge that our focus here is on the work and not the life—at least as much as the two can be separated.

Anyone who undertakes the task of getting to the bottom of Woody Allen's filmography risks coming off like the blowhard in line behind Alvy and Annie in *Annie Hall*, pontificating loudly while knowing nothing of his work, or the pompously overreaching restaurant critic in Allen's satirical piece "Fabrizio's: Criticism and Response." ("Who can forget his scampi: four garlic-drenched shrimp arranged in a way that says more about our involvement in Vietnam than countless books on the subject?") But that's a risk worth taking. In forty-five years and as many films, Woody Allen created a comic persona, discovered how to construct films around it, and transformed himself from a comedian into a distinctive cinematic voice. No one is more surprised than the man himself. "It's an amazing thing when I think back on the awful days in that little school, and coming home and sitting at the oilcloth-covered table, that one day I would actually be in a movie with Charles Boyer or direct Van Johnson. It's so unimaginable to me, and I guess you can say in a certain way that I get the full value of appreciation of all that's happened. Such an astonishing fact has retained its power to amaze me. Sometimes when I look in the mirror I'll see myself back there and I'll say, 'You're Allan Konigsberg from Brooklyn. Shouldn't you be eating in the basement?'"

For a discussion of *Magic in the Moonlight* and other future Woody Allen projects, visit **www.jason-bailey.com/p/woody-allen-book.html** for updates and new essays.

The "Reasonably Happy" Early Life and Career of Allan Stewart Konigsberg

I t squares nicely with the contradictions and paradoxes of the comedian who wanted to make dramas, the genius who claims he's never achieved greatness, and the confessor who says his work isn't autobiographical to note that famed Brooklynite Woody Allen was actually born Allan Stewart Konigsberg, in the Bronx. Both parents were the children of immigrants. Mother Nettie Cherry and father Martin Konigsberg wed in 1931 and spent the rest of their marriage battling (they "did everything except exchange gunfire," Allen joked).

The family lived in Brooklyn throughout his childhood, staying with and taking in a nonstop parade of relations. "My mother always used to say I was a very sweet, happy kid, right from the start," he recalled, "and then somewhere around five or so I turned grumpier or sour. I can only think, when I became aware of my mortality, I didn't like that idea. 'Whaddaya mean, this ends, this doesn't go on like this?' No, it ends, you vanish, forever. Once I realized that, I thought 'Hey, deal me out. I don't wanna play in this game.' And I never was the same after that."

When Allan started school at P.S. 99, he took an immediate dislike to it, playing hooky and pursuing other interests instead. Contrary to his clumsy onscreen persona, he was an expert athlete, playing football, stickball, basketball, and baseball. He acquired a magician's kit for his tenth birthday, and he subsequently used his skill with cards and sleight of hand for ends both honorable (his first performance, at age sixteen, was as a magic act) and sketchy ("I hustled millions of kids out of money when I was in high school"). As a teen, he developed a love for traditional, New Orleans–style jazz, listening to records obsessively, trying his hand at the soprano saxophone before switching to the clarinet.

But more than anything else, the young Allan loved movies. His mother took him to see *Snow White and the Seven Dwarfs* when he was three years old, and he was so enraptured by the experience, he ran up to the screen to touch the animated figures. Woody subsequently spent as much time as he could at the two dozen movie houses within walking distance of home. He soon discovered the comedies of Bob Hope, W. C. Fields, and the Marx Brothers; the latter became his gateway to the humorous writings of

Allan Stewart Konigsberg spent much of his youth at movie theaters like the RKO Prospect in Brooklyn, pictured here in 1940. *Underwood Archives/Getty Images*

George S. Kaufman, S. J. Perelman, and Robert Benchley. His love of comedy and understanding of the mechanics of humor prompted his decision to try his hand at writing jokes.

At the urging of a cousin in the public relations business, sixteen-year-old Allan Konigsberg started sending gags to the columnists at the eight major New York newspapers. The first to bite was Nick Kenny at the *Mirror*; Earl Wilson, at the more prestigious *Post*, soon followed suit. As his lines began to show up in print, he decided it was time to think up a stage name—the shy Master Konigsberg thought it would be embarrassing for his classmates to see his name in the papers. But there was more to it than that: He was getting into show business, and a stage name was part of the process. His rechristening as Woody Allen was the beginning of a carefully cultivated reinvention that would continue throughout his life.

Not long after the pseudonym debuted late in 1952, Woody got his first steady work as a comedy writer. Every day when he got out of school (on the days he went, anyway), Woody took the subway from the modesty of Brooklyn to the zazzy splendor of midtown Manhattan, where he wrote jokes for three hours, pithy one-liners for his press-agent bosses to feed to columnists, who in turn attributed them to their celebrity clients. The job paid $20 a week. "I was doing about fifty jokes a day for a long time," he said. "It was not hard." Some days, he'd already thought up half his gags on the train before he even stepped into the office.

Woody knew right away that this, unlike school or traditional work, was something he was good at. But his mother wanted him to go to college, so he enrolled in the motion picture production program at New York University. As a college student, Woody was a disaster. He was dismissed from NYU after two semesters ("You are not good college material," he was told by one of his deans), and a night course at City College of New York went even worse. But his career was blooming. By the spring of 1954, he was writing for radio, which led to a gig working for TV and radio emcee Herb Shiner. That job got him a spot on NBC's new development program for young writers, and as part of that program, Woody went to Hollywood to write for *The NBC Comedy Hour*.

Throughout his film career, Woody has seldom missed an opportunity to disparage California or television. "I was always very careful not to get seduced into TV writing," he told *Time*. "I was making a lot of money and knew it was a dead end; you get seduced into a lifestyle, move to California, and in six months you become a producer." But he's also quick to note the value of that first trip, primarily for the education he got from head writer Danny Simon (brother of Neil). "Everything I learned about comedy writing, I learned from Danny Simon," he's said. At Simon's urging, Woody took his next major step

By the early 1960s, Woody abandoned television writing to pursue a career as a performer at night clubs and in front of the TV cameras. *Bill Ray/Time & Life Pictures/Getty Images*

Woody with costars Peter O'Toole and Romy Schneider in *What's New Pussycat?*. Woody loathed the film: "They were taking my script and mangling it." *API/Gamma-Rapho via Getty Images*

after the show was canceled: In 1956, Woody did the first of his three summers at Tamiment, an upscale resort in the Pocono Mountains of Pennsylvania.

For $150 per week, Allen and his fellow writers were charged with creating an original live revue show every week for the resort's guests. The comedy sketches were eight to ten minutes long, spoofs and burlesques in the style of TV stars Sid Caesar and Imogene Coca (who were alumni of Tamiment). "You couldn't sit in a room waiting for your muse to come and tickle you," Allen said of the intense schedule. "Monday morning came, there was a dress rehearsal Thursday, you had to get that thing written. It was grueling, but you learn to write." By his second summer, Woody was directing as well.

In 1958, Allen moved from Caesar's old home to his new one. Writing for Caesar, he later said, "was the highest thing you could aspire to—at least as a TV comedy writer." Other members of the staff included Larry Gelbart (later to bring *M*A*S*H* to television) and Mel Brooks. Woody's first credit with Caesar, a special dubbed *The Chevy Show*, aired in November 1958. His contributions included a scathing parody of *American Bandstand* called *Teen Time*, with Art Carney as a Dick Clark–style deejay ("I'm especially fond of this record because I get an awful lot of money plugging it!"). Twenty-three-year-old Allen already had the contempt for rock music of a man many years his senior.

Within a couple of years, however, Woody was frustrated. Though busy as a staff writer for *The Garry Moore Show*, an occasional contributor to *The Tonight Show*, and a hired gun for various nightclub comics, he wanted new challenges. He approached Jack Rollins and Charles H. Joffe, whom he called "the Rolls-Royce of management," and asked if they'd take him on. They told him they didn't represent writers, but Woody kept at them. When he read the pair a handful of his jokes, something clicked. Rollins suddenly envisioned Woody as "the first triple-threat man since Orson Welles." They didn't want to represent him as a writer; they thought he had the goods to be a performer. Though he initially rejected the notion, Allen was also tired of being, in his words, a "paid hack." Rollins and Joffe were willing to take a chance on him. So he decided to take a chance on himself, and they made a handshake deal that stood for decades.

And that's how, in 1960, Woody came to quit his job on *The Garry Moore Show* and go from a $1,700 per week salary to anywhere from nothing to $100 a night, six nights a week, three shows a night as a nightclub comic in Greenwich Village. He would perform at small clubs like the Duplex, for indifferent audiences of ten to twelve. Most nights he bombed. Some nights Rollins and Joffe (and at least one of them was there for every gig) had to literally push him out on stage.

Somehow, by the end of his second year as club performer, Woody had arrived. He was reviewed in the *New York Times*. He was booked into clubs in Chicago, San Francisco, Los Angeles, and Las Vegas. He appeared on *Ed Sullivan*, *Hootenanny*, *The Jack Paar Show*, even *Candid Camera*. ("Now I'm trying to do Dostoyevsky," he later joked, "trying to live down this shit.") Rollins's plan to was to saturate the country and make Allen a household name.

In 1964, Allen was performing at the Blue Angel, for an audience that included producer Charles Feldman. As Woody later said in his act, "Mr. Feldman . . . just adored me on sight. He thought I was attractive, and sensual, and good-looking—just made for motion pictures. He's a little short man, with red hair and glasses." Feldman was developing a hip sex comedy, the story of a modern Don Juan, with Warren Beatty tapped for the lead. The following Monday, Feldman's office offered Allen $35,000 to write what became *What's New Pussycat?*.

The picture, which was released in 1965, was a commercial smash and an artistic nightmare for its young scribe (who also appeared in a supporting role, which became so big with each passing draft that Beatty ultimately left the project). "They were taking my script and mangling it," Woody said, finally reaching a point late in the six-month European shoot where he refused to do any more revisions.

The film's quality didn't matter—what was important was that it made truckloads of money, and that meant more work for Woody. Producer Henry Saperstein hired him to direct a spy spoof, *What's Up, Tiger Lily?*. Feldman gave him a giant paycheck to play a small role in his all-star disaster *Casino Royale*. The first of Allen's short humorous prose pieces—or "casuals," as they were called—was published in *The New Yorker* in 1966. That same year, his first foray into playwriting, *Don't Drink the Water*, opened on Broadway, kicking off a successful eighteen-month run.

But Woody wanted to make films, and after the frustrations of *Pussycat*, he would only do so under the condition of total control. Fortunately, Hollywood money men were in a daring and giving mood. The astonishing success of *Easy Rider* kicked off the "New Hollywood" movement of the 1970s, and in that environment, the director was king. Charles H. Joffe explained the sweetheart of a deal they made with Palomar Pictures for their client's first full-fledged feature thus: "Put two million dollars in a paper bag, give it to us, go away, and we'll bring you a picture." And that's basically the deal Woody Allen has maintained for forty-five years.

Poster from Allen's first Broadway play, *Don't Drink the Water. Poster from the Voyageur Press Collection*

What's Up, Tiger Lily?

RELEASE DATE: November 2, 1966

WRITERS: Woody Allen, Julie Bennett, Frank Buxton, Louise Lasser, Len Maxwell, Mickey Rose, Bryan Wilson

CAST: Allen, The Lovin' Spoonful, Tatsuya Mihashi, Akiko Wakabayashi, Mie Hama, Tadao Nakamaru

IN A NUTSHELL: Phil Moskowitz, superspy and "lovable rogue," finds himself at the center of an international plot to steal the world's greatest egg salad recipe.

RECURRING THEMES: Prostitution ("Remember, no hickeys," one is warned); Jewish mothers (when one of the prostitutes is revealed to be a character's mother, she tells him "You never write!")

Kokusai himitsu keisatsu: Kagi no kagi (*International Secret Police: Key of Keys*) was a 1965 Japanese spy thriller from director Senkichi Taniguchi, one of many international pictures cashing in on the ubiquitous Bond phenomenon. The Eastern film returned to its Western roots when cheapie outfit American International Pictures (AIP) picked it up for American distribution, only to realize (too late) that its convoluted plot and turgid style would likely leave their drive-in audiences scratching their heads. So AIP head honcho Henry G. Saperstein hatched the notion of redubbing the dialogue entirely, turning the spy thriller into a spy spoof, and hiring Woody Allen—fresh off the success of *What's New Pussycat?*, the title of which was none too subtly recalled by the moniker of this effort.

Allen and a crew of actor and comedian friends wrote (but mostly ad-libbed) the new dialogue track and provided the voices themselves, while Woody directed and appeared in wraparound sections, explaining the premise and providing a bit of additional comedy. For his effort, he received his first directorial credit—though he would later distance himself from the film when Saperstein and AIP took his original 60-minute cut (intended for television use only) and padded it out with additional scenes and incongruent inserts featuring The Lovin' Spoonful. (A rock band in a Woody Allen movie! Perish the thought.)

The picture is awfully juvenile—probably a foregone conclusion, considering the premise—

> " I think that, if you know me at all, you know that death is my bread and danger my butter—oh, no, danger's my bread, and death is my butter. No, no, wait. Danger's my bread, death—no, death is—no, I'm sorry. Death is my—death and danger are my various breads and butters.
>
> —Woody Allen (as himself) "

Posters for *What's Up, Tiger Lily?*, Allen's first foray as writer-director-actor, presented Woody as the hapless lover that would come to define his onscreen persona. *Poster from the Voyageur Press Collection*

but that doesn't mean it's not funny. Woody makes an excellent host, slyly sending up cinematic conventions and assuring us he harbors no illusions about the picture's arrant inanity. And while the goofy-spoofy nature of the thing doesn't lend itself to high wit, the Allen touch is present in lines like, "They kill, they maim, and they call information for numbers they could easily get from the book" and "I was going to marry her! I already put a deposit on twin cemetery plots!"

What's Up, Tiger Lily? is something of a curiosity in the Allen filmography. Its one-joke premise sputters out before the film does, with the final product bearing little resemblance to the rest of his work (though clearly an early influence on the bad film "riffing" of *Mystery Science Theater 3000* and its spinoffs). It seems, instead, to be one of the few cinematic reminders of his television roots: Allen and his funny friends doing a big, broad spoof, much like he did in the writers' room at the Caesar show or, even earlier, at Tamiment. None of these enterprises involved the most sophisticated satire; they certainly weren't noted for the subtlety and nuance that would come to define the Allen oeuvre.

Here, Woody's still finding his comic voice—or, at least, trying to find one that translates to film. But the entire exercise hints at the experimental instincts that will serve him well in the years to come; he's up for just about anything, willing to go to great lengths (especially early on) for a laugh.

Woody on Woody

"I never thought that the film was anything but insipid. It was a sophomoric exercise."

Take the Money and Run

RELEASE DATE: August 18, 1969

WRITERS: Woody Allen, Mickey Rose

CAST: Allen, Janet Margolin, Ethel Sokolow, Henry Leff, Jacquelyn Hyde, Louise Lasser, Jackson Beck

IN A NUTSHELL: A pseudo-documentary account of the life and crimes of Virgil Starkwell, an incompetent purse-snatcher, thief, bank robber, and prison escapist.

RECURRING THEMES: Groucho idolatry (the "disguises" worn by Virgil's parents); psychoanalysis (the pointed testimony of Dr. Epstein, interviewed with another client on the couch, explaining that Virgil's dream "was genuine and clean, not like *some* patients I know"); crime; parental disappointment

In the opening moments of *Take the Money and Run*, the tough-voiced, *Dragnet*-style narrator gives protagonist Virgil Starkwell's date of birth as December 1, 1935—the same as Woody Allen's. It's an appropriate date, since the film marked a rebirth of sorts: his first full-fledged effort as a writer/director. "That's really where I feel my career in films began," he told Stig Björkman. "Before that it was all reasons not to go into the cinema."

Allen wrote the script with longtime pal Mickey Rose, with the idea of parodying the *cinéma vérité* documentary style that had become prevalent in the 1960s thanks to the availability of handheld cameras and portable audio-recording equipment. But he wasn't looking to make an aesthetic, social, or satirical statement. His modest goal for *Take the Money and Run* was simply to transfer the persona he'd cultivated on stage to celluloid. "I always thought of myself as a comedian," he later explained. "Not to be pretentious about this, but the way you take the Chaplin character or the Keaton character or the Bob Hope character, I thought of my character on screen." (Or maybe Jerry Lewis, whom Woody asked to direct the film before he was certain about helming it himself.)

So *Take the Money* (and *Bananas* and *Sleeper*—all of his pre–*Annie Hall* output, frankly) is best viewed as a "Woody Allen picture," a vehicle for a defined comedic character, exacerbated by its placement in unexpected or incongruent situations. At this early point in his career, Woody is experimenting with different comic styles and approaches, from pure visual silliness (the cello in the marching band, his ticklishness during the prison pat-down) to Buster Keaton–inspired mechanical ingenuity (manipulating the water in his cheapo

> " • • • • • • • • • • • • • •
>
> After fifteen minutes I wanted to marry her, and after half an hour I completely gave up the idea of stealing her purse.
>
> —Virgil Starkwell
>
> • • • • • • • • • • • • • "

apartment's bathroom) to slapstick (the bit with the laundry-folding machine) to running gags (the stomping of his glasses) to wordplay (the justifiably beloved "holdup note" scene). And his absurd voice-over during the romantic interludes with Louise (Janet Margolin) could be lifted directly from his standup act.

That subversion notwithstanding, the romantic scenes are hampered by the dated, lyrical photography and the unfortunate lack of chemistry between the leads—the picture's only real flaw, aside from the rough, almost homemade quality of the filmmaking. But that wasn't accidental; as Allen told Dick Cavett in 1971, "I like my movies to look sloppy." That would change as his aesthetic evolved, but his aim in 1969 was to get laughs. When asked why he thought he could direct the film, his answer was succinct: "I think I can make it funny." And that he did.

"I haven't seen *Take the Money and Run* in a long time, so I don't know, but I can't imagine it would be among my favorites."

The illegible-holdup-note gag in *Take the Money and Run* is classic early Woody.
Cinerama Releasing Corporation/Getty Images

Bananas

RELEASE DATE: April 28, 1971

WRITERS: Woody Allen, Mickey Rose

CAST: Allen, Louise Lasser, Carlos Montalban, Natividad Abascal, Howard Cosell

IN A NUTSHELL: Fielding Mellish, a mild-mannered product tester, responds to a breakup with his campus-activist girlfriend by traveling to the banana republic of San Marcos, where he participates in the revolution and becomes the nation's leader.

RECURRING THEMES: Psychoanalysis (Fielding describes a vivid dream while on the psychiatrist's couch); parental disappointment (his parents are again in disguise—this time, rather than Groucho glasses, they wear surgical masks); celebrity (Nancy will only sleep with Fielding after he's a celebrated dictator); anti-authoritarianism; fear of machines

"*Wide World of Sports* is in the Republic of San Marcos, where we are going to bring you a live, on-the-spot assassination!" Thus begins *Bananas*, Allen's second major feature and second writing collaboration with Mickey Rose. The duo was originally engaged years earlier to adapt Robert Powell's satire *Don Quixote U.S.A.* into a Robert Morse picture, but the *How to Succeed in Business* star passed, and so it morphed into a Woody vehicle when they returned to the script after *Take the Money and Run*. It would become his first film for United Artists, the start of a fruitful partnership that continued when the company's top execs left to form Orion Pictures. The two companies would, between them, release all but one of Allen's films for twenty years.

The picture is Woody's most direct tribute to the Marx Brothers, a broad political satire in the vein of the 1933 classic *Duck Soup*. (The niggling over engaging the proper tailor for counterfeit rebel uniforms recalls Groucho's insistence that Fredonia and Sylvania go to war since he's already paid two months' battlefield rent.) There's also a generous helping of Allen's other comic hero, Bob Hope, whose proud coward character is more than a little present in Fielding Mellish.

Before Fielding arrives in the little dictatorship of San Marcos, we're treated to Woody's first cinematic glimpses of his beloved New York, then in its early '70s hellhole phase. This is the portrait of the urban man: at work (as a product tester, in a scene inspired by Chaplin's *Modern Times*), on the subway, on the street, and behind the many deadbolt locks of his low-rent apartment.

At that door appears Nancy, played by former Mrs. Allen, Louise Lasser. The principal romantic entanglement this time around is a big step up from the drag of *Take the Money and Run*. Lasser's zonked comic timing is a good fit with Woody's; they get a Nichols and May rhythm going that motors the entire first act. Once she dumps him and he heads off to San Marcos, Allen gets considerable comic mileage out of transposing urban tropes into the Latin

> " I object, your honor! This trial is a travesty. It's a travesty of a mockery of a sham of a mockery of a travesty of two mockeries of a sham.
>
> —Fielding Mellish

American revolutionary setting: the aforementioned in-demand tailor, dividing up the check following the presidential dinner, a giant deli order to feed the rebels, and delicatessen-style "take a number" and "now serving" signs at the mass executions.

With big comic set pieces and throwaway background gags (the baby carriage rolling down the steps, an homage to Eisenstein's *Battleship Potemkin*, is a nice touch), there's a black-out-sketch quality to the entire enterprise—the picture literally stops at one point for a TV commercial parody ("New Testament Cigarettes: I smoke 'em. *He* smokes 'em. . ."). *Bananas* is a cherished title among those who prefer Allen's pure comedies. It, like much of the early work, has a charmingly scattershot feel matched by a rapid pace. Most of the bits work, and if one doesn't, well, another one will be along soon enough.

WATCH OUT FOR

A very young Sylvester Stallone as one of the subway thugs.

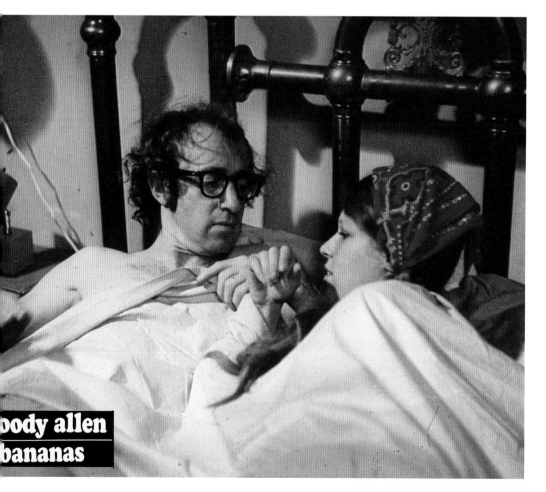

ody allen
bananas

Allen cast his ex-wife Louise Lasser as his girlfriend in *Bananas*. *Lobby card from the Voyageur Press Collection*

Woody on Woody

"I never think of it. It was boring being in Puerto Rico. There wasn't anything to do. The food wasn't good. The weather was hot and humid. The movie house leaked and I found a dead mouse in my room. I don't like to dwell on the past."

• Woody the Film Student •

> "I found myself in an odd position where I was influenced by
> Groucho Marx and Bob Hope and Ingmar Bergman,
> and there was no rationality to it."
>
> **—Woody Allen**

Allen is seldom lumped in with Steven Spielberg, Martin Scorsese, Brian De Palma, and the other "Film Brats" who found success in the New Hollywood of the 1970s—he's sort of an island unto himself. But like those filmmakers, Woody learned about making movies not from working his way up through the studio system (as the previous generation of moviemakers had) but by growing up watching, studying, and breathing in film. His pictures are littered with echoes and homages to the movies he loves. This is but a partial listing of a career spent repurposing themes, ideas, and imagery through the prism of his distinctive style and voice.

FILM	DIRECTOR	ALLEN INFLUENCE
Just Imagine (1930)	David Butler	Biographer John Baxter notes that this sci-fi comedy with a Rip Van Winkle element bears a striking resemblance to *Sleeper* (and, in an odd coincidence, it features Mia Farrow's mother, Maureen O'Sullivan, in the female lead).
Duck Soup (1933)	Leo McCarey	This is one of several Marx Brothers movies that Woody says he will "always laugh at," and the spirit of this anarchic war satire is all over *Bananas*. *Duck Soup* was also a big influence on the character of Mickey in *Hannah and Her Sisters*. Allen (as Mickey, in *Hannah*) on *Duck Soup*: "I always loved it. . . . Look at all the people up there on the screen, they're real funny, and what if the worst is true. What if there is no God and you only go around once and that's it. Well, ya know, don't you wanna be part of the experience?" *Poster from the Voyageur Press Collection*
Double Indemnity (1944)	Billy Wilder	Allen has called Wilder's film noir classic one of the "great American films," and his protagonists go to a revival screening of it at the beginning of *Manhattan Murder Mystery*. The "getting away with murder" plotline is replicated not only in that film, but also in *Crimes and Misdemeanors*, *Match Point*, and *Cassandra's Dream*.
Monsieur Beaucaire (1946) / *Casanova's Big Night* (1954)	George Marshall / Norman Z. McLeod	Woody's two favorite Bob Hope films both parachute Hope's contemporary, urbane persona into a period, costume setting—much as Woody did in the admittedly Hope-inspired *Love and Death* ("I was doing him all over the place").
Born Yesterday (1950)	George Cukor	Allen has called *Born Yesterday* one of the finest American film comedies and "the best all-time American stage comedy." The character of Olive in *Bullets Over Broadway* seems inspired by Judy Holliday's Billie, and her relationship with the gruff Cheech (particularly in the scene where they're running her lines) echoes the dynamic between Billie and Harry Brock in Cukor's classic.

FILM	DIRECTOR	ALLEN INFLUENCE
A Streetcar Named Desire (1951)	Elia Kazan	*Sleeper* features an inspired comic riff on Tennessee Williams's classic play (filmed by Kazan), but *Blue Jasmine*, with its story of a fancy yet delusional broken woman "slumming it" with her earthier sister, was not only a clear riff on *Streetcar*, but Allen even cast Cate Blanchett, who had just played Blanche DuBois on stage, as the film's star.
The Seventh Seal (1957)	Ingmar Bergman	One of Allen's absolute favorite films, he used this film's personification of Death, for comic purposes, in *Love and Death*, *Deconstructing Harry*, and *Scoop*. Of his biggest influence, Ingmar Bergman, Allen said, "in the end he was a great entertainer. *The Seventh Seal*, all of those films, they grip you. It's not like doing homework." *Poster from the Voyageur Press Collection*
Wild Strawberries (1957)	Ingmar Bergman	Bergman's story of a professor reevaluating his life via nightmares, daydreams, and revelations clearly influenced *Another Woman*; its structural device, a car trip to the protagonist's alma mater (in a Volvo, no less, a sly visual joke referring to Bergman's native land) is used in *Deconstructing Harry*.
La Dolce Vita (1960)	Federico Fellini	Fellini's Marcello, a somewhat corrupt Roman journalist, becomes New York celebrity profiler and hanger-on Lee Simon in *Celebrity*, which even replicates *La Dolce Vita*'s elegant black-and-white photography.
L'eclisse (1962)	Michelangelo Antonioni	Allen admires Antonioni greatly, though his influence is less obvious than Fellini's or Bergman's. But the iconic opening montage of *Manhattan* bears a striking similarity to the closing of Antonioni's classic.
8½ (1963)	Federico Fellini	Every film critic in the business pointed out *Stardust Memories'* debt to Fellini's semi-autobiographical, surrealistic, black-and-white take on the woes of a celebrated filmmaker. *8½* is one of Allen's favorites by the Italian auteur. *Poster from the Voyageur Press Collection*
Juliet of the Spirits (1965)	Federico Fellini	A housewife with a cheating husband finds her life transformed by a series of fantasies, memories, and indulgences—similar to the journey taken by the title character in Allen's 1990 film *Alice*.
Persona (1966)	Ingmar Bergman	Allen's *Interiors* (1978) owes a significant debt to *Persona*. Also, its signature shot is parodied at the end of *Love and Death*.
Amarcord (1973)	Federico Fellini	Allen's *Radio Days* was, by his own admission, styled after Fellini's free-form collection of nostalgic comic vignettes concerning childhood and family.
Scenes from a Marriage (1973)	Ingmar Bergman	Allen's *Husbands and Wives* mirrors the scathing and emotionally exhausting tone of Bergman's masterpiece, which begins by using an interview device that Allen adopts throughout his film.
Autumn Sonata (1978)	Ingmar Bergman	The mother/daughter tension of this film seems to have weighed particularly heavily on Allen, and clearly influenced his 1987 film *September*.

Everything
You Always Wanted to
Know About
Sex*
(*But Were Afraid to Ask)

RELEASE DATE: August 6, 1972

WRITER: Woody Allen (from the book by Dr. David Reuben)

CAST: Allen, John Carradine, Louise Lasser, Tony Randall, Lynn Redgrave, Burt Reynolds, Gene Wilder

IN A NUTSHELL: Seven vignettes about sex, each inspired by a question from Dr. Reuben's bestselling 1969 sex manual.

RECURRING THEMES: The rabbi as punch line; sexless relationships; Italian cinema; standup comedy (his hacky court jester: "That plague is really something, isn't it?")

Though the film was a box office success, Woody Allen has long derided his adaptation of *Everything You Always Wanted to Know About Sex* (*But Were Afraid to Ask)*, and it's easy to see why—it's a wildly inconsistent and uneven picture, its weaker segments barely more developed than the dirty jokes they seem inspired by, the entire enterprise low and smutty in a way his films seldom were again.

But it's a vitally important transitional work for the filmmaker, between the anything-goes quality of his early movies and the smoother, more disciplined pictures that followed. Several of the visual cues of the Allen style appear here for the first time, most notably in the opening credits: the cast listed alphabetically in a typewriter font, to the accompaniment of a vintage popular song (in this case, "Let's Misbehave"). The film's approach is a burlesque, both in its low comedy and teasingly hinted sexuality. ("I thought I was going to have a million comic ideas on sex," he said, "but it wasn't as fertile a notion as I'd imagined, and I had about six.") But the vignette structure affords Allen the opportunity, via direct parody, to work in several established styles: Gothic horror, 1960s Italian cinema, television game shows, and science fiction.

The latter is the format of the film's final, and finest, segment, "What Happens During Ejaculation?," which dramatizes the act of intercourse through the male body's NASA-style mission control: a headset-clad operator (Tony Randall) barks orders ("Can we please have an erection? What the hell's going on down there?"), as the laborers taxed with keeping the penis erect sing "The Battle Hymn of the Republic," paratrooper sperm await their departure (Woody, among them, worries: "What if he's masturbating? I'm liable to wind up on the ceiling!"), and the operator recites names of baseball players to delay the orgasm.

> "
> Before you know it,
> the Renaissance
> will be here and we'll
> all be painting.
> —The Fool
> "

UN FILM DE WOODY ALLEN
TOUT CE QUE VOUS AVEZ TOUJOURS VOULU SAVOIR SUR LE SEXE...
SANS JAMAIS OSER LE DEMANDER
(Everything you always wanted to know about sex* but were afraid to ask)

Tony Randall and Burt Reynolds toast a successful launch in the segment, "What Happens During Ejaculation?"
Lobby card from the Voyageur Press Collection

In that segment, Allen goes for big, broad laughs. But the film's other highlight, "What Is Sodomy?," plays out in a far more muted, naturalistic vein. The joke of the segment—that Gene Wilder's well-to-do doctor embarks on a sexual affair with a sheep—is so wild that it only works if done totally straight. And that's what Wilder does, masterfully; the way he softens to "Daisy" when first meeting her, and his quiet playing of the later "seduction," is matched by Allen's refusal, as director, to overplay the gag. The same goes for "Why Do Some Women Have Trouble Reaching an Orgasm?," which gets its laughs not from the wink-wink-nudge-nudge premise but from its spot-on stylistic aping of Italian cinema (Allen's first cinematic acknowledgment that his personal viewing habits extended beyond the works of Hope and Marx).

Everything You Always Wanted to Know misses as often as it hits. Some scenes are funnier in conception than execution (like the "giant boob" sketch, in which, in a strange bit of reappropriation, Woody reprises the name of his *What's New Pussycat?* character, Victor Shakapopulis), while others fizzle well before the fade-out. But the crassness of the humor is mostly offset by Allen's growing sophistication as a filmmaker. The roughness of his initial efforts is gone, replaced by a slick, pliable sense of visual skill.

Woody on Woody

"In retrospect, I don't think it was a very good idea. . . . If I had it to do over, I would not do it again."

Play It Again, Sam

RELEASE DATE: May 4, 1972

DIRECTOR: Herbert Ross

WRITER: Woody Allen (based on his play)

CAST: Allen, Diane Keaton, Tony Roberts, Jerry Lacy, Susan Anspach, Jennifer Salt

IN A NUTSHELL: Newly divorced film critic Allan Felix attempts to return to the dating world, with the help of his best friends and the ghost of Humphrey Bogart.

RECURRING THEMES: Infidelity; psychoanalysis; Bogart idolatry; hypochondria; art vs. life ("It's from *Casablanca*. I waited my whole life to say it!"); magic realism; Italian cinema

The incorporation of *Play It Again, Sam* in this volume is arguable, because unlike all the other films considered at any great length, Woody Allen wrote and stars in *Sam* but did not direct it. "I didn't want to spend a year making it into a movie," he explained (*Sam* was released during the same busy fifteen-month stretch in which *Bananas* and *Sex* hit theaters). So he whipped up a quickie screenplay adaptation and passed it to Herbert Ross, who'd recently had a hit with *The Owl and the Pussycat* and would become a regular director of Neil Simon's comedies.

But *Play It Again, Sam* is worthy of inclusion and consideration, as even the most casual viewer can see it as not only a turning point for the Woody character (he is, for the first time, a romantic leading man), but as an influence on his evolution as a filmmaker. Ross's direction is simple but elegant. In contrast to the herky-jerky rhythms of Allen's filmography to this point, Ross's use of long two-shots and medium-wides foreshadows what would become Allen's signature style. And *Sam* pointed, for the first time, away from the filmed monologue, all-jokes-all-the-time approach. "Even though it's an antiquated comedy," he later said, "in a way it had a freshness to it. It was based more on character. But will it always seem fresh? Probably not, because it lacks genius. I mean it lacks a lot and also genius."

Woody wrote much of the play in Chicago in 1968, during a long standup stint at Mister Kelly's nightclub, inspired both by his then-current split with Louise Lasser and his divorce from first wife Harlene Rosen (the ex-wife character is based, at the very least, on the version of her that he was presenting in his act). Producer David Merrick brought it to Broadway, and it was at the auditions for that production that Woody met a beautiful young actress named

> 66 ....
>
> I wonder if she actually had an orgasm in the two years we were married, or did she fake it that night?
> —Allan Felix
>
> 99

Diane Keaton. "Keaton was in a class by herself," he recalled. They would end up sharing the screen six times (and Keaton costarred in two more Allen films that he only directed). Also making the first appearance of many was Tony Roberts, who had acted in the stage production (but not the film) of *Don't Drink the Water*. Their fictional friendship became a real one; he would turn up in five more Allen films.

But *Play It Again, Sam* isn't just notable for the soon-to-be familiar faces in its cast. Themes and devices that would become routine appear here for the first time: the breaking of the fourth wall (done in both voice-over and by talking to camera), the matter-of-fact magic realism of the Bogart character (Bogie was in the midst of a huge revival, motored by college students enamored of his anti-authoritarian cool), the added ripple of hypochondria to the Woody character. Most importantly, the film is the first of Allen's explorations of the wide and sometimes damaging gulf between the fictional worlds we romanticize—or, in some of his later films, the ones we create—and the real world we must reconcile them with.

Add in some of Woody's finest, most adroitly executed pure slapstick, and you've got one of the best of his early comedies. The fact that it bears another director's signature is incidental. To a modern fan, *Play It Again, Sam* looks, sounds, and feels much more like a "Woody Allen movie" than the pictures that came before it, and its considerable success at the box office (it was his biggest hit yet) ensured that more would follow in the same mold.

Woody on Woody

"Long after I'm dead people will be able to curl up in bed and watch *Sam* on TV and say, 'Oh, that's a cute kind of story from the sixties,' just as we watch *It Happened One Night* or that genre of films now. Not that I think *Sam* is very good—it's not. More likely they will curl up in bed and say, 'What else is on?'"

Allan looks to Humphrey Bogart (played by Jerry Lacy) for guidance during one of his romantic encounters in *Play It Again, Sam. Lobby card from the Voyageur Press Collection*

• Woody the Writer •

P*lay It Again, Sam* was the last time Woody Allen would turn his words over to another filmmaker. Looking over the previous attempts by others to translate his vision to the screen, it's not hard to figure out why.

What's New Pussycat?: a huge hit, and one of Woody's greatest embarrassments. *Poster from the Voyageur Press Collection*

Brian Hamill/Getty Images

What's New, Pussycat?

Woody made his screenwriting debut with this flaccid, dated, and overlong 1965 sex comedy starring Peter Sellers, Peter O'Toole, Romy Schneider, Capucine, "and introducing . . . Woody Allen." Although Woody wrote off the product of his mishandled script as "a moronic enterprise from start to finish," there are a few lines that maintain the oddball surrealism of his stand-up and early prose material (like a call to a hotel's front desk for "twelve loaves of bread and one Boy Scout uniform"). And this embryonic version of the Woody character—emphasizing the horny bumbler element—is remarkably close to the final version, while also allowing Allen several opportunities to show off his skills as a physical comedian.

Casino Royale

Pussycat producer Charles Feldman, costar Peter Sellers, and Allen reunited for this notorious 1967 boondoggle, the result of Feldman's acquisition of the rights to Ian Fleming's first James Bond book well before the rest of the series was brought to the screen by Eon Productions. Rather than compete directly, Feldman orchestrated a broad spoof, employing five directors and even more screenwriters. The results are about as choppy and desperate as you'd expect, and aside from a brief early scene, Allen's unlikely supervillain doesn't even show up until the last eighteen minutes. He gets off a few good lines—mostly of his own creation, the result of an uncredited rewrite of his scenes—but this one is for completists (of Bond and Woody) only. Allen summed up the project best himself during its production: "It's like a bad fashion show, and they could just as well have Bob Hope emcee it as me."

THEY'RE CAUGHT IN A SECURITY LEAK!
A Flood Of Laughs, With Hot And Cold Running Spies, And A Drip From The Embassy!

Joseph E. Levine presents AN AVCO EMBASSY FILM

Jackie **Gleason** · Estelle **Parsons**

"Don't Drink The Water"

IN COLOR

CO-STARRING TED BESSELL · JOAN DELANEY Based on the play by Woody Allen R.S. ALLEN SCREENPLAY BY HARVEY BULLOCK PRODUCED BY CHARLES H. JOFFE · HOWARD MORRIS Produced on the New York Stage by David Merrick Music by Pat Williams Photo by Phil Lathrop A JACK ROLLINS–CHARLES H. JOFFE PRODUCTION AN AVCO EMBASSY RELEASE

Allen had no involvement in the first, 1969 film version of *Don't Drink the Water*—and it shows. *Poster from the Voyageur Press Collection*

WOODY ALLEN
JAMES BOND 007
CASINO ROYALE

URSULA ANDRESS
JAMES BOND 007
CASINO ROYALE

Allen would reunite with *Pussycat*'s producer, and much of its cast and crew, for the big-budget debacle *Casino Royale. Poster from the Voyageur Press Collection*

Don't Drink the Water

Though his longtime managers Charles H. Joffe and Jack Rollins are credited as producers, Woody wasn't involved in this 1969 adaptation of his long-running play; the screenplay is credited to *With Six You Get Eggroll* scribes R. S. Allen and Harvey Bullock. Their attempts, as well as those of director Howard Morris, to "open up" the script frequently serve to make it broader and goofier—and it's already a far from subtle piece of work—while the zoom-ins and frenetic cutting date it poorly. But there are some big and genuine laughs, especially from Estelle Parsons, Michael Constantine, and Jackie Gleason, miscast though he may be. ("He's a genius," Allen said of Gleason's casting, "but he's the wrong guy.")

Sleeper

RELEASE DATE: December 17, 1973

WRITERS: Woody Allen, Marshall Brickman

CAST: Allen, Diane Keaton, John Beck, Marya Small, Susan Miller

IN A NUTSHELL: Health food store owner Miles Monroe goes into the hospital in 1973 for a minor procedure—and wakes up 200 years in the future.

RECURRING THEMES: Fear of machines; anti-authoritarianism; Woody the Great Lover

I n the fall of 1972, Woody Allen bid farewell to standup comedy. He worked up no new material for his six-week, six-city standup tour (culminating in Las Vegas); he did the old act, to the delight of audiences across the country. And then he retired it—and himself. He easily could have continued to pack houses as a stage performer, but films were his primary preoccupation now, and by the time he was preparing his next picture, he was already keenly aware of his need to evolve. "People go see you because they expect you to be a certain way," he said in 1973. "But after four or five films they suddenly say, 'That's the same old stuff.' You have to present a moving target. If you hold still long enough, someone will get you."

His next picture, written with new collaborator Marshall Brickman (they would go on to pen *Annie Hall* and *Manhattan* together, among others), was advertised as "a nostalgic look at the future." The tagline was apt; in spite of the visionary setting, this was Allen's most retro film to date, its dystopian-future storyline a framework for a direct homage to silent comedy. That tribute could have been even more explicit, as Brickman and Allen initially toyed with the idea of a future where no one spoke at all. (They also had the ambitious idea of doing it as a three-hour, two-part film with an intermission, with the first half set in contemporary New York, but Allen quickly abandoned it and opted to focus on the futuristic part.)

Indeed, several sequences seem pulled straight from the days of silent cinema: Miles-as-robot's inept food prep, his cavorting with guests, the escape from the Domesticon lab, the epic banana peel, the inflating "hydrovac suit." If the physical chaos of those sequences recalls Chaplin, his facial expressiveness (and dark glasses) echo Harold Lloyd, while the mechanics of the gags are straight out of Buster Keaton. The throwback qualities of these scenes are heightened by the old-timey music provided by Allen, with the help of New Orleans' legendary Preservation Hall Jazz Band and his own New Orleans Funeral Ragtime Orchestra.

> " I don't know what I'm doing here. I'm 237 years old, I should be collecting Social Security.
> —Miles Monroe "

Woody channels silent-cinema comedy legends Buster Keaton and Harold Lloyd in *Sleeper*—or, as the French translated it, "Woody and the Robots." *Lobby card from the Voyageur Press Collection*

But *Sleeper* simultaneously shows unmistakable maturity from the blackout-sketch quality of his earlier comedies. In those films, the minimal plot is to be tolerated but mostly ignored, whereas *Sleeper* (due in no small part to Brickman's influence) sets up a traditional three-act structure, in which a protagonist has a complication and a goal that is eventually reached—and the most successful bits, no matter how far out they may be, are in service of that plot. *Sleeper* may have the look of science fiction and the feel of a silent comedy, but when you get down to it, Allen and Brickman are telling the Hitchcockian tale of an innocent man wrongly accused and the pretty girl who is his (initially) reluctant accomplice.

And what a girl she is. Diane Keaton had made an impression in *Play It Again, Sam*—and she was lovely and charming in the role—but it was a role that Allen wrote for anyone and that Keaton found herself cast in. *Sleeper*'s Luna, on the other hand, was a role written *for* her, with her unique gifts and zizzy comic timing in mind, and it shows. She's not just "The Girl" here, but a fully engaged accomplice, she and Allen forming, for the first time, a great comedy team. Hints of her uproarious weirdness are sprinkled through the first half: the oddball montage of her living in the woods, the way she tops Woody's Blanche DuBois by doing Brando-as-Kowalski. But when the duo goes "undercover" in the third act, they're comic equals, tuned in to each other's peculiar energy, bouncing and sparking off the other. *Sam* showed that she could support Allen; *Sleeper* was proof that she could top him.

Woody on Woody

"I have no outstanding memory of *Sleeper*. I don't think of it very much. Again, it's one of those films. It seems to have worked out fine."

Love and Death

RELEASE DATE: June 10, 1975

WRITER: Woody Allen

CAST: Allen, Diane Keaton, James Tolkan, Olga Georges-Picot, Henri Czarniak, Jessica Harper

IN A NUTSHELL: In this parody of Russian literature, cowardly Boris Grushenko falls in love with his cousin, who convinces him to join her in a plot to assassinate Napoleon.

RECURRING THEMES: God (or lack thereof); obsession with death; infidelity; morality; suicide; sexless relationships ("Leonid, I know I could have been a better wife to you. Kinder. I could have made love to you more often. Or once, even"); Woody the Great Lover

Woody Allen was stuck. He'd written the first incarnation of a script that eventually would become both *Annie Hall* and *Manhattan Murder Mystery*, but he was desperately unhappy with it. "I was pondering around in the living room in my penthouse," he recalled, "and I saw a book on Russian history and I thought, Hey, why not do *Love and Death*? I've always said those are two subjects I'm interested in and it would be like *War and Peace*." So he put the other script aside, wrote this one "in no time at all," and that was that.

Love and Death would prove to be the last, for a while, of Allen's purely comic pictures—the end of the "early, funny ones." But there are hints here of what's to come. Most obviously, the film's Eastern European setting and milieu allows Allen his most organic opportunity yet for both quotation and parody of the foreign films that had become staples of his movie-going diet. The most explicit homage comes in the picture's penultimate scene, when the Bermanesque compositions and trancelike line readings of Sonja and Natasha directly quote *Persona*. But there are little homages throughout, visually and stylistically, particularly the presence of a Death character straight out of *Seventh Seal* and the searching, direct-to-camera monologues of both Allen and Keaton's characters.

The film is not just a love letter to Ingmar Bergman, of course. Much as *Sleeper* was a tribute to his favorite silent comics, *Love and Death* is his most direct valentine to the talking comedians he idolized. His first introduction to Napoleon ("A greater honor for me!") recalls Groucho Marx's round-robin of "Mr. Gottlieb, Mrs. Claypool" in *A Night at the Opera*, while the quibbling over "my seconds" and "my

> " All I could think of was Sonja. I wanted to hold her close to me, weep tears on her shoulder, and engage in oral sex.
> —Boris Grushenko "

In a film that reflects influences ranging from the Marx Brothers to Ingmar Bergman, Woody plays a Russian soldier who bumbles his way into heroism. *Ernst Haas/ Getty Images*

thirds" is vintage Groucho nonsense. More clear than that, however, are his tributes to Bob Hope. *Love and Death* falls squarely in the tradition of Hope's costume comedies, and in several scenes—the rapid-fire responses to taunts of cowardice from his family ("Thanks a lot, Mom. My mother, folks!"), his face-off with the Countess' lover ("Well, I mean a much *shorter* man"), and his response to her jaw-dropping sleepwear ("I'd prefer something sexy, but. . .")—he's all but doing a Hope imitation. He admitted as much while working on it: "I've got scenes that just one after the other Hope should do—it would be a better movie than if I did it."

Yet it works. *Love and Death* has the pacing and wit of a farce but also a real visual flair—courtesy of Ghislain Cloquet, the great cinematographer behind such classics as *Au hasard Balthazar* and *Night and Fog*—from the picturesque countryside shots that open the film to the delightful image of Woody and Death dancing down the lane at its conclusion. Like *Bananas*, it pulls many of its laughs from the transposition of moments in contemporary metropolitan life to an unexpected setting. In between, Boris and Sonja discuss, albeit mockingly, the concepts of God, death, and absolute morality that (though usually more seriously) become consistent thematic concerns. "I was trying to do a film with philosophical content, if you can believe it," he later said. "And I learned that it's hard to do a film with philosophical content if you're too broad."

With each passing film, Allen adds a new and vital element to his toolbox: visual style (*Everything You Always Wanted to Know About Sex*), semi-serious romance (*Play It Again, Sam*), attentiveness to narrative (*Sleeper*), and a pronounced art film influence (*Love and Death*). With all those qualities at his fingertips, he was now ready to make his most sophisticated picture to date.

Woody on Woody

"It was one of my funniest films, as I recall. I much prefer it to *Take the Money and Run* and *Bananas.*"

Annie Hall

RELEASE DATE: April 20, 1977

WRITERS: Woody Allen, Marshall Brickman

CAST: Allen, Diane Keaton, Tony Roberts, Paul Simon, Carol Kane, Shelley Duvall, Colleen Dewhurst

IN A NUTSHELL: Standup comedian Alvy Singer sifts through the pieces of his failed relationship with singer/actress Annie Hall.

RECURRING THEMES: Infidelity; obsession with death; Brooklyn childhood; Jewish mothers; psychoanalysis ("I'm gonna give him one more year and then I'm goin' to Lourdes"); California hatred ("I don't cultural advantage is being able to make a right turn on a red light"); television hatred ("It's because they turn it into television shows"); rock music hatred; anti-authoritarianism; show business; standup comedy; sexless relationships; masturbation ("It's sex with someone I love!"); younger women ("Twins, Max. Sixteen-year-olds"); jealousy; Judaism; the rabbi as punch line; past vs. present

The path to Woody Allen's first masterpiece is nearly as twistily circuitous as the layout of the film itself. He and Mickey Rose originally wrote a comic murder mystery, in which Woody and Diane Keaton would play lovers who come to believe that their neighbor has killed his wife. But "it didn't come out to my liking," so he put the project on hold while he made *Love and Death*. When he and Marshall Brickman returned to the script, they decided to keep the main characters of Alvy and Annie but jettison the mystery angle.

Still, the original script they wrote was far from the film they ended up with. Titled *Anhedonia* (the medical term for the inability to experience pleasure), it was originally "something that goes on in my mind, and the love story with Annie was one big part of it, but it was only one big part" of what Allen called, at the time, a "stream of consciousness showing one individual's state of mind, in which conversations and events constantly trigger dreams, fantasies and recollections." But, he recalls, "when Marshall saw my first cut with [editor] Ralph Rosenblum, he just didn't think it was coherent—and he co-authored the story!"

Brickman found the picture funny but "non-dramatic and ultimately uninteresting, a kind of cerebral exercise." Woody took it like a champ: "It was good criticism. We worked to make it coherent."

That work meant carving the 140-minute cut Brickman saw (culled from a shoot that lasted nearly ten months) into a ninety-four-minute version in which the free-floating structure remains, but all the sidebars and transgressions fall within the orbit of Annie and Alvy's "nervous romance." Though that wildly experimental first

> " A relationship, I think, is like a shark. You know? It has to constantly move forward or it dies. And I think what we've got on our hands is a dead shark.
> —Alvy Singer "

The creatively attired Annie Hall and the chronically neurotic Alvy Singer are classic characters from one of Woody Allen's most beloved and highly regarded films. *United Artists/Getty Images*

pass became something more conventional, the film was still a risky departure from the joke-joke-joke style of Allen's work to that point. "I thought I'll sacrifice some of the laughs for a story about human beings," he said, "and they will get involved in the story in a way that they had not ever been involved before. And it will be richer, and it'll be a better experience for them, and fun for me to try. And the worst that'll happen is I'll make a fool of myself." Suffice it to say, he did not make a fool of himself.

The film opens with Allen speaking directly into the camera, almost as a sort of comfort—here is Woody the comedian, telling jokes and delivering a "monologue," less like the star of a movie than the emcee of a variety show. But his gags aren't greeted with reassuring laughter from a delighted audience (as we'll discover later, he is no fan of artificial laughs), only the rather eerie silence that accompanies the opening credits. It's a striking choice, a sharp contrast to the scenes we'll see later of Alvy performing standup at a college or on television. There, he is a performer looking for laughs—just as Allen was in those early films. But in the opening scene, and throughout *Annie Hall*, he's not performing for us; he's talking to us, sharing of himself, making a personal connection.

He's also establishing, in that first scene, the film's unconventional structure, explaining that "the strangest things have been going through my mind," which tends to "jump around a little, and have some trouble between fantasy and reality." The setting down of those terms allows Allen to play with all kinds of toys, cinematically speaking: split-screen, animation, subtitles, special effects, man-on-the-street interviews, and breaking the fourth wall. Chiefly, though, it allows him to tinker with chronology, inserting

31

'ANNIE HALL'

"casi" una historia de amor

Una Producción de JACK ROLLINS · CHARLES H. JOFFE

WOODY ALLEN · DIANE KEATON · TONY ROBERTS · CAROL KANE · PAUL SIMON
SHELLEY DUVALL · JANET MARGOLIN · CHRISTOPHER WALKEN · COLLEEN DEWHURST

Escrita por WOODY ALLEN y MARSHALL BRICKMAN · Dirigida por WOODY ALLEN
· Producida por CHARLES H. JOFFE   V.O. Subtitulada

DISTRIBUIDA POR UNITED INTERNATIONAL PICTURES

The tagline on this Spanish-language poster calls the film "Almost a love story." The English-language poster called it a "nervous romance." *Poster from the Voyageur Press Collection*

flashbacks, flash-forwards, and the intersection of past and present, all at the service of "sifting the pieces of the relationship through my mind," as Alvy says in his opening monologue.

Perhaps the most remarkable thing about the stories of *Annie Hall*'s complete overhaul in the editing room is how little it bears the mark of such labor. The picture hopscotches nimbly through Alvy's life, taking its cues not from an A-leads-to-B-leads-to-C chronology, but from key words and themes that trigger new detours. Alvy's mother talks of how he's never trusted people, which leads to him and Rob (Tony Roberts) discussing his suspicions of anti-Semitism. His disgusted withdrawal from an aborted sexual encounter with his second wife ("I'm gonna take another in a series of cold showers") prompts Rob's boast that his tennis serve "is gonna send you to the showers." Annie asks (at a rather inopportune moment), "Were you always funny?," and, as if to answer, Alvy's agent tells the hack comic (and the audience, and her?), "This guy is naturally funny." And so on.

Allen's not just showing off. On an instinctual level, he's replicating the flights of fancy and strange nostalgic cubbyholes that the human mind can disappear into on a moment's notice. But he's also separating his film from the conventional boy-meets-girl narrative, jumbling up the pieces so that the audience is lulled out of the complacency of preconceived notions.

And those notions are most spectacularly subverted by the story's resolution. It should not come as a surprise; Alvy says right off the bat, in that first monologue, "Annie and I broke up," and sure enough they do. They do not reconcile at the film's end, which means that although *Annie Hall* is often cited (and rightfully so) as the template for the modern romantic comedy, it has what most of its imitators dare not attempt: an unhappy ending.

The sophistication of storytelling and willingness to confound expectations aren't the only major leaps here. *Annie Hall* marked the first of Allen's eight collaborations with director of photography Gordon Willis, one of the two men (along with editor Rosenblum) whom Woody credits for his cinematic education. Willis's suggestions and innovations managed to change Allen's preference for merely photographing the gag, with memorable results: the tracking shot across his grade-school classmates, timed to their names; the slow pan in the car from Annie's brother Duane (Christopher Walken) to Annie to the terrified Alvy; the lovely image of Annie and Alvy kissing near the Brooklyn Bridge (a forerunner of the most iconic image in *Manhattan*); the 360-degree tracking shot as Alvy paces around Allison's (Carol Kane) bed, working through the JFK assassination.

That latter scene is one of many done in what would become Allen's signature style: the single scene (or large portion of one) done "all in one," without edits, cutaways, or other "coverage." Willis also suggested that the split-screen scene of Alvy and Annie's simultaneous therapy sessions be done practically rather than optically, with the "split" created by a wall between two sets. This delighted Allen, because it allowed him and Keaton to do the scene live, working off of each other, rather than having to create their rhythms in the editing room.

In spite of all this talk of narrative scaffolding and inventive cinematography, it's important to note that Woody never stopped delivering the comic goods. But the laughs in *Annie Hall* are of a different sort. It's the first film he directs that takes place entirely in the "real world," the laughs borne from relatable comic situations rather than absurdity and parody.

Much of that reality is a result of Keaton's delightful and deservedly iconic performance. The eccentric wardrobe was hers ("Let's just leave her alone, let her wear what she wants," Woody told his costume designer. "If I really hate something, I'll tell her."), as was the distinctive delivery and cheerful manner. But Annie is a fully formed character—one that grows, changes, and matures through the story's timeframe, in sharp contrast to Alvy, who seems basically immovable. When they meet, she's a charming drip, not yet sure of who she is or what she wants to be. Alvy, fancying himself a Professor Higgins, encourages her creativity and growth, gives her dense tomes about death, and puts her into analysis. He thinks that he's grooming her to be his perfect woman. (In real life, Allen similarly introduced Keaton to new experiences: "I showed her films that she had not seen, that

WATCH OUT FOR

Christopher Walken as Annie's brother Duane; Beverly D'Angelo on the monitor in the "laugh track" scene; Jeff Goldblum as the guy at the party who's forgotten his mantra; Sigourney Weaver as Alvy's date when he bumps into Annie one last time.

Allen and his editor, Ralph Rosenblum (left), toiled for months in the editing room to get the unruly film down to its final ninety-four-minute running time. *Brian Hamill/ Getty Images*

33

"Annie Hall was a much-adored picture. I mean, it's fine, but I've done better pictures than that, though it may have had a warmth, an emotion, that people responded to."

Annie Hall won the 1977 Academy Award for Best Picture, beating out (clockwise from top right) *The Turning Point, The Goodbye Girl, Star Wars,* and *Julia. ABC Photo Archives/Getty Images*

I thought were great," and he encouraged her to go into therapy.) But in reality, Alvy is helping her to outgrow him, and when she starts to slip away, he's both jealous and resentful—an inclination most present in the sad scene where he torpedoes a genuine networking opportunity for her by making up (badly) an excuse not to socialize with music producer Tony Lacey (Paul Simon), whom she later moves in with.

It takes a bit of bravery for Allen to write and play that character, even if he hadn't guessed the degree to which the picture would be presumed as autobiography. "It's really a work of fiction," he told the *New York Times* in 1977, while allowing, "details are picked from life." That's an understatement; after all, he was a comedian, twice divorced when he and Keaton (who was born Diane Hall, and had a "Grammy Hall" of her own) dated and lived together, often spending time in the company of Tony Roberts, who had a habit of calling Woody "Max," just as Roberts's character, Rob, does to Alvy in the film. Roberts's character emigrates to California, as did Woody's pal and collaborator Mickey Rose; so does Keaton's, at the urging of Lacey, just as Keaton herself had when she fell in love with Al Pacino (an actor similar in diminutive stature to Simon).

But, as Allen has noted, those are just the broad strokes, which ignore the specifics of these characters and situations, to say nothing of the contributions of Brickman. It seems safer to presume that *Annie Hall* is Allen's version of the play Alvy writes at its conclusion, another case of "always trying to get things to come out perfect in art because, uh, it's real difficult in life." Or, as he tells us earlier in the film, "Boy, if life were only like this."

In the end, life worked out pretty well for the forty-one-year-old filmmaker in the wake of the film's release. *Annie Hall* was an unqualified smash—a critical and commercial success that won four Oscars, including Best Screenplay, Best Director, and Best Picture. Allen (in what would become a tradition) did not attend the Academy Awards ceremony, staying instead in New York and keeping his regular weekly gig playing clarinet with his jazz band.

"I know it sounds horrible, but winning that Oscar for *Annie Hall* didn't mean anything to me," he said in 1979. "I have no regard for that kind of ceremony. I just don't think they know what they're doing. When you see who wins those things—or who doesn't win them—you can see how meaningless this Oscar thing is. It has nothing to do with artistic merit. It's a sort of popularity test. When it's your turn, you win it."

"Jew Eat?"
Jews and Judaism in Allen's Films
by Ezra Glinter

There's a scene in *Annie Hall* in which Woody Allen, playing his fictional alter ego Alvy Singer, is about to perform at a dinner in support of Democratic presidential contender Adlai Stevenson. Just before going onstage, Alvy strikes up a conversation with the stage manager, a young woman named Allison Portchnik (Carol Kane). After she tells him that she's doing her thesis on "political commitment in twentieth century literature," he asks: "Were you, like, New York, Jewish, left-wing, liberal, intellectual, Central Park West, Brandeis University, the socialist summer camps, and the father with the Ben Shahn drawings and the really strike-oriented. . . . I'm stopping before I make a complete imbecile of myself."

"No, that was wonderful," she responds. "I love being reduced to a cultural stereotype."

Almost four decades after drawing that indelible picture of American Jewish life, Allen has himself become a cultural stereotype. His comedy and persona, channeled through the Woody Allen–esque character he plays in many of his movies, have become synonymous with Jewish humor and have influenced Jewish comics from Larry David to Lena Dunham. For viewers who grew up on movies like *Annie Hall* and *Manhattan*, Allen, with his small-frame, neurotic temperament, and sly wit, has become the quintessential Jewish-American comedian and filmmaker of the twentieth and twenty-first centuries.

If Allen is credited with a particularly Jewish sensibility, however, it's one of his own making. The bumbling slapstick figure he played in early films like *Take the Money and Run* (1969) and *Bananas* (1971) typifies the *schlemiel*—Yiddish, roughly, for "buffoon"—which was a common trope of Jewish folklore and literature. At the same time, his cerebral jokes connected him to comics like Mort Sahl and Lenny Bruce, whose intellectual styles were upending the nightclub routines of the Borscht Belt. Most important to his Jewish bona fides, Allen managed to poke the ribs of the very community he came from.

In fact, Allen's most Jewish films tend to be those that are at least somewhat autobiographical. They often feature portrayals of his working-class Brooklyn upbringing, and of peers who became Manhattan's upwardly mobile intelligentsia. In his 1983 mockumentary, *Zelig*, these included real people like Saul Bellow, Irving Howe, and Susan Sontag who, like Allen, were the Jewish children or grandchildren of immigrants. And the movie itself, with its shape-shifting protagonist, tackled the idea of passing—something that many Jewish intellectuals of Allen's generation were trying to do.

It wasn't just the people in Allen's films that embodied Jewish characteristics, but also the world in which they lived. In *Bananas*, Fielding Mellish stops at a newsstand to buy a pornographic magazine along with a copy of *Commentary*, a highbrow periodical published by the American Jewish Committee. (References to *Commentary* surfaced elsewhere in Allen's work, as in his *Annie Hall* joke that *Commentary* and *Dissent* had merged to form "Dysentery.") Behind the magazines, you can spot a copy of Leo Rosten's *The Joys of Yiddish*. Such scenes don't address Jewish themes exactly, but they occur within a Jewish milieu.

While Mellish is only Jewish by implication, Allen's characters soon became more overt about their identity. In *Annie Hall*, Alvy Singer not only complains repeatedly about anti-Semitism, but also experiences it firsthand through Annie's grandmother, Grammy Hall. In one of the film's most famous scenes, Alvy visits the Hall family for Easter and imagines himself, in Grammy's eyes, as a Hasidic Jew in black coat, hat, beard, and side locks. Here we see Allen's Jewish identity, as well as his self-consciousness about that identity, presented in one unforgettable picture.

It's ironic, however, that this image, often considered one of the most overtly Jewish in Allen's oeuvre, illustrates precisely the kind of Jew Allen is not. As far as Allen is concerned, the Hasidic way of life is about as foreign to his identity as that of the blond-haired, all-American Midwestern family with whom he is eating dinner. Only undistinguishing bigots, like the racist grandmother, would think of him as Orthodox.

In contrast, Allen's sense of Jewishness is rooted in the hothouse atmosphere of a heavily ethnic, but not necessarily religious, Brooklyn childhood.

"You're what Grammy Hall would call a real Jew."
United Artists/Getty Images

Such reminiscences show up in *Annie Hall*, where his thinly fictionalized family is portrayed as loud and argumentative, and most notably in *Radio Days* (1987), which is entirely devoted to a similar depiction of childhood. In *Crimes and Misdemeanors* (1989), Judah Rosenthal (Martin Landau) recalls a family Passover Seder at which his relatives bickered over the existence of absolute morality. This freethinking conversation around a ritual holiday dinner illustrates the cultural, but not necessarily religious, nature of Allen's Jewish sensibility.

Given how contextual Jewishness is in Allen's films, it isn't surprising that as the American Jewish community charted a path of upwardly mobile assimilation, Judaism disappeared from Allen's films as well. Like many of his contemporaries, Allen left the ethnic environment of his childhood behind, and the midcentury intellectual culture that emerged from it isn't the same as it was, either. Yet in at least one case, Allen managed to portray the disappearing immigrant past within a contemporary setting, creating one of the most poignant films of his career.

In *Broadway Danny Rose* (1984), Allen plays an unsuccessful talent manager whose only client is Lou Canova (Nick Apollo Forte), a singer and entertainer specializing in popular Italian songs. Here, Allen's character is a distinctly Jewish, if not particularly successful, showbiz figure—he repeatedly holds his hands up, proclaiming "It's the *emes*" (that is, "it's the truth")—but what's more interesting is the comparison to a different ethnic group. Although much of the movie's comedy derives from the contrast between Woody's diminutive Jewish persona and physically intimidating Italian mobsters, both character types belong to the same disappearing moment. In Allen's film, Jewish and Italian identities are equally subject to assimilation, and both Lou Canova and Danny Rose are members of a vanishing species.

The Carnegie Deli, a renowned gathering place for New York's comics and agents, and the centerpiece of *Broadway Danny Rose*. Lobby card from the Voyageur Press Collection

Indeed, this prognosis is borne out in Allen's later films, which have far less Jewish content than his earlier work. Even a movie like *Anything Else* (2003), which exhibits marked similarities to earlier films, lacks the same obsession with Jewish identity. Though it has not one but three Woody Allen–esque figures—including Jason Biggs as comedian Jerry Falk and Danny DeVito as his agent, Harvey Wexler—the most Jewish of them all is Falk's mentor, David Dobel, who is played by Allen himself and who, tellingly, is the oldest of the bunch.

Of course, Jewish filmmaking has continued to evolve, and after Jerry Seinfeld and Sarah Silverman, Seth Rogen and Judd Apatow, Allen is no longer the last word on Jewish humor. But his movies documented a particularly Jewish time and place—New York from the 1930s to the 1970s—and his neurosis-ridden style defined a Jewish sensibility for a whole generation. If Woody Allen still seems like what Grammy Hall would call a "Real Jew," that's hardly surprising. It's not so easy, after all, to shake such a successful stereotype.

Ezra Glinter is the deputy arts editor of the Jewish Daily Forward. His writing has appeared in the *Los Angeles Review of Books*, the *Paris Review Daily*, and *Bookforum*, among other publications. He received a master's degree from the Cultural Reporting and Criticism program at New York University's Arthur L. Carter Journalism Institute.

Interiors

RELEASE DATE: August 2, 1978

WRITER: Woody Allen

CAST: Diane Keaton, Geraldine Page, Mary Beth Hurt, E. G. Marshall, Kristin Griffith, Richard Jordan, Maureen Stapleton, Sam Waterston

IN A NUTSHELL: The separation of their parents rocks three troubled adult daughters and drives their unstable mother to suicide.

RECURRING THEMES: Infidelity; divorce; familial attraction; obsession with death; psychoanalysis; frustrated artists; writers; sibling rivalry; neurotic actresses

The success and recognition for 1977's *Annie Hall* gave Woody Allen the opportunity to take his biggest artistic leap yet: to make a serious drama in which, for the first time, he would not appear. "I was indulged by them," he later said of his bosses at United Artists. "They said, well, you've earned the right to make any film you want to make, so if you want to make a very serious drama, go ahead and make one."

He certainly did. Set in the world of Manhattan-and-Hamptons WASPs, *Interiors* is an unblinkingly straight-faced affair, told in impeccably designed and stiflingly clean rooms, often in wide shots and backed by deafening silence. (Like *Annie Hall*, there is no score to speak of, only occasional music from a clearly identifiable source.) His characters are creative types: writers, poets, actors, designers. They live in an insular world, a bubble, in which their personal woes and psychological struggles are their defining characteristics.

Those who disliked *Interiors*—and reaction, among both critics and moviegoers, was decidedly mixed—wrote it off as a clumsy and too obvious homage to the European filmmakers Allen fancied, particularly Ingmar Bergman. Allen insisted, shortly after the film's release, that "a critic that doesn't see a difference between my film and Bergman's is just not sensitive enough to be allowed to talk about movies." But he's kidding himself if he thinks the picture's photography doesn't recall the Swedish master, most explicitly in its closing image of the sisters at the window. Allen *had* to know he was aping *Persona*; after all, he'd parodied those very shots just three years earlier in *Love and Death*.

The foreign influence may also explain what some critics deemed a stilted, too-written quality in the dialogue. Allen later provided a possible explanation: "When you see, say, a Bergman film, you're reading it because you're

I think you're really too perfect to live in this world. I mean, all the beautifully furnished rooms, carefully designed interiors, everything's so controlled. There wasn't any room for any real feelings. None, between any of us.

—Joey

following the subtitles. And when you read it, the dialogue has a certain cadence. . . . Because of my exposure to foreign films, in my ear for dialogue, was I really writing subtitles for foreign films?" It's possible, but the issue dims with age, its disparity from contemporary idiom far less noticeable from a distance of thirty-five years.

In fact, time has softened the initial view of *Interiors* considerably. The shock of a serious-minded Allen picture no longer prevents the viewer from appreciating, for instance, the picture's sly use of voice-over, or Gordon Willis's understated yet powerful photography of the sequence with Eve and the gas oven. And it marked the first of several fruitful explorations (including *Hannah and Her Sisters*, *Cassandra's Dream*, and *Blue Jasmine*) of the sibling dynamic. "Sisters are great," Allen told Richard Schickel, "because, whether it's two or three, you know, there's always dramatic possibilities. I just feel you have a natural conflict all the time when there's a sibling around."

There's also an argument to be made that this—rather than *Annie Hall* or *Radio Days* or *Husbands and Wives* or any of the usual suspects—is Allen's most personal film. The character of the mother, Eve (Geraldine Page), though somewhat inspired by Louise Lasser's mentally unstable mother (who had attempted and finally committed suicide in

Woody on Woody

"I think I could do that film much better now, much better. I know I could. But I did the best I could at the time. . . . It's a wonderful idea that I just wasn't fully up to. I got some juice out of it but nowhere near what it should be."

"INTERIEURS"

In his first attempt at serious drama, Allen told a family story centered on three sisters, played by (left to right) Diane Keaton, Kristin Griffith, and Mary Beth Hurt. *Lobby card from the Voyageur Press Collection*

WATCH OUT FOR

The costumes of Joel Schumacher, who would later direct such critically reviled films as *Batman & Robin*.

the early 1960s), is one Allen claims to identify with closely. She is, in his words, "a kind of disciplinarian, obsessive, wants everything just right, controlling things, making things perfect." Eve is a character who (per her ex-husband) "created a world around us that we all existed in," prone to demanding that things be (in Michael's words) "done and redone, two and three times over," as Allen has often done, reworking and reshooting scenes, subplots, and once an entire film. Joey (Mary Beth Hurt) is a frustrated artist with ambition and "a real need to express myself" but "none of the talent" to do so—and Allen has often complained that the great films he admires are simply out of his grasp. And while Renata (Diane Keaton) is talented, her work is not good enough; she constantly dismisses her poems as unimportant throwaways, never satisfied in her quest to create "fine work that means something in the long run."

Interiors feels so personal perhaps because it is (contrary to its reputation for sterility) so raw and candid. Allen is not hiding his concerns, obsessions, and neurosis under the protective layer of jokes; he is putting it all out there, as Arthur (E. G. Marshall) states, "so everything is as direct and open as possible." As a result, the picture is a bit on the nose. But it also offers a fascinatingly unfiltered glimpse into Allen's psyche. Shortly after making it, he dubbed *Interiors* "an interesting failure." But as the years pass, the second half of that description seems less and less accurate.

Allen takes a moment of serious reflection during a break in filming on *Interiors*. Brian Hamill/Archive Photos/ Getty Images

Diane Keaton

"Keaton is basically an actress with a great, great comic gift. And having known her personally so well, I [was] able to tap into some of her strengths; so I could write things for her that I knew she could play well, and she did."

—Woody Allen

Allen and Keaton on the streets of New York during their dating days, circa 1970. *Ron Galella, Ltd./WireImage/ Getty Images*

When Diane Keaton (she had to change her name because there was already a Diane Hall in Actors' Equity) came to audition for the female lead in Woody Allen's Broadway production of *Play It Again, Sam*, she had only recently moved up from understudy and chorus member in *Hair*—where she was best known as being the one cast member who wouldn't go nude in the show's finale. She immediately developed a crush on Woody, and he soon felt the same, attracted both to her looks and her talent. (Jack Benny came to a performance and told Woody after, "That girl is going to be gigantic.")

Their relationship—the sunny Midwestern gentile in the roach-infested apartment, given an education of sorts by the Jewish comic from New York—would inspire *Annie Hall*, a film about which she confessed to being "afraid that, unconsciously, I might stop myself from showing the truth because it made me uncomfortable." But more importantly, the opportunity to write roles worthy of her talent— whether as the daffy comic partner of *Sleeper*, the morose artist of *Interiors*, or the hard-edged intellectual of *Manhattan*—forced Allen to expand the male gaze of his early work and

attempt to write female characters that were more than ingénues and comic props.

"One of the things I gained was a female perspective," he reflected, "and it was more interesting to me than the male perspective." Decades later, Woody was still singing Keaton's praises: "First of all, she has flawless instincts. She is very lucky. She's a very gifted person. She was very beautiful. She could sing, she could dance, she could draw, she could paint, she could take photographs. She could act. I mean, she had so much talent. And quite good in every department."

Manhattan

RELEASE DATE: April 25, 1979

WRITERS: Woody Allen, Marshall Brickman

CAST: Allen, Diane Keaton, Michael Murphy, Mariel Hemingway, Meryl Streep, Anne Byrne

IN A NUTSHELL: Comedy writer Isaac Davis leaves his lucrative television gig and falls for the mistress of his best friend.

RECURRING THEMES: Infidelity; obsession with death; morality ("It's very important to have some kind of personal integrity!"); psychoanalysis ("You call your analyst Donny?"); television hatred (the drug-addled sketch comedy show seems inspired by *Saturday Night Live*, which his friend Jean Doumanian worked on); Groucho idolatry (he's the first name on Ike's list of things that make life worth living); younger women ("I'm dating a girl who does homework")

"Chapter one. He adored New York City. He idolized it all out of proportion." So begins Woody Allen's second true masterpiece, and seldom have a film's opening words been more accurate. *Manhattan* is Woody Allen's valentine to the city he loves—a romanticized representation of a city that was, at that moment, not exactly at its best. But Woody didn't care. "I wanted to show the city the way I felt about it," he said.

Manhattan is best considered alongside the two films that immediately preceded it, since it seems such a cunning fusion of their sensibilities: the romanticism and quirkiness of *Annie Hall* mated with the serious undercurrents of *Interiors*. This was the mold he would spend the next several years working in, and he explained it thus: "It's more of a foreign film influence—in foreign comedies, you don't get those kind of joke comedies very often. What you get more is regular dramatic stories, with a little light touch to them here and there."

The straighter face with which Allen (and thus, his audience) approached these characters and their foibles manifests itself in several ways. Most obvious was his choice to shoot in black and white, for the first time. Allen said he made that choice "because that's how I remember [New York] from when I was small." In sharp contrast to *Annie Hall*, the film would be a straight narrative, as he noted during preproduction. "There's no screwing around in time, and there's no special gimmicks, there's no dream sequences, no fantasies, no voiceovers, nothing. It's a very spartan kind of story." He and director of photography Gordon Willis also decided to shoot in 2.35:1 "Scope" widescreen, almost on a lark: "We were talking about how they did all those war pictures, with tanks and airplanes, and we thought it would be very interesting to do an intimate picture like that."

Some of those aggressive aesthetic choices may have been, more than anything, to prevent the movie from being perceived as *Annie Hall II*. But those fears were put to rest by Diane Keaton, whose Mary is a 180-degree shift from the affable Annie. Mary is a hard-edged New York neurotic, a "creep" who crashes into the movie and wrecks two relationships, a

Well, I don't believe in extramarital relationships. I think people should mate for life, like pigeons or Catholics.

—Isaac Davis

WOODY ALLEN
DIANE KEATON
MICHAEL MURPHY
MARIEL HEMINGWAY
MERYL STREEP
ANNE BYRNE

"MANHATTAN" GEORGE GERSHWIN
Une Production JACK ROLLINS - CHARLES H. JOFFE Réalisé par
Écrit par WOODY ALLEN et MARSHALL BRICKMAN WOODY ALLEN
Produit par Directeur de la photographie
CHARLES H. JOFFE ROBERT GREENHUT GORDON WILLIS s.c.
Distribué par LES ARTISTES ASSOCIÉS United Artists

MANHATTAN

This iconic image from the film *Manhattan* has come to represent Woody Allen and his love for the city. *Lobby card from the Voyageur Press Collection*

woman cursed with the kind of snobbish intellectualism that would seemingly make her an ideal date for the McLuhanite in line in *Annie Hall.* It's a wonderfully complicated character, alternately likable and cringe-worthy, and admirably self-aware. "I'm young, I'm highly intelligent, I've got everything going for me!" she insists, yet admits mere breaths later, "I'm all fucked up."

Her personality—and, even more importantly, Allen and Brickman's presentation of it—created a markedly different dynamic between the Allen and Keaton characters this time around, morphing from hostility to warm dislike (with kidding-on-the-square insults like the Great Dane/penis substitute bit) to, eventually, affection. The arc of their relationship means the black and white makes even more sense; this is a classic screwball-comedy relationship, along the love/hate lines found in *Bringing Up Baby* or *It Happened One Night.*

That's not the only romantic entanglement in a film that, as Charles Champlin wrote, is imbued with the "mournful sense of the avoidable loss of love." "She's seventeen," Ike explains in the first scene, of his date, Tracy. "I'm forty-two and she's seventeen. I'm older than her father." This specific clip was aired on the news the day that Woody's relationship with Mia Farrow's twenty-one-year-old adopted daughter, Soon-Yi Previn, was first revealed, and this much must be said: It is difficult to watch *Manhattan* without

The Allen and Diane Keaton characters shared a different dynamic from their previous onscreen roles, but the chemistry was still strong. *Brian Hamill/Getty Images*

at least some mild level of discomfort about this fictional storyline, considering what we know about Allen's personal life. In fact, the Tracy character was supposedly inspired by actress Stacey Nelkin, an NYU student who says she dated Allen when she was seventeen. (Allen has never confirmed this.)

Throughout his career, Woody has revisited the notion of judging the artist rather than the man, and it's not that our knowledge of what happened outside the frame prevents us from appreciating what transpires inside it. But little moments—the line about the sixteen-year-old twins in *Annie Hall*, the argument about Charlotte Rampling's thirteen-year-old cousin in *Stardust Memories*—give the viewer pause and provide a window into Allen's mind that we'd probably rather not consider. Or, as critic Pauline Kael put it, "What man in his forties but Woody Allen could pass off a predilection for teenagers as a quest for true values?"

But whatever red flags the character of Tracy raises, it's hard to find any fault with Mariel Hemingway's work in the role. (It netted her an Oscar nomination.) Her performance feels less like Allen's directing her than capturing a presence. It is a model of understated, behavioral performance, in which every line is unaffected by anything but honesty and truth. When she and Ike break up (at a soda fountain, no less, which seems like exactly where an arrested adolescent like Ike would go to end it with a good girl) and those big tears roll down her cheeks, the movie becomes more than a comedy.

If anything, the character of Tracy triumphs at the picture's end because she knows what we've suspected from the beginning: Age be damned, she's far wiser and more *emotionally* mature than her forty-two-year-old suitor (or any of his comparably aged friends). That Ike asks her to cash in her trip to London for an eternity of late movies and comfort food with him is unforgivable—but it's important to note that while Ike wants her to stay, Woody knows that she cannot. Like Alvy Singer, Ike is the educator/sculptor of his younger lover (helping her keep straight *his* boyhood crushes, Rita Hayworth and Veronica Lake), and Ike knows what Alvy discovered by the end of *Annie Hall*: that great women change, and then you're screwed. "In six months you'll be a completely different person," Ike despairs, and he's right, whether he "has faith" or not.

The slight ambiguity of that ending—encapsulated in a wonderful, *City Lights*–echoing final closeup—revealed Allen's further growth as well as his further reluctance to pander to his audience. When the film was released, Roger Ebert wrote, "I think it goes wrong in the very things the New York critics like the most—when, in the last forty-five minutes or so, Allen does a subtle turn on his material and gets serious about it." Ebert usually got it right, but not here—or, more precisely, he missed what made the picture a step forward for Allen. The story had to be taken seriously because the characters took it seriously, even if (as Ike says into his tape recorder) they were doing so because "it keeps them from dealing with the more unsolvable, terrifying problems about the universe." Even when *Manhattan* is at its most serious, the jokes are still there. But Woody was selective this time, snipping out one-liners and sight gags that "were very funny . . . but in the context of the film, they looked like they had dropped down from the moon." The jokes

Woody on Woody

"They put me on the cover of *Time* and of *The New York Times Magazine*, and they said it was the greatest. But two weeks before that happened, if United Artists had said, 'Well, tell you what we'll do. If you'll do two films for us for nothing, we'll burn the negative of this one,' I would have said, 'Okay, you have it.'"

WOODY ALLEN
DIANE KEATON
MICHAEL MURPHY
MARIEL HEMINGWAY
MERYL STREEP
ANNE BYRNE

MANHATTAN

"MANHATTAN" GEORGE GERSHWIN
JACK ROLLINS · CHARLES H. JOFFE
WOODY ALLEN and MARSHALL BRICKMAN WOODY ALLEN
CHARLES H. JOFFE ROBERT GREENHUT GORDON WILLIS
LES ARTISTES ASSOCIÉS United Artists

Mariel Hemingway's performance in *Manhattan* earned her an Academy Award nomination. *Lobby card from the Voyageur Press Collection*

45

WATCH OUT FOR

Legendary *Saturday Night Live* writer Michael O'Donoghue as Mary's friend Dennis; Karen Allen as an actress on Ike's TV show; Mia Farrow's sister Tisa as Polly, the girl who had the wrong kind of orgasm.

that remain are reactive, responsive, the characters' coping mechanism for their petty insecurities and betrayals—or their method of softening their genuine anger with and distrust of each other.

And for that reason, scoring their tiny problems with the lushness of Gershwin music and framing them in the epic wide screen becomes a wry aural and visual commentary. The former idea came to Allen early on and marked one of the few occasions in which he wrote "specifically to accommodate music. . . . A number of times I would stretch things out so I could leave myself a lot of room to do a big dose of Gershwin." One such moment was his dash across town for Tracy near the end; another was the opening montage, a remarkable mosaic of New York portraits scored to "Rhapsody in Blue," culminating in a spectacular display of fireworks over Central Park and the Manhattan skyline. (To get that shot, a cameraman hung out the window of a production member's parents' Central Park West apartment.)

The images of that montage are relatively minor compared to the photographic miracles Willis accomplishes in what may be his most beautiful film for Allen. His signature use of darkness, or hard shadows and soft light, creates several jaw-dropping frames: the silhouettes of Ike and Mary in the planetarium, the pools of late-night light in Ike's apartment, and perhaps the most iconic shot in any of Woody's films, Ike and Mary on a park bench near the Brooklyn Bridge as the sun rises. "It was a pain in the neck to do!" Allen said. "I had to wake up at 3:00 in the morning. Plus we had to bring our own bench, because there's no bench there." Of the final product, he shrugs, "I didn't know it would be iconic. I knew it'd be pretty."

One year after earning an Academy Award nomination for her role in *The Deer Hunter* and in the same year as her Oscar-winning performance in *Kramer vs. Kramer*, Meryl Streep played the role of Woody Allen's ex-wife-turned-lesbian in *Manhattan*. © Moviestore collection Ltd / Alamy

• Woody Allen's New York •

"He adored New York City. He idolized it all out of proportion. Eh, uh, no, make that he, he romanticized it all out of proportion. Better—New York was his town, and it always would be."

—Ike Davis (Woody Allen), *Manhattan*

When I was a very young kid," Woody Allen told Eric Lax, "it was not the pirate pictures I liked or the cowboy pictures, which *thrilled* my friends. I fell asleep at them. What turned me on at the *youngest* age was when the credits finished and the camera panned across the skyline of New York." His impression of the real thing was no less rhapsodic. Crossing over from his home borough of Brooklyn to The City was "an *explosion* of everything that you only knew from Hollywood movies." From childhood, "all that I ever wanted to do was live in Manhattan and work in Manhattan," and that's exactly what he did.

His first film set in New York, *Bananas*, differs starkly from the version of the city he would come to embrace. As is typical of 1970s New York pictures like *The French Connection* and *Taxi Driver*, Manhattan is portrayed as dirty, grimy, and dangerous. But from *Annie Hall* forward, Woody's take on the city was romanticized—sanitized, some would say. Martin Scorsese, another legend of the NYC film scene, said Allen's New York "is not another world, it's another planet."

"I love the city and have always loved it," he confessed, "and whenever I have a chance to show it in a flattering way, I do." Sometimes that flattering requires a bit of deception; New York circa 1979, for example, was certainly not the sparkling wonderland of *Manhattan* (and indeed, Allen excised a gag about a mugging from the carriage ride sequence, lest he spoil the mood). But Joe Klein may have put it best when he wrote, in 1986, that Allen's New York "commingles with the real one."

It's recognizable, occasionally, but is often as far removed from the genuine article as those artificial versions of the city, created on soundstages with painted backdrops, that he fell in love with as a child.

"The New York that Hollywood showed the world," Allen explained, "which never really existed, is the New York that I show the world because that's the New York I fell in love with." That fantasy-vision of Manhattan, all white telephones and penthouse suites and sparkling nightclubs, fused with Allen's own rarified Upper East Side existence—of chatty, intellectual, financially comfortable writers, filmmakers, architects, and academics—to create a vision of the city as specific to its creator as Fellini's Rome or Bertolucci's Paris (or, for that matter, Scorsese's New York).

Klein again: "Woody Allen's New York City—the city of his movies—has a peculiar geography. It ends at 96th Street, where Harlem begins. It extends south to SoHo, but not as far as Wall Street. It allows, grudgingly, for one outer borough, Brooklyn. In fact, there are only two *crucial* neighborhoods in his New York: Times Square and the quiet, elegant Upper East Side, where he and the characters he plays usually live. Manhattan's two other main residential areas—the Village and the Upper West Side—exist primarily as foils for his humor. The Village (and SoHo, in *Hannah and Her Sisters*) is where silly, trendy, artsy things happen; the Upper West Side is where the insufferable intellectuals hang out." A survey of the films, and where they were shot, mostly bears Klein out.

UPPER EAST SIDE

1. Mickey gets some tests, Mount Sinai Hospital, 1184 5th Avenue and East 101st Street (*Hannah and Her Sisters*)
2. Ray and Frenchy's ritzy apartment, 1169 Park Avenue and East 92nd Street (*Small Time Crooks*)
3. Ike picks up Tracy, The Dalton School, 108 East 89th Street and Park Avenue (*Manhattan*)
4. Double date opening scene (*Manhattan*) and where Lee and Bonnie meet friends (*Celebrity*), Elaine's, 1703 2nd Avenue and East 88th Street
5. Amanda's brownstone, 441 East 87th Street (between 1st Avenue & York Avenue) (*Anything Else*)
6. Jerry Falk's apartment, 52 East 82nd Street and Park Avenue (*Anything Else*)
7. Holden sings to Skylar, near the Metropolitan Museum of Art, 1000 5th Avenue and East 82nd Street (*Everyone Says I Love You*)
8. Ray, Frenchy, and David look at art, Metropolitan Museum of Art, 1000 5th Avenue and East 82nd Street (*Small Time Crooks*)
9. Brandon is mobbed by paparazzi, Stanhope Hotel, 995 5th Avenue and East 81st Street (*Celebrity*)
10. Larry and Carol's apartment, 200 East 78th Street and 3rd Avenue (*Manhattan Murder Mystery*)
11. Lee picks up the supermodel, The Cherokee, 517 East 77th Street and York Avenue (*Celebrity*)
12. Val and Ellie meet for a drink, The Carlyle Hotel, 35 East 76th Street and Madison Avenue (*Hollywood Ending*)
13. Laurel and Cassie eat, Café Boulud, 20 East 76th Street and Madison Avenue (*Melinda and Melinda*)
14. Sally spies Jack buying lingerie, La Lingerie store, 845 Madison Avenue and East 70th Street, Manhattan (*Husbands and Wives*)
15. Annie Hall's apartment, East 68th Street and Madison Avenue (*Annie Hall*)
16. Alvy and Annie almost go to the movies, Beekman Theatre, 1254 2nd Avenue at 66th Street (*Annie Hall*)
17. Ike and Mary watch the sunrise, Brooklyn Bridge overlook, Sutton Square and Sutton Place (*Manhattan*)
18. Lenny and Linda meet again, FAO Schwarz, 767 5th Avenue and East 59th Street (*Mighty Aphrodite*)
19. Supermodel has a smoke, Queensboro Bridge, East 59th Street (*Celebrity*)

UPPER WEST SIDE

20. Frenchy's Cookie Shop, West 145th Street and Amsterdam Avenue (*Small Time Crooks*)
21. Harry and Joan argue, West 92nd Street and West End Avenue (*Deconstructing Harry*)
22. Alvy and Annie go to the movies, meet Marshall McLuhan, The New Yorker Theater, 2409 Broadway (between 88th & 89th) (*Annie Hall*)
23. Jerry meets with Harvey, Isabella's, 359 Columbus Avenue and West 77th Street (*Anything Else*)
24. Danny Rose gets kidnapped, West 73rd Street and Broadway (*Broadway Danny Rose*)
25. Hannah's apartment (also Mia Farrow's apartment), 135 Central Park West and West 73rd Street (*Hannah and Her Sisters*)
26. Alvy and Annie meet again at *The Sorrow and the Pity*, Thalia Theatre, 2537 Broadway and 72nd (*Annie Hall*)
27. Linda's old apartment, West 72nd Street and Amsterdam Avenue (*Mighty Aphrodite*)
28. Cliff and Wendy meet with Lester (*Crimes and Misdemeanors*) and Lisa meets Sheldon's mother (*New York Stories: Oedipus Wrecks*), Tavern on the Green, Central Park West and 67th Street
29. Alvy and Annie say goodbye, outside Lincoln Center, West 63rd St & Columbus Avenue (*Annie Hall*)

CENTRAL PARK

30. Jerry and Dobel walk and talk, Reservoir Bridge and Greywacke Arch (*Anything Else*)
31. Alvy and Annie people-watch (*Annie Hall*) and Alice meets Joe (*Alice*), Central Park Zoo
32. Melinda, Laurel, and Cassie talk, Bow Bridge (Mid-Park at 74th Street) (*Melinda and Melinda*)
33. Ike and Mary go boating, Boating Lake (*Manhattan*)
34. Mickey talks to a Hare Krishna, Sheep Meadow (*Hannah and Her Sisters*)
35. Mel's movie set, Bethesda Terrace (*Deconstructing Harry*)

MIDTOWN

36. Ike and Yale talk about the future, Rizzoli Bookstore, 31 West 57th Street (between 5th & 6th Avenues) (*Manhattan*)
37. Alvy buys Annie books, Doubleday bookstore, 724 Fifth Avenue between 56th & 57th (*Annie Hall*)
38. Holden buys a ring, Harry Winston, 718 5th Avenue and West 56th Street (*Everyone Says I Love You*)
39. Danny's apartment, 200 West 54th Street and 7th Avenue (*Broadway Danny Rose*)
40. Fielding helps a driver park, East 54th Street and 1st Avenue (*Bananas*)
41. Jerry and Dobel eat lunch, Stage Deli, 834 7th Avenue and West 53rd Street (*Anything Else*)
42. Nicole's movie premiere, Ziegfeld Theatre, 141 West 54th Street and 6th Avenue (*Celebrity*)
43. Benny's apartment, Washington Jefferson Hotel, 318 West 51st Street and 8th Avenue (*Small Time Crooks*)
44. Hypnotist Show, Rainbow Room, Floor 64, 30 Rockefeller Plaza (*Curse of the Jade Scorpion*)
45. Ike and Jill argue about her book, Rockefeller Center, West 50th Street and 6th Avenue (*Manhattan*)
46. Little Joe and Bea's day in the city, Radio City Music Hall, 1260 Avenue of the Americas and 50th Street (*Radio Days*)
47. Danny gets dumped, Waldorf Astoria Hotel, 301 Park Avenue (between East 49th & 50th Street) (*Broadway Danny Rose*)
48. Ben's daughter's wedding, Waldorf Astoria Hotel, 301 Park Avenue (between East 49th & 50th Street) (*Crimes and Misdemeanors*)
49. Olive's apartment, Edison Hotel, 228 West 47th Street and 7th Avenue (*Bullets Over Broadway*)
50. Lee gets drunk after losing a role, Joe Allen, 326 West 46th Street and 8th Avenue (*Melinda and Melinda*)
51. Little Joe gets a chemistry set, Macy's, 151 West 34th Street (between 6th and 7th Avenues) (*Radio Days*)

52. Larry and Carol go to a hockey game, Madison Square Garden, 4 Pennsylvania Plaza (8th Avenue & 33rd Street) (*Manhattan Murder Mystery*)
53. Carol and Ted walk and talk, Gramercy Park, between 20th and 21st street (between Third and Park Avenue) (*Manhattan Murder Mystery*)
54. Carol and Ted's wine tasting, National Arts Club, 15 Gramercy Park South (*Manhattan Murder Mystery*)

DOWNTOWN

55. Alvy and Annie meet, Wall Street Racquet Club, South Street at Piers 13 & 14 (*Annie Hall*)
56. Jerry and Amanda go to the movies, Quad Cinema, 34 West 13th Street (between 5th and 6th Avenues) (*Anything Else*)
57. Hobie goes to the movies with Stacey, Cinema Village, 22 East 12th Street and 5th Avenue (*Melinda and Melinda*)
58. David's apartment, 43 East 5th Avenue and 11th Street (*Small Time Crooks*)
59. Alvy and Annie's first kiss, 9 Greenwich Avenue between 10th and Christopher Streets (*Annie Hall*)
60. Melody meets Perry, East 10th Street and Stuyvesant Street (*Whatever Works*)
61. Elliot and Lee browse for books, Pageant Book & Print Shop, 109 East 9th Street and 3rd Avenue (*Hannah and Her Sisters*)
62. Alvy and Annie break up and Alvy talks to passerby, West 4th Street between MacDougal Street & Sixth Avenue (*Annie Hall*)
63. Ray, Frenchy, and David walk and talk, Washington Square North and Waverly Place (*Small Time Crooks*)
64. Lee meets Nola at midnight, Franklin Street Subway and West Broadway (*Celebrity*)
65. Cliff and Jenny's favorite movie theater, Bleecker Street Cinema, 144 Bleecker Street and LaGuardia Place (*Crimes and Misdemeanors*)
66. Ike and Tracy eat pizza, John's Pizzeria, 278 Bleecker Street and Jones Street (*Manhattan*)
67. Boris and friends talk, Caffe Vivaldi, 32 Jones Street and Bleecker Street (*Whatever Works*)
68. Val and Lori bump into Ellie and Hal, Balthazar Restaurant, 80 Spring Street and Crosby Street (*Hollywood Ending*)
69. Boris and Melody get a knish, Yonah Schimmel Knish Bakery, 137 East Houston Street and Forsyth Street (*Whatever Works*)
70. Marion bumps into Claire, Cherry Lane Theatre, 38 Commerce Street and Bedford Street (*Another Woman*)
71. Alvy tells Annie he "lurvs" her (*Annie Hall*) and Ginger and Augie go sightseeing (*Blue Jasmine*), South Street Seaport
72. Boris and Melody get married, courthouse, 1 Centre Street (*Whatever Works*)

BROOKLYN

73. Alvy's childhood home, under the Thunderbolt, Coney Island (*Annie Hall*)

QUEENS

74. Little Joe's home, Beach 115th Street off Rockaway Boulevard, Rockaway (*Radio Days*)
75. Woody's favorite studio: Kaufman Astoria studios, 34-12 36th Street, Long Island City (*Shadows and Fog, Radio Days*, and many others)

Stardust Memories

RELEASE DATE: September 25, 1980

WRITER: Woody Allen

CAST: Allen, Charlotte Rampling, Jessica Harper, Marie-Christine Barrault, Tony Roberts, Laraine Newman

IN A NUTSHELL: Comedy director Sandy Bates, frustrated by his failed attempts to make serious films, reassesses his life during a weekend retreat for movie lovers.

RECURRING THEMES: Celebrity; obsession with death ("I will trade that Oscar for one more moment of life"); filmmaking and filmmakers; magic; anti-authoritarianism; younger women; neurotic actresses; kamikaze women; Groucho idolatry (a still from *A Night at the Opera* is, at one point, Sandy's wallpaper); God (or lack thereof); Judaism; art vs. life; past vs. present

In February 1973, Woody Allen was driven an hour north of Manhattan to Tarrytown, where he was the guest of honor at one of several film weekends organized by Judith Crist, critic for *New York* magazine. "I thought, this would be such a funny idea," he later said. "A guy who was going away on a film weekend and everybody up there is asking me for autographs and asking me if I'll help them with this and will I read this and can I do this, and I'm completely out of my depth and over my head. I'm up there doing the best I can as a favor to Judith Crist, who I liked very much, and I thought that would make a funny movie."

That instinct was right, but *Stardust Memories* has more on its mind than merely being "a funny movie." It opens with a ghostly quiet, starkly stylized black-and-white sequence in which our hero finds himself on a grim railway car filled with terrifying passengers. Across the tracks, the beautiful people are laughing, drinking, and carrying on. Once again, Woody is repulsed by the kind of club that would have someone like him for a member.

But the sequence is revealed as a scene from the new picture by Allen's character, Sandy Bates, and the studio types are not pleased. "I thought this was supposed to be a comedy!" bleats one. "He's not funny anymore!" says another. Sandy, for his part, doesn't care. The world is too bleak to make funny movies anymore. "I don't feel funny!" he says. "I look around the world, and all I see is human suffering!"

When we look around his world, all we see is the grotesque. *Stardust Memories* marks a return to black and white, but the look of the film is worlds away from *Manhattan*. That previous film's cinematography had a glistening beauty, where here Gordon Willis uses a baroque style—blinding lights, hard shadows, tight closeups—to emphasize the fact that everyone around Sandy, from his employees to

> " ....
>
> You wanna do mankind a real service? Tell funnier jokes.
>
> —Og
>
> .... "

Stardust Memories

Woody Allen as disillusioned filmmaker Sandy Bates—not, he insists, as disillusioned filmmaker Woody Allen. *Lobby card from the Voyageur Press Collection*

his fans, looks just a little off. Their faces are grim and gaunt or round and fat; every pair of glasses seems constructed from Coke bottles.

A picture speaks a thousand words, and it may well have been these gawking, giant images of freakish followers and sycophants, more than the autobiographical details of his struggle to tackle serious topics, that fostered the perception that *Stardust Memories* is the nakedly hostile gesture of a filmmaker who has all but had it with those who love his work. Allen disagreed: "The audience in the movie was just an exaggerated depiction of what somebody who couldn't appreciate his success might imagine under the pressure of being a hit and yet still being unable to stave off life's tragedies or have a good love relationship." In other words, sure, that's how a guy struggling with his station as an artist might see his audience, but hey, I'm not *that* guy!

The other, and perhaps more credible, explanation for the way in which Woody/ Sandy presents the world around him is a simple one: As critics noted immediately and have reiterated since, *Stardust Memories* is a self-conscious riff on Federico Fellini's 8½, another gorgeously stylized tale of a filmmaker in crisis, and those are exactly the kinds of faces Maestro Fellini showcases. The Fellini influence may have also led Allen to experiment with his most surrealistic and abstract filmmaking to date. The shuffled chronology, flash cut-ins, and flights of fancy seem awfully close to the original version of *Anhedonia* before it was scaled back to the relatively more straightforward *Annie Hall*—except this time Allen went through with it. He plays with the subjective camera in both the scenes of Sandy's arrival and his first conversation with Dorrie (Charlotte Rampling), and in both, he steps out of that subjective frame and becomes part of the scene. The picture also contains some of Allen's most daring intertwining of fantasy and reality, most notably in the big reveal of the cast and crew watching the film (and critiquing it, of course) at its conclusion.

Woody on Woody

"I still maintained for years that it was my favorite movie because I was just being honest. I felt I had set out to make a certain kind of movie and had made it, and whether I had a blind spot or not, I felt it worked. . . . Maybe it worked for no one but me."

Sharon Stone made her film debut as one of the "beautiful people" across the platform from Woody's character in his grim train car. Director Allen and cinematographer Gordon Willis are at left in the photo. *Brian Hamill/ Getty Images*

It's Allen's most dreamlike filmscape, fantastical images intermingling with flatly realistic ones, the present cueing the past cueing the fictional. Allen has a perfectly logical explanation for this cohabitation. "It's a dream film," he told Eric Lax. "He sees the dead rabbit on the kitchen table and as he looks at it, the sight of death leads him to a series of thoughts. From then on, the whole film takes place in his mind. It's shot in exaggerated form because it's in the mind."

Of course, that admission doesn't mean that we can take everything he says about the film at face value, or that we can't come away from it with other readings. Allen seems to predict the chatter about an 8½ influence right there in the movie; when a fan asks Sandy about homage (and gives his buddy a self-satisfied wink), Tony (Tony Roberts) responds, "An homage? Not exactly. We just stole the idea outright."

Allen insisted that Sandy's struggle to make serious movies was a "total fabrication," since he had no such difficulties with the carte blanche-granting United Artists execs, but the lines he has the studio executives deliver in the film weren't pulled from thin air. "He's pretentious," complains the studio executive Walsh about Sandy's work. "His filming style is too fancy. His insights are shallow and morbid. I've seen it all before. They try to document their private suffering and fob it off as art."

The suits in charge of *Interiors* might not have made such complaints, but other people did. When *Stardust Memories* was released, Pauline Kael wrote, "If Woody Allen finds success very upsetting and wishes the public would go away, this picture should help him stop worrying." That's overstating it—maybe. But this would be the first of many Allen films that made its money in Europe rather than in the United States. Perhaps, subconsciously or not, Allen was happy to shed those who wanted him to keep grinding away in the same vein. Free of their expectations, he was ready to begin the most fruitful and versatile period of his career.

WATCH OUT FOR

Sharon Stone—in her film debut— blowing Woody a kiss across the trains.

Dreams in Black and White

"He's very arty, pretentious.
One of those assholes who shoots
all his films in black and white."
—Tony Gardella (Joe Mantegna), *Celebrity*

The thematic explanation for Woody Allen's decision to shoot *Manhattan* in black and white—the first time he ever made that call—is provided in Ike's opening voice-over about the city of its setting: "No matter what the season was, this was still a town that existed in black and white and pulsated to the great tunes of George Gershwin." *Manhattan* is a visualization of that ethos, and one that asks us to consider the contradictions of Ike's statement. The film is set in the present, but it filters Woody's world through the past—this was *still* a town that was in black and white, and for Allen, black and white doesn't just symbolize the past but all that was wonderful *about* the past. By lensing the picture in such a way, F. X. Feeney notes, Allen creates a "nostalgia for the present."

For Allen, the decision to use black and white is not schematic or intellectualized; it's organic, the way the material feels. *Manhattan*, *Broadway Danny Rose*, and *Celebrity* were all originally conceived in black and white. "To me, whether a film is in black and white or color is of no import," he told Eric Lax. "Hundreds of the films you've loved in your life are in black and white, hundreds are in color. It's one kind of aesthetic you're using when you tell your story."

What's striking, when considering the films for which he's used that aesthetic, is how Allen has (with the exception of *Shadows and Fog*) dodged the traditional thinking that monochromatic photography is strictly for films *set* in the past. Modern-day black and white films such as *Schindler's List*, *Good Night and Good Luck*, and *The Man Who Wasn't There* use the look to trigger the feel of an earlier era, and pictures such as *The Artist* and *The Good German* include it in their toolbox to explicitly re-create the film styles of the time. But Allen's period pictures, from *The Purple Rose of Cairo* and *Radio Days* to *Sweet and Lowdown* and *Curse of the Jade Scorpion*, don't make that easy play. As Allen notes, he prefers to invoke the past with "cartoon-like costumes and amber lights and red velvet," which "just has a beautiful, nostalgic feel to it."

The decision to shoot without color is often, it seems, less motivated by the setting of the film than by the pictures that inspired it. Of *Broadway Danny Rose*, Allen said, "I saw that as a black-and-white Italian comedy. And that's probably why I made it in black and white." It also seems reasonable to conclude that he just "saw" *Stardust Memories* in the black and white of the similarly themed *8½*, and ditto *Celebrity* to *La Dolce Vita*.

As of this writing, Allen hasn't made a black and white picture since 1998's *Celebrity*, whose box office failure was partially blamed on the general audience's indifference to the monochromatic style. Not that Allen buys that excuse: "Some segments of the audience just won't go to see black and white; they think it's inferior or you don't have enough money for color, or they just don't like black and white. Yet that's not the audience I want anyway. I figure I'm better off without them."

A Midsummer Night's Sex Comedy

RELEASE DATE: July 16, 1982

WRITER: Woody Allen

CAST: Allen, Mia Farrow, José Ferrer, Julie Hagerty, Tony Roberts, Mary Steenburgen

IN A NUTSHELL: Three couples spend a weekend in the country before one is to be wed; complications (and new pairings) ensue.

RECURRING THEMES: Infidelity; magic; obsession with death (in a lighter way—Maxwell's profession leads him to see so much death that he chooses to live for the moment); sexless relationships

It was the spring of 1981, and Woody Allen had some time on his hands. He'd just finished the script for *Zelig*, an ambitious mock documentary, and was waiting around for the (more complex than usual) budget numbers and production details. "I had nothing to do," he recalled, "and I was home and I thought, 'Wouldn't it be fun to do just some little tiny summer picture?'" So in two weeks, he knocked out a modest pastoral, drawing inspiration from Bergman's *Smiles of a Summer Night* and Shakespeare's *A Midsummer Night's Dream*. "I thought it would be fun to get some people in a country house and just celebrate summer, and make it very beautiful, with butterfly nets and badminton courts and picnicking and butterflies." When the picture was released the following summer, critics summarily dismissed it as lightweight piffle. It is that—purposefully. This is Woody making a modest, sweet little charmer, in contrast to the ambition of the films bookending it.

And if Allen's aim was to "make it very beautiful," the picture is a resounding success. Gordon Willis's picturesque, sun-kissed country photography is gorgeous throughout, with a couple of the Mendelssohn-and-nature montages amounting to a rustic reimagining of the "Rhapsody in Blue" sequence in *Manhattan*. As their first color film since *Interiors*, it also provides a hint of the exquisite warmth that will define Allen's subsequent color pictures. And by now, the scenes shot "all-in-one" are more the rule than the exception (in one scene, Allen leaves his closeup and Mary Steenburgen takes his seat in the same shot, without a cut), though Allen will occasionally break into coverage for more intimate conversations.

A Midsummer Night's Sex Comedy is very much an actor's showcase, more so than the

> " We can't have intercourse where we eat oatmeal! . . . There's a man in the other room singing the Lord's Prayer! We'll go blind!
> —Andrew "

flashy *Stardust* or the forthcoming *Zelig*. This is the first time Woody is part of an ensemble, rather than the lead—though, yes, he does give himself most of the best lines. And that's the direction he would continue to follow in *Radio Days*, *Hannah and Her Sisters*, and *Crimes and Misdemeanors*, among others. He's terrific, finding the gentle sight gags in his character's wobbly inventions and scoring one of the film's biggest laughs with his way-overdone reaction to the arrival of Ariel (Mia Farrow) and the revelation that they know each other. Steenburgen is a good match, particularly in the late scenes where she goes after him sexually with a stubborn, forceful single-mindedness. José Ferrer is appropriately stuffy, while Julie Hagerty is dizzy and delightful. And this may be the best work Tony Roberts (named "Maxwell"—shades of *Annie Hall*) ever did for Allen. His desperation and lovesickness give him the chance to play a juicy variation on his usual laidback observer.

But the key new cast member of note is Farrow, who had recently become Mr. Allen's off-screen romantic interest. Unsurprisingly, he originally wrote the role for Diane Keaton, but she was too busy with *Reds* and *Shoot the Moon* to take it on, so Woody broke his usual rule and cast a current paramour as his leading lady. She'd influenced the script greatly; as biographer John Baxter notes, the film plays less like one written by a man in love than one "written by a man who found himself in love and distrusted the feeling profoundly." On screen, the duo have a sweet, unforced chemistry, and right away he subverts the pixieish purity that plagued Farrow's film persona, casting her as an unabashedly (and unashamedly) sexual creature. This was just the beginning of the versatility she would reveal in their decade-long collaboration.

Woody on Woody

"I wanted it to be light. I just wanted it to be a small intermezzo with a few laughs. I don't say this was a great picture at all, but in general this atmosphere is something that nobody cares about here in the United States. For me it was fine. I had a great time doing it."

In her first Woody Allen role, as Ariel, Mia Farrow demonstrated her acting range and her onscreen chemistry with her off-screen love interest. *Orion/Getty Images*

Zelig

RELEASE DATE: July 15, 1983

WRITER: Woody Allen

CAST: Allen, Mia Farrow

IN A NUTSHELL: A cleverly contrived "documentary" account of Leonard Zelig, the "human chameleon" who fascinated the world in the 1920s and 1930s with his ability to blend in with those around him.

RECURRING THEMES: Celebrity; psychoanalysis; rabbi as punch line; Judaism; infidelity; art vs. life (Zelig's escape "was nothing like it happened in the movie," *The Changing Man*)

Woody Allen's run of outright masterpieces, a five-year, five-film stretch of perfect motion pictures seldom matched in American cinema, began with a bang. *Zelig* was his most technically challenging picture to date, a fictional story told in documentary style. But he wasn't merely using nonfiction as a narrative framework, a la *Take the Money and Run*. This was a painstakingly constructed period documentary, in which Allen, cinematographer Gordon Willis, editor Susan E. Morse, and a team of effects experts created utterly convincing footage that not only re-created the 1920s and '30s, but inserted Allen's character of Leonard Zelig into existing footage from the era.

When *Zelig* was released in summer of 1983, those technical innovations—which involved use of vintage lenses and cameras, detailed re-creation of locations and costumes, and careful distressing of new footage to look weathered and aged—were the primary focus of its coverage. Allen, ever the contrarian, insisted, "the technical part of *Zelig* was not hard. . . . We'd turn on the kind of lights the newsreel would have and shoot. So the technical part of it and making it look old was not hard."

In other interviews, he did admit that it was, if nothing else, a time-consuming process (the months he spent watching documentary footage and revising the script for promising clips help explain the uncharacteristic two-year gap between *Stardust Memories* and *Midsummer Night's Sex Comedy*). But he's correct in suggesting that too much attention was paid to the picture's mechanical elements, at the expense of its remarkable thematic and narrative achievements. "*Zelig* got a very positive response here critically," he said, a decade or so later, "but the

For the Ku Klux Klan, Leonard Zelig, a Jew that could turn himself into a Negro and an Indian, was a triple threat.

—Narrator

content of the film has not even to this day been evaluated properly. . . . The technique was fine. I mean, it was fun to do, and it was a small accomplishment, but it was the content of the film that interested me."

The subtext was far richer than your average '80s comedy. "I wanted to make a comment with the film on the specific danger of abandoning one's true self," Allen explained, "in an effort to be liked, not to make trouble, to fit in, and where that leads one in life in every aspect and where that leads on a political level." *Zelig* also marks a continuation of *Stardust*'s examination of the disparity between celebrity and identity. Leonard Zelig becomes famous and beloved for what he is rather than who he is (which is, through much of the film, a void). Fame is not Zelig's goal, but his other aim—to be accepted, to be liked, even to be loved—isn't that far from the aim of a performer like Woody Allen himself, who constructed a persona with which to ingratiate himself to the public.

However, *Zelig* is most intriguing to consider as Allen's most explicit portrait of the Jewish experience. It's an undercurrent that has run throughout his work, but usually as an easy joke at the expense of an overbearing mother or an Orthodox rabbi. Yet Irving Howe's commentary within the film itself is spot-on; this is a story of assimilation, of hiding what is individualistic in order to fit in with the herd, to draw attention away from that which makes him unique (and thus dangerous) by melting into whatever amorphous cultural mass is nearby. And in the film's most brilliant logical curlicue, that's what leads his Jewish hero to join the Nazis. "Fascism offered Zelig that kind of an opportunity," the narrator explains. Allen's characters often share his anti-authoritarian streak, but in *Zelig*, he imagines someone who leans clear in the other direction, who smothers his own identity to please those around him.

Likewise, therapy and psychoanalysis—perhaps the only topic Allen has considered comparably fertile comic soil to Judaism—is not only taken seriously, but trumpeted. It is the dedication of psychiatrist Dr. Eudora Nesbitt Fletcher (Mia Farrow) and the brilliance of her technique that saves Zelig's mind, and his life. The moment when she turns the tables on him, about halfway into the

"It was one of my more successful films. Successful meaning that I had a vision of something and I brought it off."

Leonard Zelig pictured with presidents Calvin Coolidge (left) and Herbert Hoover (right). *Lobby card from the Voyageur Press Collection*

COPYRIGHT © 1983 BY ORION PICTURES COMPANY/WARNER BROS. INC. (ALL RIGHTS RESERVED) CONSENT IS HEREBY GIVEN TO NEWSPAPERS AND MAGAZINES TO REPRODUCE. COUNTRY OF ORIGIN U.S.A. IMPRIME AUX ETATS-UNIS D'AMERIQUE

'ZELIG' WOODY ALLEN

film, is when it stops being a lark and becomes a genuine, if unconventional, narrative. This is smart; Allen knows he can only coast on the gimmick so long. And it's in that second half that *Zelig* truly achieves greatness, because he keeps the artifice intact and tells the secondary story of their romance entirely in the background and as subtext.

Allen fills out the film with interview testimonials, both by known commentators playing themselves and unknowns playing characters in the story. But actors don't fill even the latter roles, and the hesitancy of these "civilians" is infinitely more convincing than the smooth delivery typical of polished actors. Farrow, for her part, makes the brilliant choice to make Dr. Fletcher ill at ease on camera, halting in her delivery and never quite comfortable in the spotlight.

She is only at home in the sessions, and the use of those sequences is a masterstroke. It also came out of necessity. Allen was determined not to cheat, to only create footage that could conceivably exist from his characters' public lives. "You can only show them walking up steps or going into cars or at a banquet," he explained. But there was a problem: "When I finally put it all together, the movie was forty-five minutes. I couldn't stretch out the newsreel and documentary shots because I was unable to do scenes between people." So he hatched the "White Room Sessions," where his camera eavesdrops on Zelig and Dr. Fletcher's sessions, providing a window (literally) into those private interactions.

Dr. Eudora Fletcher first cures then falls in love with the chameleon-like Leonard Zelig. *Orion/Getty Images*

Miraculously, it all works. The editing and immersion is astonishing, culminating in one of Woody's greatest onscreen moments: waving to Eudora from the platform of a Nazi rally, totally upstaging the Fuehrer. The little touches of authenticity (the fuzz on the original songs, the way the on-the-street interview subjects talk just a little too loudly, the popping and skipped frames of the "archival" footage) are spot-on. The parodies of documentary convention (like the newsreel interview with Eudora's wholly uncooperative mother) are uproarious. And the picture's not a moment too long at seventy-nine minutes. *Zelig* is sheer perfection.

Woody the Mockumentarian

"I thought it was an ideal vehicle for doing comedy, because the documentary format was very serious, so you were immediately operating in an area where any little thing you did upset the seriousness and was thereby funny."

—Woody Allen

I started my career doing a documentary," Woody Allen said in 2005, and it's one of the stylistic constants of an ever-evolving career: the idea of telling stories via the scaffolding of the faux-documentary form. In *Take the Money and Run*, Woody sends up the new vogue for news-related documentaries, using talking-head interviews, archival footage, and a stern-voiced narrator to tell the story of bumbling bank robber Virgil Starkwell (while also calling upon those devices to smooth over the rough edges of this early effort).

Three years later, he returned to the form for the one Woody Allen movie that's never seen a television airing or video release—in fact, it's only been seen by a handful of PBS execs and those who make the pilgrimage to The Paley Center for Media in New York or Los Angeles. *Men of Crisis: The Harvey Wallinger Story* is a brilliantly funny short film, made for PBS, with Allen as a Henry Kissinger–inspired advisor to President Nixon. The program was pulled at the eleventh hour, in fear that a satire of the administration would adversely affect the funding for public television. But it remains a droll, ingenious film, using clever juxtapositions (Allen cuts from footage of George Wallace defending himself to a shot of his audience: all Klansmen), selective archival pulls (clips of Nixon using the "him" pronoun about Kissinger make it seem like he's talking about Wallinger), and photographic tricks (Allen is pasted into a photo of Nixon's inauguration) to create a "real" documentary about a fictional character.

In other words, it was a decade-earlier dry run for *Zelig*. When Allen made his acclaimed 1983 "mockumentary," he wasn't interested in the technical innovations and post-production wizardry that so many of its reviews focused on—the newsreel footage, masterfully re-created with vintage equipment and aged by hand. He wanted to tell a real story, an honest-to-goodness romance, but within the boundaries of the documentary form. Due to those limitations, he explained, "We didn't have access to the private lives of the real people Zelig is shown with." Some of these constraints are used for comic effect (e.g., the long, wide, distant shot of his fistfight with the doctors). But the "raw footage" from Eudora Fletcher's sessions with Zelig, wherein she treats the man while simultaneously falling in love with him, uses the documentary form for narrative ends: it's film that would exist for one purpose but, within the context of the narrative, serves another.

Allen returned to the form in 1992 when he adopted a rough, *cinéma vérité* style, complete with talking-head interviews and an omniscient narrator, for *Husbands and Wives*. He later modified it somewhat by employing doc-style "experts" to augment the otherwise traditional *Sweet and Lowdown*. At the base level he describes, the documentary does inspire richly comic possibilities; the pomposity of the form allows parody and social satire, the hyper-serious narration bringing ironic counterpoint to onscreen action (in *Zelig* and *Take the Money*). But Allen also uses the form, and its inherent "truth," against itself—manipulating filmed "reality" to create the fictional Leonard Zelig, most obviously. And if his fake documentaries tell the truth even when their characters don't (such as in the matter of Jack and his hookers in *Husbands*), they're also capable of the opposite, such as the so-called experts who are blissfully unaware of reality but tell their versions of stories with utter certainty (the much-debated resolution to the gas station story in *Sweet and Lowdown*). Woody Allen knows that even in the seemingly unimpeachable documentary form, a story is only as reliable as the one who's telling it.

Broadway Danny Rose

RELEASE DATE: January 27, 1984

WRITER: Woody Allen

CAST: Allen, Mia Farrow, Nick Apollo Forte, Milton Berle

IN A NUTSHELL: A group of aging comics and show-biz insiders tell their favorite stories about Danny Rose, legendary bottom-rung New York talent agent.

RECURRING THEMES: Show business; organized crime; celebrity; infidelity; standup comedy; magic (particularly his client the hypnotist)

Most of Woody Allen's films begin with a concept. *Broadway Danny Rose* began with a character. He and Mia Farrow often ate at Rao's, a famed uptown Italian eatery, and they were fascinated by Mrs. Rao, "a great character" who had big blond hair, wore sunglasses, and always wielded a cigarette between her fingers. "Mia mentioned it would be fun to play that kind of woman—just to try, and I took her seriously," Allen told the *New York Times*. "I'd always wanted to do something about that whole milieu, and when she mentioned that, one thing led to another in my mind over a period of time and it sort of fell into place." Farrow also drew some inspiration for the character from her time spent with those who circled her first husband, Frank Sinatra.

Most of the film's acclaim, initially and in the years since, focused on Mia's miraculous transformation into the brassy gangster's moll Tina Vitale—and deservedly so. She's all but unrecognizable, with her thick accent and pile of bleached-blond hair and extra weight ("I rounded her out with a little padding," Allen confessed) and giant shades, which are removed only in the rare moments when she softens up (while discussing her dreams of decorating, or in a moment of doubt at the bathroom mirror). The sunglasses are both prop and protection, which Farrow used to create a tough exterior and keep out the vulnerability that defined so much of her screen work. But there was a flip side; as Woody pointed out, "she had to act without using her eyes." Considering

> " If you take my advice, you'll become one of the great balloon-folding acts of all time. Really, 'cause I don't just see you folding balloons in joints. You listen to me, you're gonna fold balloons in universities and colleges.
>
> —Danny Rose "

In a true departure from type, Mia Farrow played a brash, tough character, while Woody takes on the role of a sleazy, tacky agent always looking for an angle. *Lobby card from the Voyageur Press Collection*

what an indispensable tool the eyes are for any actor, the achievement is all the more impressive.

She's not the only one doing new things here. On one hand, this is the most exaggerated variation on Allen's regular character: big gestures, wild vocalization, "Woody" at his broadest and funniest. But he's also playing beyond the bounds of his usual neurotic New York intellectual. Danny is a bit of a lowlife, a fast-talker clad in loud jackets and the smallest of gold chains, throwing around words like "didactic" and "facetious" incorrectly, constantly working an angle. He's a rogue, but a lovable one. We laugh at his sleaziness, yet feel sympathy for the poor lug, particularly when the director walks him into a tight closeup at the moment when he finds out exactly what all his hard work for client Lou Canova (Nick Apollo Forte) is going to get him.

As usual, Gordon Willis's black-and-white photography is used for nostalgia, not for period. *Broadway Danny Rose* is a contemporary picture, but one filled with remnants of a bygone era: the crooning of Lou, the clowning of Milton Berle (whom Woody had met as a kid in his favorite magic shop), the novelty acts in Danny's office, and the comics and kibitzers talking shop in the Carnegie Deli. Among them is Woody's manager and producer, Jack Rollins; biographer Eric Lax surmised that *Broadway Danny Rose* is a "valentine" to Rollins and his partner Charles H. Joffe. Woody knew their world well—he had spent many of those long nights at the Carnegie himself as a young comic, getting tips and hearing stories. (There's a throwaway reference to Weinstein's Majestic Bungalow Colony, where young Woody made his first-ever appearance as a performer, doing magic.)

But Rollins was a much higher roller than Danny Rose. If anyone, the character was inspired by Harvey Meltzer, the garment salesman and would-be agent who first represented Allen. Woody's love of that era and of the men who lived through it is all over this wild, affectionate picture, his most raucous comedy since *Love and Death* and still one of his warmest and funniest films.

Woody on Woody

"I can play a seedy character. I could play a good bookmaker. I could play a Runyonesque character. . . . And *Broadway Danny Rose* was an opportunity for me to play that kind of character."

The Purple Rose of Cairo

RELEASE DATE: March 1, 1985

WRITER: Woody Allen

CAST: Mia Farrow, Jeff Daniels, Danny Aiello, Stephanie Farrow

IN A NUTSHELL: A movie-crazy housewife in Depression-era New Jersey escapes her grim life by spending all her time at the movies, but things get complicated when one of the actors notices her in the audience, and steps out to join her.

RECURRING THEMES: Art vs. life; celebrity; filmmaking and filmmakers ("So that's what popcorn tastes like! I've been watching people eat it for all those performances. . ."); actors and acting; magic realism; infidelity; class; prostitution ("I'd be surprised if all you ladies weren't married soon. Especially by the way you dress. It's so seductive to a man!")

For Cecilia (Mia Farrow), it's not just the movies that offer an escape—it's the mere promise of them. In the opening scene of *The Purple Rose of Cairo*, she stands in front of her neighborhood movie house, staring agog at the poster for that week's attraction. She's caught up in the idea of its music and glamour, and the theater manager promises her, "You're gonna like this one. It's better than last week's. More romantic!" She knows all the stars, their backstories and romances, and when she comes to the theater, the ticket seller and concession girl know her by name.

Her brief vacations from reality are understandable. She's got a lousy job as a diner waitress, which she supplements by doing laundry. Meanwhile, her no-good bum of a husband is unemployed, shoots craps all day, and drinks and smacks her around all night. In the middle of the Depression, she can only imagine a life of martinis and dinner at the Copa and the other pleasures of a white telephone, "drinks, anyone?" picture like *The Purple Rose of Cairo*. But the fantasy is vivid enough that when Tom Baxter, one of its characters, notices her watching the movie for a fifth time, he can't help but stop the movie and join her.

The tension between fiction and reality is one of Woody Allen's favorite topics, but he seldom addresses it as directly or as effectively as in *Purple Rose*. From the contrast of madcap music to the events on screen—a jazzy song follows a serious fight between Cecilia and her husband Monk, and another one is used as score when Cecilia and Tom visit a soup line—to its observation of audiences in the Great Depression eating up these fluffy stories of the idle rich, the film is a subtle commentary on the idea of cinema as escape. (That we're also watching these events adds an additional, unspoken layer of meta-commentary.) And while Allen's early comedies scored laughs

> I just met a wonderful man. Fictional, but you can't have everything.
>
> —Cecilia

LA ROSE POURPRE
DU CAIRE

The Jewel Theater provided
Cecilia with a fantasy getaway,
until that fantasy entered her
world. *Lobby card from the
Voyageur Press Collection*

by surprising us with the intersection of incongruous worlds—the screaming drill sergeant in *Love and Death*, the deli order for the rebel army in *Bananas*—that becomes the entire subject of *Purple Rose*.

As such, Allen's screenplay is a marvel of comic efficiency, in which each variation on the gag is considered and intricately worked out. After stepping off the screen, Tom Baxter must reconcile his world with the real one: his money is fake, cars require keys, and kisses aren't followed by a fade out. Once those jokes are told, Allen introduces the character of actor Gil Shepherd, who created the role. This turn introduces both the tension between man and character and the notion of the smugly self-satisfied actor, full of babble about his "early work" and the influence of his dialogue coach, whose grilling of Cecilia is easily sidetracked by her compliments. And the second that deviation hints of sputtering out, Allen flips the whole scenario by sending Cecilia into the film-within-the-film, and plays with that for a while.

Years after *Stardust Memories* was released, Allen explained that most of that movie took place in Sandy's head. It seems entirely possible that the same thing happens in *Purple Rose*, that its fantastical turns are all a daydream conjured up by Cecilia in the midst of her marathon, daylong trip to the picture at her lowest emotional point. In such a daydream, the handsome explorer from the fantasy world of celluloid could not only step out of the screen, but would make the trip specifically to rescue her; he would love her on sight and only have eyes for her, no matter what. "You kiss perfectly," he tells her. "It's what I *dreamed* kissing would be like."

And in that vision, the actor would also fall for her, a visitor from that magical land of Hollywood who would profess his love and promise to take her away to that perfect place. Given the choice, she understandably selects the real man rather than his fictional avatar, and the moment of Tom's rejection ("I'm devastated") is heartbreaking. But it is merely a warm-up for Cecilia's own crestfallen expression when she finds out that Gil has

The Spanish-language poster for *The Purple Rose of Cairo* depicts Tom Baxter coming through the screen to kiss Cecilia. *Poster from the Voyageur Press Collection*

"That's the closest I've come to a feeling of satisfaction. After that film I thought, 'Yes, this time I think I got it right where I wanted to get it.'"

left without her, that his endearments were a lie. The fantasy is over; she is stuck, with no love and nowhere to go. "I have to choose the real world," Cecilia has told Tom, and by the end of her daydream, that's exactly where she remains.

Its unconventional, unsentimental, and ultimately unhappy ending was, Woody later said, "the whole reason for *Purple Rose*." He got a phone call from Orion Pictures after its first test screenings, tentatively asking, "Is that definitely the ending?" But it was. "It would have been a trivial movie with the other ending," Woody said, and he's right. If the audience feels cheated by Cecilia's heartbreak, it is merely because we too have been seduced by the movies, our thinking skewed by the happy endings they promise.

But it's not all misery, of course. With nowhere else to go, Cecilia wanders back into the Jewel Theater, where Fred Astaire is singing "Cheek to Cheek" in *Top Hat*, and then he and Ginger Rogers dance. And it's all so lovely and inspiring that she can't help but get lost in it, her look of heartbreak slowly fading as she stares up at the screen in wonder. "Most movies about the movies are either giddy with nostalgia or grim with star-is-born melodrama," writes Richard Schickel. "*The Purple Rose of Cairo* alone tries to address the most basic way the medium works on us." They transport you, the movies, and for the next hour and half, poor Cecilia will go somewhere else, and be someone else, leaving her life and her troubles far, far away.

Mia Farrow

"She's just a very good, realistic actress, as opposed to someone like Diane Keaton who is a great comedian, who has a single personality, a very strong single personality. She's always the same, but always great. Like Katharine Hepburn. Mia is different all the time."

—Woody Allen

In April 1979, the *New York Times Magazine* ran a profile of Woody Allen, with a cover photo of him looking over Central Park from the terrace of his apartment. Mia Farrow cut it out and stuck it in a scrapbook; she thought he looked "interesting." The stories vary as to who actually introduced them, but the tidiest is that it was Michael Caine—whose *Hannah and Her Sisters* character would romance Lee, as Allen did Farrow, with the poems of e.e. cummings.

As we all well know, there was no Hollywood ending for Allen and Farrow. After more than a decade, their relationship would end in scandal, when Allen embarked on an affair with Farrow's adopted daughter, and in allegations of sexual abuse. No charges were filed in the latter, but he was no longer allowed to visit the children he'd adopted with Farrow, and he could only visit his biological son with a third party present. Those visits ceased in 1995. In the ensuing years, Farrow changed the children's names and insisted they sever all ties with their father.

Yet there is no denying the effect of Mia on his work, and vice versa. After the heights of *Peyton Place* and *Rosemary's Baby*, her career had stalled after *The Great Gatsby*. But Allen wrote for her an astonishing variety of rich, complex roles. Writing

Allen wrote many complex roles for Mia Farrow, including the character Judy Roth in his 1992 film *Husbands and Wives*. *Woody Allen Film Company Tristar 14, © AF archive / Alamy*

from the set of *Radio Days*, journalist Thierry de Navacelle observed, "You have a feeling that Woody is proud of her, and impressed by her, too." His desire to showcase Farrow's gifts combined with the desire to shift the focus from his own persona, and such masterpieces as *The Purple Rose of Cairo* and *Broadway Danny Rose* were born. (Shockingly, Farrow received not even an Academy Award nomination for her work in Woody's movies.)

Years after their ugly breakup, even after so much bad blood, Allen still speaks highly of her gifts. "Oh, she's wonderful," he told Richard Schickel in 2003. "I always thought she was underrated because she was raised in Hollywood and sort of taken for granted. But I found her to be a terrific actress with a very good range."

Hannah and Her Sisters

RELEASE DATE: February 7, 1986

WRITER: Woody Allen

CAST: Allen, Michael Caine, Mia Farrow, Carrie Fisher, Barbara Hershey, Lloyd Nolan, Maureen O'Sullivan, Daniel Stern, Max von Sydow, Dianne Wiest

IN A NUTSHELL: The romances, hopes, fears, and disappointments of a large New York family are glimpsed over the course of three Thanksgivings and the two years between them.

RECURRING THEMES: Infidelity; hypochondria; obsession with death; suicide; Judaism; morality; God (or lack thereof) ("How the hell do I know why there were Nazis? I don't know how the can opener works"); rock music hatred ("I had a great time tonight, really, it was like the Nuremberg trials"); television hatred; Groucho idolatry (*Duck Soup* saves Mickey's life); art vs. life; familial attraction; sibling rivalry; writers; frustrated artists

God, she's beautiful." These are the first words spoken (and the first of several intertitles, most of them pulled from dialogue) in *Hannah and Her Sisters*, heard in a voice-over by Elliot (Michael Caine), husband of Hannah (Mia Farrow), obsessed with her sister Lee (Barbara Hershey). That it is a voice-over is significant, because those inner monologues will dominate the picture—Hannah and Lee each get at least one of their own, as does third sister Holly (Dianne Wiest), and Hannah's ex-husband Mickey (Allen). The device is often the crutch of the lazy screen-writer, but it feels appropriate here; these neurotic and self-reflective Manhattanites can't get out of their own heads, and neither can we.

If Woody Allen wrote *Broadway Danny Rose* and *The Purple Rose of Cairo* to create great roles for Mia Farrow, *Hannah* seems like a trade-off, Farrow allowing Allen to mine her life for material as he had, for so long, his own. Her mother, legendary film actress Maureen O'Sullivan, played her mother in the film; her relationship with Evan (Lloyd Nolan) is somewhat inspired by that of O'Sullivan and Mia's father, director John Farrow. Farrow has three sisters, two of them actresses, both appearing in minor roles in Allen pictures (some connected Elliot's attraction to Lee with Woody's rumored flirtation with Mia's sister Tisa, who appeared in *Manhattan*). Her apartment doubled as Hannah's in the film—leading to the surreal experience of once happening upon the film on television and watching a scene on the screen in the room in which it was shot. And several of her adopted children pop up in nonspeaking roles, including Soon-Yi Previn.

With that in mind, it seems appropriate that the character of Holly is chastised so severely by Hannah for writing a play that is "obviously based on me and Elliot," filled with

> "For all my education, accomplishments, and so-called wisdom—I can't fathom my own heart.
> —Elliot

"intimate details" of their life. The scene is played straight, drawing on the real pain and anger of those who find their lives turned into the fodder of an artist (a theme that would return, most notably in *Deconstructing Harry*). But Allen also kids the notion, both with the delighted response of Holly and Hannah's mother ("I especially loved the character of the mother!") and his own character's inquisitiveness about how Holly "got the idea" of the brutal fictional murders of the friend and would-be beau who did her wrong.

In all this etymology of character and situation, there is one key question to consider about Farrow/Hannah herself: How genuine is she? "Hannah was a character neither Mia nor I understood at the start, and at the finish," Allen told Eric Lax. "Mia looked to me for guidance, and I could never give it to her. I could just say to her, 'Well, play this scene and let me see you play it instinctively and maybe I could change something.' But I'm in the dark a lot of times that way." His ambivalence is fascinating; here is a character who is, at least on the surface, very much like the woman who had been his lover for at least five years now, but he could not make a clear judgment of her nature and motives. Ultimately, that hesitancy is for the best, placing the character in a gray area between saint and passive-aggressive manipulator. (Her character in *Husbands and Wives* six years later was similarly malleable.) Later on, Woody would confess, "I think she's not so nice. If you look closely, she's not as nice as you imagine."

The story of sisters Holly (Diane Wiest), Lee (Barbara Hershey), and Hannah (Mia Farrow) brought in elements from Farrow's real life and combined them with some classic Allen film elements. *Orion/ Getty Images*

WATCH OUT FOR

Julia Louis-Dreyfus, John Turturro,
Lewis Black, and J. T. Walsh in the
backstage scene at Mickey's
TV show; Richard Jenkins (with
hair!) as the doctor he calls from
the phone booth.

It would be a mistake, of course, to view *Hannah* solely as Allen's take on the Farrow family. As a comic story with wrenchingly serious moments, it plays like a lighter take on *Interiors*, with the basic types of the three sisters revitalized: the grounded, successful one (Renata/Hannah), the troubled beauty (Finn/Lee), and the frustrated, neurotic artist (Joey/Holly). As with that film, Allen and cinematographer Carlo Di Palma—replacing Gordon Willis, who was unavailable—create compositions and camera movements to link the sisters physically as well as psychically, most memorably during a tense lunch scene shot in a series of 360-degree circular movements. It's a terrific flourish, capturing not only the flow of the dialogue, but the often-pained reactions of Hershey's Lee, who's agonizing over her affair with Hannah's husband.

Neither Elliot nor Frederick, the man Lee was cheating on, were intended to be played by foreign-born actors. But casting director Juliet Taylor suggested Bergman favorite

Michael Caine won his first Oscar for playing Elliot, who lusts for his sister-in-law Lee, played by Barbara Hershey.
Orion/Getty Images

Allen earned nominations for Best Director at the Academy Awards and the Golden Globes. He is seen here during filming of a scene in Central Park. *Brian Hamill/ Getty Images*

Max von Sydow—which of course delighted Allen—for the role of artist Frederick, while he realized Caine was a good choice for Elliot because "there is no American actor who could be a regular man who is an accountant." It's a wonderful performance, sensitively capturing the complexities of a man who can love his wife with all his heart while still desiring another woman to the point of distraction, and if his actions are unlikable, his natural charm (and the boyish thrill of his "I have my answer" scene) wins the audience over. And the Academy, for that matter, which rewarded Caine with a Best Supporting Actor statue and gave the Best Supporting Actress counterpart to Wiest. Allen's novelistic script won the Oscar for Best Original Screenplay, his first since *Annie Hall*.

Roger Ebert declared *Hannah* "the best movie he has ever made," while Charles Champlin called it "his warmest and most optimistic film," comparing the picture favorably to Bergman's *Fanny and Alexander*. It was a popular hit as well, Allen's first since *Manhattan*, and it remains one of his highest grossing pictures domestically (even before adjustment for inflation).

And maybe this was an accidental outcome, but it does seem curious that Woody followed his unhappiest movie ending with his happiest—though he would later insist, "The characters sort of *resign* themselves at the end. But people see this as great happiness!" Still, being Woody, he never forgave himself for that nod toward conventionality. "I copped out a little on that film, I backed out a little at the end," he later said of the third Thanksgiving scene, added in reshoots. "I tied it together at the end a bit too neatly. I should have been a little less happy at the end than I was." Yes, God forbid Woody should allow himself to get away happy.

"*Hannah and Her Sisters* is a film I feel I screwed up very badly, but people who like me choose to like my work."

Radio Days

RELEASE DATE: January 30, 1987

WRITER: Woody Allen

CAST: Mia Farrow, Julie Kavner, Michael Tucker, Dianne Wiest, Seth Green, Allen (narration only)

IN A NUTSHELL: Allen's memories of his childhood, via the songs and radio programs of the era.

RECURRING THEMES: Nostalgia ("Forgive me if I tend to romanticize the past—I mean, it wasn't always as stormy and rain-swept as this, but I remember it that way, because that was it at its most beautiful"); Brooklyn childhood ("We're poor but happy. But definitely poor"); celebrity; actors and acting; infidelity; Judaism; art vs. life; organized crime ("You know, this is a funny coincidence. I don't meet nobody from the old neighborhood in years. I finally do, and I gotta kill her")

O nce upon a time, many years ago," begins Woody's first voice-over for this memory film, the words casting it as not just a reminiscence but a fairy tale. This distinction is important, since even Allen will admit that *Radio Days* is one of his most autobiographical efforts. Though his onscreen avatar (played by Seth Green, in his first major role) is credited as "Joe," he's never called by that name in the film, and Allen's narrator gets no credit at all. The implicit assumption, from the personal nature of the narration, is that this is Woody's story, and much of it is taken from his childhood: the unemployable father's get-rich-quick schemes, the incident with the Communist neighbors, the uncle bringing home bags of fish, the dyeing of his mother's coat, even some of the names.

Whatever fascination *Radio Days* may hold as one of his few admitted autobiographies, there's much more to it than that. This is also one of his most purely pleasurable pictures, a tapestry of family situational humor, absurd stories, backstage comedy, and glorious music. Structurally, it's vignette-based, contrasting Allen's family in Rockaway with the glamorous celebrities broadcasting from Manhattan. The radio stars and most of their programs are fictional, though loosely based on fact, while real-world incidents—the *War of the Worlds* broadcast, the attack on Pearl Harbor, the attempted rescue of Kathy Fiscus (here renamed Polly Phelps)—are woven in.

Though Allen has never stooped to making a sequel to an earlier hit, *Radio Days* sometimes plays like a reworking of the childhood scenes in *Annie Hall*: the arguing parents, the classroom scenes, jokes about the "pretty" sister. Interestingly, the gags are sharper this time around. This is a riotously funny film, benefitting from the full range of Allen's comic gifts. The household scenes are cracklingly good

> Boy, what a world. It could be so wonderful, if it weren't for certain people.
> —Joe's mother

character—and insult—humor, Sally's (Mia Farrow) stories work as broad farce, and several of the blackout bits (like the opening scene with the burglars, or "Bill Kerns's Favorite Sports Legends") have the cuckoo humor of his best *New Yorker* casuals.

But the film has a serious streak, too. The confession of Bea's gay date isn't played for laughs but as quiet, understated melancholy, while the tragedy of Polly Phelps is rendered more moving by the way Allen cuts back to the Brooklyn family, the chaotic spanking disrupted, Martin now clutching his son tightly. Elsewhere, Allen allows his film to simply create a mood and resonate in it: the evocative sequence of little Joe's first visit to Radio City Music Hall (a scene that pulses with Allen's own feelings of falling in love with The City and the movies), the warm scene in which he recalls his parents' only kiss, the touching memory of Aunt Bea waking him up to ring in 1944.

In those scenes, and particularly the simple yet disarming ending, Allen is addressing what would become one of his primary preoccupations in the years to come: nostalgia. It seems no coincidence that so much of the *Radio Days* cast is drawn from earlier Allen films, and when they gather on that midtown rooftop on New Year's Eve, their concerns about being forgotten (because "after enough time, everything passes") could be his own. He knows as much, from the other side of the equation, as he notes with a bit of sadness in his final narration: "I've never forgotten any of those people, or any of the voices we used to hear on the radio. Although the truth is, with the passing of each New Year's Eve . . . those voices do seem to grow dimmer and dimmer."

WATCH OUT FOR
Larry David and William H. Macy, heard but barely seen as the Communist neighbor and the New Years' Eve announcer, respectively.

One of Allen's most personal films, *Radio Days* is a nostalgic look at a working-class family in New York in the 1940s. *Woody Allen Film Company MGM,* © *AF archive / Alamy*

Woody on Woody

"A purely pleasurable, self-indulgent thing. . . . You know, somebody puts twenty million bucks in the bank—whatever the budget was, fifteen, sixteen million—and you get a chance to re-create your childhood, or a facsimile of it."

• The Woody Allen Rep Company •

Over the course of his forty-five-year (and counting) career, Woody has frequently reused the same personnel, on both sides of the camera. Part of it is convenience; at the rate he works, it's easier to have a stock company—almost akin to the old studio system—to call upon. Moreover, it makes his work simpler: "When you know the people, I do feel that, for me, it relaxes me more and I feel more confident." This was even more the case when he acted in his work. "I also think there's a chemistry between Diane and me, just as there is with Mia, and Tony Roberts," he explained in 1989. "If I'm doing a film with them or with Dianne Wiest or Judy Davis, I feel loose as a goose as an actor because I feel they've played with me and were willing to do another movie with me, so they couldn't have hated it that much." Here are the most-seen faces in Allen's films, from recurring extras to featured players:

Mia Farrow

A Midsummer Night's Sex Comedy
Zelig
Broadway Danny Rose
The Purple Rose of Cairo
Hannah and Her Sisters
Radio Days
September
Another Woman
New York Stories: Oedipus Wrecks
Crimes and Misdemeanors
Alice
Shadows and Fog
Husbands and Wives

Diane Keaton

Men of Crisis: The Harvey
Wallinger Story
Play It Again, Sam
Sleeper
Love and Death
Annie Hall
Interiors
Manhattan
Radio Days
Manhattan Murder Mystery

Simpsons star Julie Kavner is a veteran of seven Allen pictures.
Brian Hamill/Getty Images

Wallace Shawn, Mia Farrow, and Tony Roberts, seen here in a scene from *Radio Days*, have two dozen roles in Allen's movies among them. © Moviestore collection Ltd / Alamy

Tony Roberts

Play It Again, Sam
Annie Hall
Stardust Memories
A Midsummer Night's Sex Comedy
Hannah and Her Sisters
Radio Days
Sounds from a Town I Love (short)

Julie Kavner

Hannah and Her Sisters
Radio Days
New York Stories: Oedipus Wrecks
Alice
Shadows and Fog
Don't Drink the Water (1994)
Deconstructing Harry

John Rothman

Stardust Memories
Zelig
The Purple Rose of Cairo

Renée Lippin

Stardust Memories
Radio Days
Celebrity

Fred Melamed
Hannah and Her Sisters
Radio Days
Another Woman
Crimes and Misdemeanors
Shadows and Fog
Husbands and Wives
Hollywood Ending

Judy Davis
Alice
Husbands and Wives
Deconstructing Harry
Celebrity
To Rome with Love

Sam Waterston
Interiors
Hannah and Her Sisters
September
Crimes and Misdemeanors

Alan Alda
Crimes and Misdemeanors
Manhattan Murder Mystery
Everyone Says I Love You

Philip Bosco
Another Woman
Shadows and Fog
Deconstructing Harry

Isaac Mizrahi
Celebrity
Small Time Crooks
Hollywood Ending

Louise Lasser
What's Up, Tiger Lily?
Take the Money and Run
Bananas
Everything You Always Wanted to Know About Sex* (*But Were Afraid to Ask)
Men of Crisis: The Harvey Wallinger Story
Stardust Memories

Wallace Shawn
Manhattan
Radio Days
Shadows and Fog
The Curse of the Jade Scorpion
Melinda and Melinda

Caroline Aaron
Crimes and Misdemeanors
Alice
Husbands and Wives
Deconstructing Harry

Blythe Danner
Another Woman
Alice
Husbands and Wives

Victor Argo
New York Stories: Oedipus Wrecks
Crimes and Misdemeanors
Shadows and Fog

Larry Pine
Celebrity
Small Time Crooks
Melinda and Melinda

David Ogden Stiers
Another Woman
Shadows and Fog
Mighty Aphrodite
Everyone Says I Love You
The Curse of the Jade Scorpion

Tony Sirico
Bullets Over Broadway
Mighty Aphrodite
Everyone Says I Love You
Deconstructing Harry
Celebrity

Scarlett Johannson
Match Point
Scoop
Vicky Cristina Barcelona

Alec Baldwin
Alice
To Rome with Love
Blue Jasmine

Jack Warden
September
Bullets Over Broadway
Mighty Aphrodite

Frances Conroy
Manhattan
Another Woman
Crimes and Misdemeanors

Rosemary Murphy
September
Don't Drink the Water (1994)
Mighty Aphrodite

Dianne Wiest
The Purple Rose of Cairo
Hannah and Her Sisters
Radio Days
September
Bullets Over Broadway

Diane Wiest, veteran of five Allen films, accepting her Academy Award for *Bullets Over Broadway.* Don Emmert/AFP/Getty Images

Larry David
Radio Days
New York Stories: Oedipus Wrecks
Whatever Works

Zak Orth
Melinda and Melinda
Vicky Cristina Barcelona
You Will Meet a Tall Dark Stranger

Irving Metzman
Stardust Memories
The Purple Rose of Cairo
Deconstructing Harry

September

RELEASE DATE: December 18, 1987

WRITER: Woody Allen

CAST: Mia Farrow, Dianne Wiest, Sam Waterston, Elaine Stritch, Jack Warden, Denholm Elliott

IN A NUTSHELL: Hearts are broken and long-buried secrets are revealed as summer comes to an end at a Vermont country house.

RECURRING THEMES: Show business; infidelity; jealousy; murder; magic realism (via the Ouija board)

Coming off five straight masterpieces in as many years—a run of brilliance all but unparalleled in modern American cinema—Woody Allen decided the time was right to take another shot at an all-out, straight-up drama. The strictures were simple: "I wanted this to be like a little short story. I wanted it to be realistic. I wanted one set—one house—six people, and in the present, completely in the present, unfolding in front of you in a brief period of time."

The result was his most troubled production to date. He originally cast Mia Farrow in the lead role of Lane, Dianne Wiest as Lane's best friend, Maureen O'Sullivan again playing Mia's on-screen mother, Denholm Elliott as O'Sullivan's husband, Charles Durning as the neighbor, and Christopher Walken as the writer. A few days into the shoot, Sam Shepard was brought in to replace Walken ("We just couldn't get copacetic on what to do," Allen explained). The film was shot and edited, and once it was done, Allen decided he had to start all over. From a production standpoint, this was easy enough (the set was still standing). But O'Sullivan was too ill to return, and Durning and Shepard had previous commitments. So Allen moved Elliott into the Durning role and brought in Jack Warden to play Elliott's original part. Elaine Stritch replaced O'Sullivan, and Sam Waterston became the third actor to take on the writer role. He then rewrote the script and shot the whole thing again.

September is one of his most theatrical efforts, from the single location to the searching monologues to the direct duets, from the long takes capturing the element of performance to the high drama inherent in the material. This isn't, in itself, a flaw; the trouble is, the accordant three-act structure (the setups and introductions, then the conflicts and tension during the blackout, followed by the meltdowns and big reveal the next day) is ultimately too schematic, lacking the spontaneity and spark of his best work. Farrow is given an all but impossible character to play, and she struggles with it—although she has one incredible moment, a cry of "I'm so lonely" that's thick

> " The Richmonds are flooded, the electricity's off, God is testing us, and I for one am gonna be ready. Where's the vodka?
> —Diane "

74

September

ORION   DISTRIBUÉ PAR TWENTIETH CENTURY FOX FRANCE

Sam Waterson, who appeared in four Woody Allen movies during his career, was the third actor to assume the role of Peter in *September*. *Lobby card from the Voyageur Press Collection*

Woody on Woody

"September is a picture that I think I shot better than any before. I did it with more sophistication, because we were all in that house and the camera was moving constantly and there were tons of things happening off camera, which is a way I never would have shot my early films . . . . Of course I know going in that there's not much of a market for these films."

with raw desperation. And the dialogue, particularly the expositional passages early on, is frequently clunky.

The three old pros come off best, their decades of delivering stage dialogue carrying them through—especially Stritch, who is easily the best thing in the picture. "I like her energy!" Waterston says, echoing the sentiments of the audience, and it's not just that her whiskey-soaked line readings lend some much-needed levity to the film ("I am too young for liver spots—maybe I could merge them into a tan"). She also has the two most poignant and effective monologues: her early speech into the mirror ("It's hell getting older, especially when you feel twenty-one inside") and her plea to her late husband over the Ouija board.

There are other worthwhile moments in the film, which is flawed but far from the disaster critics—spoiled by the work before it—proclaimed it to be. Years later, Charles Champlin wrote, "If the film does not entirely escape the impression of proscenium theatricality, it achieves real emotional power as the characters struggle with their various anguishes." Though not altogether successful (and his lowest-grossing film to date), *September* was still a vital transitional film, moving Allen toward a pair of dramatic efforts that would prove more rewarding for both the filmmaker and his audience.

• Buried Treasures •

As of this writing, forty-five feature films directed by Woody Allen have been released on DVD, and not one of them has included what has become, for most other directors, a *de rigueur* bonus feature: deleted scenes, shot and edited but not included in the final cut. He sometimes recycles unused ideas or sequences (see "The Black Reels"), but most of it is gone forever; one legend has it that Woody disliked a sequence in *Annie Hall* so much that he gathered up the reels and threw them into the Central Park reservoir. Over the years, through set reports and interviews, we've heard about other bits and pieces of classic films that are now nothing but fish food. Woody probably knows best, but they still sound awfully tantalizing.

Bananas

According to biographer John Baxter, the film's first cut included a revolution sequence that ran nearly an hour. (It's about thirty seconds in the final cut.) The return of Howard Cosell replaced Allen's original ending, in which Black Power activists attempt to assassinate Fielding during a speech at Columbia University. "The explosion blackens his face," Baxter wrote, "and his three putative assassins immediately greet him as a brother." Okay, maybe he made the right call on that one.

A still from that unfortunate deleted scene in *Bananas. Lobby card from the Voyageur Press Collection*

Everything You Always Wanted to Know About Sex

Woody spent two weeks, at considerable expense (and discomfort to himself and costar Louise Lasser), shooting "What Makes Men Homosexuals?" "I just thought it was the greatest idea," he recalled, "that I would be a spider and there would be a black widow and we would have sex and she would devour me and that would symbolically show one possible reason why men become homosexuals." But he couldn't come up with a suitable ending, and he and Lasser couldn't improvise one, so he killed the vignette.

Sleeper

In the transition from a 140-minute first cut to the final eighty-nine, the slapstick sequences of Miles hanging out of the window and battling the machines of Luna's kitchen were both "cut to the bone," according to Baxter. He also describes an elaborate dream sequence, shot in the Mojave Desert, with Miles as a pawn in a giant chess game, and another scene in which Allen trots out his old magic tricks as Miles tries to charm Luna (Diane Keaton) into sleeping with him.

Annie Hall

As has been well documented here and elsewhere, the original, *Anhedonia* version of Allen's smash was a semi-surrealist, stream-of-consciousness effort centered on Alvy rather than his relationship with Annie. Among the dropped elements from the initial 140-minute assembly: a fantasy scene in which Alvy and a pickup team that also includes Kafka and Nietzsche take on the New York Knicks, shot at Madison Square Garden with the team and fans in attendance; Alvy and a Rolling Stone reporter

(Shelley Duvall) visiting the Garden of Eden to talk with God about the female orgasm; a sci-fi/horror parody scene, with Alvy and Annie visiting a "podded" Rob in Beverly Hills; a follow-up scene to his L.A. driving arrest, in which he wins a joke-telling contest in jail; more childhood flashbacks, including one of a young Alvy's romantic encounter with a young Brooke Shields; and a scene in which the electronic billboard in Times Square gives Alvy the advice to go to California for Annie. Though a similar device would be used in Steve Martin's *Annie Hall*-in-California comedy *L.A. Story*, this last one was reportedly the scene Allen tossed into the reservoir.

Stardust Memories

The character of Nat Bernstein, only mentioned in the final cut ("Your problem is you never got over Nat Bernstein's death"), was originally an onscreen one. Stories vary as to why he was cut. Baxter writes that the scene of his death was too depressing, though a rumor persists that the actor who played the role underwent a sex change before the film was finished and was thus unavailable for reshoots. (This seems apocryphal; Allen has certainly never hesitated to recast roles.)

Hannah and Her Sisters

Allen reportedly reshot an astonishing four-fifths of *Hannah*. Among the scenes that didn't make the cut were several with Tony Roberts, a scene in which Woody's Mickey goes to confession, more sex scenes between Elliot and Lee, and a confrontation at the second Thanksgiving where Lee, rebuffing Elliot's attempt to rekindle the affair, stabs him in the hand with a pair of scissors. Added in reshoots was the third Thanksgiving bookend sequence, with the sunny ending that Allen would come to dislike.

Radio Days

The cut scenes of this film are particularly well documented, thanks to *Woody Allen: On Location*, a daily diary of its production by French journalist Thierry de Navacelle. Among the most noteworthy deletions: an elaborate opening sequence with listeners gathered around the radio to hear a stunt by "The Astonishing Tonino"; a lengthy sequence summarizing the history of radio; studio scenes of such radio programs as *Whiz Kids*, *The Amateur Talent Hunt*, *The Herbie Hanson Show*, and *The Radio Playhouse on the Air*, the latter two additional steps in the career of Mia Farrow's Sally; a scene of Sally kissing military men goodbye as they ship off to war; and a dramatization of one of radio's most enduring legends, wherein kiddie-show host Uncle Walt growls into an open microphone, "That oughta hold the little bastards."

September

Some Allen movies have deleted scenes; *September* has a deleted movie. After shooting and assembling his initial cut, featuring Mia Farrow, Maureen O'Sullivan, Dianne Wiest, Charles Durning, Denholm Elliott, and Sam Shepard (who had himself replaced Christopher Walken after a few days of shooting), Woody realized he "needed to do a lot of reshooting." Fearing he had miscast Elliot, he thought, "Well, as long as I'm going to do four weeks of reshooting, why not reshoot the whole thing and do it right?" That original "draft," as he came to consider it, isn't even in Woody's possession. "It's gone," he told Stig Björkman.

Crimes and Misdemeanors

The Martin Landau plot remained mostly intact during reshoots, but Allen totally reworked his comic thread. Initially, Farrow's character was a married social worker in a nursing home, and Allen's documentarian decides to make a film about the ex-vaudevillians there so he can spend more time with her. Alan Alda saw his small role greatly expanded in the rewrite, while Daryl Hannah's role was reduced to a cameo, and Sean Young (who played an aspiring actress that Allen's Cliff attempts to seduce by claiming to be a TV producer) was cut entirely.

Another Woman

RELEASE DATE: November 18, 1988

WRITER: Woody Allen

CAST: Gena Rowlands, Ian Holm, Mia Farrow, Gene Hackman, John Houseman, David Ogden Stiers, Sandy Dennis, Martha Plimpton

IN A NUTSHELL: A philosophy professor, subletting an office to work on a book, overhears a woman in the adjoining psychiatrist's office and is moved to reexamine her own life and relationships.

RECURRING THEMES: Eavesdropping; psychoanalysis; infidelity; past vs. present ("There are times when even a historian shouldn't look at the past")

Another Woman opens with an anomaly in the Woody Allen canon: a precredit sequence. In it, via an internal voice-over, we are introduced to Marion Post (Gena Rowlands), a prototypical Allen upper-class intellectual. Having just celebrated her fiftieth birthday, she seems successful and happy, with a good job, a doctor husband, a stepdaughter who idolizes her, and enough disposable income to rent an apartment to write her next book. And then she starts to hear the voices through the vents.

"The idea began as a comic notion," Allen explained in 1987, during the picture's production—and it would become one again, when he recycled the device a decade later for *Everyone Says I Love You*. But what's interesting about its deployment here is how carefully Allen chooses not to use it realistically. As Roger Ebert noted in his four-star review, "Not only can Marion (and the rest of us) easily eavesdrop on the conversations, but when the pillows are placed against the air shaft, they completely block out every word." The choice is unambiguous: one may choose to listen or not to listen.

Ebert floats the theory that "the cries coming in through the grillwork on the wall are the sounds of real emotions that she has put out of her mind for years." Allen goes further: that the Mia Farrow character she is choosing to block out (or not block out) is "in some way an incarnation of her own inner self." That character—called "Hope" in the credits but never called by name in the film—is pregnant, as Marion once was, and they share a passion for painting with watercolors. More importantly, her emotional intensity is directly contrary to the "cold," "cerebral" woman Marion has become.

And so Hope serves as a passageway into Marion's past and inner self, which she's previously blocked off as carefully as the vent into the psychotherapist's office. As Jill Gordon notes in *Woody Allen and Philosophy*, "All of the dialogue by all of the characters who populate her dream

> " I wondered if a memory is something you have, or something you've lost.
> —Marion Post "

comes from Marion's own psyche. All the pointed remarks about regret, passion, self-deception, and repression are Marion talking to herself, and are thus the beginning of her transformation to better self-knowledge." Some of the connections are direct, memories triggered by words and emotions seeping in through the grate. Others seem happenstance, as when a spontaneous decision to follow Hope through Greenwich Village leads to a chance encounter with her old friend Claire (Sandy Dennis).

There's a fluidity to the narrative, and to the fantasies that motor it—a kind of magic realism more often attempted on stage than screen, and much of it occurring here within an explicitly theatrical framework. It's not entirely alien to Allen's work; the scene where Marion speaks in the present to her brother in the past recalls Alvy, Annie, and Rob's trip to the old neighborhood in *Annie Hall*. It's tougher to play that kind of thing straight, but Allen pulls it off here—with considerable help from director of photography Sven Nykvist, go-to cinematographer for Allen's hero Ingmar Bergman (whose *Wild Strawberries* was mentioned by most critics as an obvious influence on this film).

Another Woman is the most successful of Allen's early dramas. As biographer John Baxter notes, "It shows Allen beginning to manipulate the tropes of Strindbergian drama, where until then he had been content simply to mimic Bergman's use of them." Though hampered by the occasional bit of stilted dialogue ("These are artifacts from a more civilized time in our lives"), *Another Woman* works: Rowlands is extraordinary, the imagery is evocative, and the film is a model of shrewd restraint.

Woody on Woody

"I could make that better now. . . . There's a kind of coldness that the lead character in *Another Woman* has that permeates the film. It's a little colder than I wanted it to be."

87/95/16 - Pictured: Woody Allen and cinematographer Sven Nykvist discuss a shot on the set of Mr. Allen's new film, "Another Woman".
Photo by Brian Hamill
©1988 Orion Pictures Corporation. All Rights Reserved.

Allen confers with cinematographer Sven Nykvist, who was the director of photography on more than twenty Bergman films. *Promotional photo from the Voyageur Press Collection*

• Woody the Dramatist •

"I can never bear seeing a headline like 'Woody Dying to Be Taken Seriously.'
It misses the point entirely. I don't want to be taken seriously.
I have to be taken seriously."
—Woody Allen

Looking back on those afternoons when he would dash off dozens of jokes during the subway ride to his first paid writing job, Woody told Richard Schickel, simply, "If you can do it, there's nothing to it. You know, it's like drawing. I can't draw, so I'm astonished at a kid sitting next to me in class who will draw a rabbit or something. I'm amazed by it. For him it's nothing, and he wonders why I can't do it. . . . Well, I could write jokes, so there was nothing to it."

That something so remarkable came (and continues to come) so easily to Woody Allen goes a long way toward explaining why, from almost the beginning of his career,

making people laugh has never been enough. As early as 1976, he was confessing his desire to do "more serious comical films and do different types of films, maybe write and direct a drama." The aim was clear: to "take chances—I would like to fail a little for the public."

When he followed up the Oscar-winning critical and box office success of *Annie Hall* with the dour *Interiors*, he certainly got that opportunity. The move came partially from a desire, seen in *Annie Hall*, to make films that were more than "just" comedies. "As soon as you start to want to say something meaningful in comedy," he explained at the time, "you have to give up some of the comedy in some

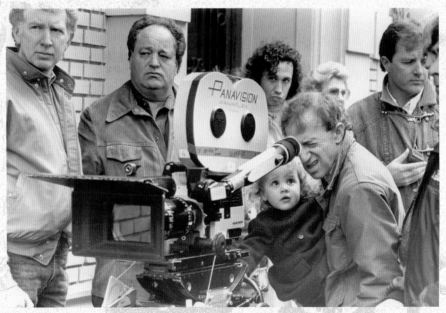

Allen on the set of *Another Woman*, his third "serious film." *Brian Hamill/Getty Images*

way." But more than anything, Allen wanted to make a film that achieved a gravitas he felt simply wasn't within the grasp of comic work. "There's no question that comedy is harder to do than serious stuff," he said in 1972. "There's also no question in my mind that comedy is less valuable than serious stuff. . . . I don't want to sound brutal, but there's something immature, something second-rate in terms of satisfaction when comedy is compared to drama."

True enough. But what made *Interiors* difficult for so many viewers to embrace was that it was such a stark departure, such a 180-degree turn from the output that had come before it. Though undeniably a film of skill and value, it also dispensed with much of what made Woody interesting, from the naturalistic, vernacular dialogue of *Annie Hall* to the rough energy of even a story-driven knockabout comedy like *Sleeper*. "He created such an original comic outlook and voice that any subsequent attempt at drama jarred the sensibilities of many in his audience," theorized biographer Eric Lax. It's not a film without humor—the character of Pearl is not only a breath of fresh air, but her no-nonsense approach to the thought-provoking play the family discusses at dinner almost seems like an inside joke, Woody having a chuckle at his own serious pretentions.

To his credit, Allen has never blamed his audience for resisting his serious streak. "I hoped they would come with me, but they didn't," he said of the reaction to the film, and he rebukes the notion that his audience left him. "I left my audience is what really happened; they didn't leave me. They were as nice as could be. If I had kept making *Manhattan* or *Annie Hall*—the same kind of pictures—they were fully prepared to meet me halfway."

But Allen has never been the kind of film artist who could keep making "the same kind of pictures." "I expect more of myself," he said, "and the audience does, too." He may have rebounded from *Interiors* with *Manhattan*, another comedy concerning the romantic entanglements of New York intellectuals, with himself back in a starring role, but he was still moving forward: His primary focus was no longer on jokes and laughs, but on conflict and character. He smuggled serious scenes and subject matter into *The Purple Rose of Cairo* and *Hannah and Her Sisters*, and cashed in their success with two more straightforward dramas, *September* and *Another Woman*. The reviews and box office were no kinder, but Allen was sanguine. "Those three dramas," he said, "were very ambitious. So when I struck out, it was apparent and egregious and not entertaining. The impulse was honorable, the attempt was honorable, I did the best I could."

Those films—which *People* magazine sneeringly dubbed "the trilogy from hell"—may be problematic, but they were vital to his development as an artist. Each film in the Allen filmography seems a necessary bridge to the next, and he simply may have needed to get those straightfaced chamber dramas out of his system in order to arrive at *Crimes and Misdemeanors*, a magnificent fusion of what he did best and what he desired so badly to do as well.

One can view *Crimes* as the amateur magician performing an epic feat of audience diversion, distracting them with the familiar comic elements while drawing them in to the serious, powerful narrative in the picture's other half. But more importantly, Allen realized that he need not cordon off his comic gifts. The serious, thoughtful stories he wishes to tell can be cut with a healthy measure of comedy (*Crimes, Melinda and Melinda*) or thriller (*Match Point, Cassandra's Dream*) to make them less drab and more palatable.

He would soon come to realize that the compartmentalization of comedy and drama, either from film to film or within the same projects, wasn't necessary either. In 1984, he voiced a desire to "constantly alternate between comedy and seriousness"; a decade later, he would confess an interest in "the attempt to try and make comedies that have a serious or tragic dimension to them." This seems the true achievement of recent pictures like *Vicky Cristina Barcelona* and *Blue Jasmine*: the filmmaker's happy discovery that comedy and drama can not only comingle, but complement.

New York Stories:
Oedipus Wrecks

RELEASE DATE: March 10, 1989

WRITER: Woody Allen

CAST: Allen, Mia Farrow, Julie Kavner, Mae Questel

IN A NUTSHELL: A successful lawyer finds his lingering problems with his mother solved by an accident at a magic show.

RECURRING THEMES: Jewish mothers ("This morning she told the entire borough of Queens that I had a hiatus hernia"); magic; magic realism; fear of fatherhood

Oedipus Wrecks marked Woody Allen's return to comedy after two years of laboring over serious dramas, but it came in a prestige package: an omnibus film for Touchstone Pictures called New York Stories. "I was working with Marty Scorsese and Francis Ford Coppola, two great directors," he explained. "I sandwiched myself in there to get, you know, acclaim by association."

Scorsese's film, most critics agreed, was the best; Coppola's was the consensus pick as the worst. Allen's fell somewhere in the middle—amusing enough, but slight, a witty premise (the kind of thing that'd make a funny New Yorker casual) not really fleshed out, even at short film length. The abbreviated form doesn't really agree with Allen. The picture feels like a gag skeleton, without any real meat on its bones in the form of characterization or genuine pathos.

But it is intriguing as a window into Allen's complex dynamic with his mother, whom he said "hit me every day when I was a child" and was a constant source of criticism as an adult. "I'm very successful," Woody tells his psychiatrist at the beginning of the film, "and I still haven't resolved my relationship with my mother." His sheer exasperation with every aspect of her personality provides the segment's biggest laughs— particularly the big closeup on his delighted face as the magician slides his swords into the box and he can only imagine her cowering inside.

WATCH OUT FOR
Larry David as the magician's stage manager; Kirsten Dunst as one of Lisa's children

Woody on Woody

"It was fun to make that film. We were working with a very limited budget and we had a very short time to shoot it, but it was only a short story. And short-story films notoriously don't do well at the box office."

> I need oxygen. I need to get out. I need fresh air. I need cyanide.
> —Sheldon

Crimes and Misdemeanors

By the end of the 1980s, Woody Allen's filmmaking had become somewhat bilineated. His light, mostly comic films (in which he frequently appeared) were met with critical praise, awards recognition, and modest commercial success, but the serious-minded, European-styled dramas that were his passion received mixed reviews and miserable box office receipts. As the decade drew to a close, Allen decided to confront this split personality by putting his two halves into the same film and letting them fight it out. He ended up making one of the finest and most sophisticated of all his pictures.

He arrived at it with considerable struggle. In his first cut, the comic story was entirely different: Mia's character was a social worker at a nursing home where Woody's Cliff was shooting a documentary about ex-vaudevillians. There was more of his sister and niece and far less of Alan Alda. Allen watched the rough cut, decided his story didn't work, and threw it all out. He rewrote and reshot a good third of the movie from scratch, incorporating ideas from Alda, whose character of Lester, a pontificating television sitcom producer, was, it is whispered, inspired by Larry Gelbart, whom Allen had written with for Sid Caesar and Alda had worked with for years on *M*A*S*H*.

It's easy to read that half of *Crimes and Misdemeanors* as the "comic relief," the spoonful of sugar that helps the medicine go down. But this was the most acidic comedy he'd done since *Stardust Memories*, and the most melancholy. Halley (Farrow) is carefully established as a kind soul and tasteful intellectual who "gets" Cliff, shares his impeccable taste, and is equally fascinated by Professor Levy (Martin Bergmann). Still, she betrays his affection by falling for Lester, whom Cliff assumed was their shared personification of all that is intellectually corrupt. Not that Allen's character is some tremendous catch; he's playing a would-be adulterer here, but without the

> It's a human life.
> You don't think
> God sees?
> —Ben Rosenthal

RELEASE DATE: October 13, 1989

WRITER: Woody Allen

CAST: Martin Landau, Allen, Mia Farrow, Alan Alda, Anjelica Huston, Jerry Orbach, Sam Waterston

IN A NUTSHELL: An extended family's two stories of deception, betrayal, and guilt—one comic, one dramatic—are interwoven.

RECURRING THEMES: Infidelity; Judaism; God (or lack thereof); filmmaking and filmmakers; show business; murder; morality; art vs. life

83

CRIMES AND
MISDEMEANORS

ORION

Judah (Academy Award nominee Martin Landau) confers with his disreputable brother Jack (Jerry Orbach), who makes a chilling suggestion. *Lobby card from the Voyageur Press Collection*

whimsy of, say, *A Midsummer Night's Sex Comedy*. And if the other half of *Crimes* has a comparable message, it's that adultery is serious business.

His other aim in the dramatic half of the picture was simple. "I just wanted to illustrate in an entertaining way that there's no God," Allen explained to Richard Schickel, "that we're alone in the universe, and that there is nobody out there to punish you, that there's not going to be any kind of Hollywood ending to your life in any way, and that your morality is strictly up to you."

To that end, the Judah Rosenthal portion (Martin Landau) of the story is unique among Allen's works in that it takes his Jewish faith seriously instead of treating it as merely a comic device or an affectation. His three serious dramas to that point were primarily concerned with the woes of WASPs; here, Woody merges the existentialist preoccupations of his adulthood with the Hebrew school principles he was raised on. The character of Ben (Sam Waterston)—the sole link between the two narratives—is not the punch-line rabbi of *Everything You Always Wanted to Know About Sex* or even *Radio Days*. He is the most moral person in either story, a kind, wise, and good man who professes—nay, *insists* on—the organizing principle of a moral structure. For his trouble, he goes blind. His secular sparring partner, meanwhile, literally gets away with murder. He comes out free of not only legal consequence, but any permanent sense of guilt.

Does Judah truly "get away with it"? Allen lets the viewer decide. In Hebrew school, we see that he is taught that the wicked "will be punished for eternity." It is certainly this kind of talk that gives Judah pause when his brother, Jack (Jerry Orbach), floats the notion of having his mistress problem "taken care of." But as Jack points out, correctly, there aren't many more assumptions to be made from the fact that he has reached out to his shady brother at that juncture. It's not just that he wants Jack to tell him what he wants to hear; he also wants to be properly revolted by the suggestion before giving him the go-ahead.

Ultimately, he makes that decision—and gets over it—by making the same choice as his aunt at the Seder dinner: to decide that there is no eternity, no absolute morality, and no God. Yet Allen does not let him, or any of his other characters, off the hook entirely. The final dialogue of the film is that of the recently departed Professor Levy, who reminds us that "we are, in fact, the sum total of our choices."

If this seems like an awfully light sentence for an adulterer and murderer, that's part of the film's genius. In the section following the murder, as Judah is wracked with guilt and visited by police, Allen is toying with us, setting up our expectation for how this kind of thing normally plays out in films. And then—it just doesn't. Judah Rosenthal's soul may be corrupted, but he's free from punishment and happy from moment to moment. He may have learned nothing. Sometimes people don't. "You've seen too many movies," Judah tells Cliff, in the brilliant scene where their threads finally intersect. "If you want a happy ending, go see a Hollywood movie." (As Ian Jarvie wryly notes in *Woody Allen and Philosophy*, "It would not be lost on the audience that Woody Allen's movies, like Cliff's, are made in New York, not in Hollywood.")

In those lines, and in the witty intercutting of ironically appropriate old movie clips, Allen is returning to the incompatibility of fantasy and reality ("This only happens in the movies," he whispers to his niece). He replicates the quiet intensity of the dramatic films and repurposes *Another Woman*'s imagined conversations and fantastical intersections of past and present. *Crimes and Misdemeanors* was the culmination of all his gifts: piercing drama, effortless comedy, and philosophical exploration. Once again, Woody Allen had topped himself.

Woody on Woody

"I think it's one of my better films. I think it's one of the more successful ones, because I felt it had some substance to chew on and it portrayed the philosophical and intellectual interest that I had in this subject matter in a reasonably entertaining way."

Alan Alda's role as a blowhard television producer was greatly expanded when Allen reworked the film after its initial edit. *Mondadori Portfolio by Getty Images*

Woody the Philosopher:
The Bad Luck Philosophy of Woody Allen
by David Detmer

Woody Allen noted in a 2010 interview with *Commonweal*'s Robert Lauder that philosophical and religious questions—on the existence of God, life after death, the meaning of life—were "always obsessions of mine, even as a very young child." He began to pursue those obsessions somewhat systematically following his marriage, at the age of twenty, to Harlene Rosen, who would shortly go on to major in philosophy at Hunter College in Manhattan. While Woody's project of reading and informally studying philosophy may have begun as an attempt to keep up with his new wife, it has long outlasted that marriage, and has continued throughout his adult life. Indeed, his friend and biographer Eric Lax lists philosophy, along with magic and the clarinet, as one of Allen's three "constant avocations."

It is clear, moreover, that Allen's interest in philosophy is not based on mere curiosity or a desire for intellectual exercise, but rather is driven by a deeper, more personal concern. As he told Lax in 1975's *On Being Funny: Woody Allen and Comedy*: "My depression is why I'm drawn to philosophy, so acutely interested in Kafka, Dostoevsky and Bergman. I think I have all the symptoms and problems that those people are occupied with: An obsession with death, an obsession with God or the lack of God, the question of why we are here. Answers are what I want."

Allen's primary philosophical interests center around the "existential" issues that troubled philosophers in continental Europe from the mid-nineteenth to the mid-twentieth centuries—questions about life and its meaning; about how to cope with its terrors and miseries; about how to avoid its corrupting temptations; about how to live a life of authenticity and integrity, filled with deep meaning and value. Accordingly, in his philosophical reading and thinking, he has primarily engaged the existentialist tradition, especially the philosophers Kierkegaard, Sartre, and Camus, together with like-minded figures in literature, notably Kafka and Dostoevsky, and his favorite filmmaker, Ingmar Bergman. His biographer reports that "the problems inherent in the existential dilemma of man" are Allen's "daily preoccupation."

Not surprisingly, Allen has regularly included these existential-philosophical preoccupations in his films. "My movies have been very self-expressive," he commented to Lax in 2007. "They're expressive of observations of mine or feelings of mine." Moreover, as he told Sara Vilkomerson of *The New York Observer* in 2009, the philosophy he expresses in his films "has been consistent over the years. . . . The ideas have always been the same."

Well then, what are those ideas? One is that our lives are governed substantially by luck. In *Whatever Works*, Boris Yelnikoff periodically turns toward the camera and addresses the audience directly. During one of these speeches, he advises his listeners to seize every opportunity available to them to find fun, love, and happiness in life. But he then cautions them: "Don't kid yourself. Because it's by no means up to your own human ingenuity. A bigger part of your existence is luck than you'd like to admit. Christ, you know the odds of your father's one sperm, from the billions, finding the single egg that made you? Don't think about it, you'll have a panic attack."

Similarly, *Match Point* begins with the following words from the narrator: "The man who said

'I'd rather be lucky than good' saw deeply into life. People are afraid to face how great a part of life is dependent on luck. It's scary to think so much is out of one's control. There are moments in a match when the ball hits the top of the net and for a split second it can either go forward or fall back. With a little luck it goes forward and you win. Or maybe it doesn't and you lose."

In interviews, Allen has confirmed that these statements reflect his views. "I'm a big believer in luck," he told Richard Schickel. "It appears in all my movies. . . . I feel that luck is the chief component in a good relationship between a man and a woman, and that luck guides our lives much more than we care to admit."

Nor is the tyranny of luck limited to the domain of interpersonal relationships. According to Allen, the success or failure of artistic creations also depends on the vagaries of fortune: "Sometimes I get lucky and the film comes out good. Sometimes I'm not lucky and it doesn't come out good." Ironically, he claims that this point holds with special force in connection with *Match Point*, his one film that deals most extensively with the theme of

Contemplating the meaning of life has been an obsession of Allen's since childhood and a consistent theme in his films.
Gerald Israel/Archive Photos/Getty Images

Allen most directly explored the inherent conflict between the joys of fantasy and the unpleasantness of reality in 1985's *The Purple Rose of Cairo*. Lobby card from the Voyageur Press Collection

luck. Speaking with Jim Schembri of the Australian newspaper *The Age*, Allen said, "*Match Point* is one of my A-films. It's arguably maybe the best film that I've made. This is strictly accidental, it just happened to come out right. You know, I try to make them all good, but some come out and some don't. With this one everything seemed to come out right. The actors fell in, the photography fell in, and the story clicked. I caught a lot of breaks. It turned out to be one of the luckiest experiences I've ever had. Every little break that we needed at every little turning point went right!"

One might argue that Allen is overstating the importance of luck in artistic creation because he is focusing on external circumstances beyond the artist's control and neglecting a much more significant factor internal to the artist, namely, the artist's talent. But Allen has a reply at the ready, one that he echoed in a 1996 interview with *The Paris Review*: Talent, too, is largely a matter of luck. "It's a nice but fortuitous gift—like a nice voice or being left-handed. That you can create is a kind of nice accident," he said.

While Allen acknowledges the existence of good luck, his dark vision holds that our luck is mostly bad. To give just one obvious example of our bad luck, we are all destined to die, and there is nothing we can do about it. In response, most of us engage in various strategies for disguising or distorting the horrors of existence. What all of these strategies come down to, according to Allen, is the attempt to exchange reality for fantasy. And the difference between fantasy and reality, he informs us, is "one big theme" of his films, telling Stig Björkman, "there's always a pervasive feeling of the greatness of idealized life or fantasy versus the unpleasantness of reality."

Because of his dismal view of reality, Allen confesses a degree of personal sympathy for the strategy of fleeing to a fantasy world. As he told John Lahr of *The New Yorker*, "I like being in Ingmar Bergman's world. Or in Louis Armstrong's world. Or in the world of the New York Knicks. Because it's not this world. You spend your whole life searching for a way out. You just get an overdose of reality, you know, and it's a terrible thing. I'm always fighting against reality."

The problem with this strategy, of course, is that it cannot be sustained. When lost in a world of fantasy, a person cannot meet real-world needs, such as paying the rent, buying the groceries, fixing the leaky faucet, or maintaining a relationship. Reality always reasserts itself.

The film in which Allen most clearly dramatizes this issue is *The Purple Rose of Cairo*, in which a character from a movie steps out of the screen and joins the real world. He embarks on a romance with Cecilia, the character played by Mia Farrow, who memorably remarks, "I just met a wonderful new man. He's fictional, but you can't have everything." Though she would dearly love to use this new relationship as a vehicle for escaping her hellish existence (she is an impoverished, Depression-era waitress married to an abusive, insufferable lout), she eventually realizes that the fictionality of her new boyfriend (who, for example, cannot pay a real-world restaurant bill because he has only "stage money") makes this impossible. So she rejects him in favor of a real man—the actor who plays him. The actor abandons her, leaving her to pick up the pieces of her unhappy life and face her bleak future.

In interviews, Allen confirmed that *The Purple Rose of Cairo* is about the choice we all must face, between fantasy and reality. He explained, to Richard Schickel, that while one must "choose reality, because if you choose fantasy, that way lies madness," if you choose reality "it crushes [you] at the end." He added that, "By choosing the real world, which we all must do, [Cecilia] is inevitably crushed by it, as we all inevitably are."

And unfortunately, if Allen is right, Cecilia's plight is also ours: "My perception is that you are forced to choose reality over fantasy and reality hurts you in the end, and fantasy is just madness. . . . Like life, it's a lose-lose situation."

David Detmer is a professor of philosophy at Purdue University Calumet. He is the author of four books and has written extensively on Woody Allen, including the essays "The Philosopher as Filmmaker" in *A Companion to Woody Allen* (2013) and "Inauthenticity and Personal Identity in Zelig" in *Woody Allen and Philosophy* (2004). He is executive editor of Sartre Studies International and a past president of the North American Sartre Society.

Alice

RELEASE DATE: December 25, 1990

WRITER: Woody Allen

CAST: Mia Farrow, Joe Mantegna, William Hurt, Keye Luke, Alec Baldwin, Blythe Danner, Judy Davis, Cybill Shepherd

IN A NUTSHELL: An upper-class New York housewife visits a Chinatown acupuncturist for back trouble, but his magical herbs prompt several unexpected discoveries about herself and those around her.

RECURRING THEMES: Magic realism ("Geez, *nothing* shocks New York cab drivers," notes Joe, while invisible); infidelity; eavesdropping; past vs. present

If *Another Woman* was innovative but widely unseen, Woody Allen wasn't content to let its themes or techniques go to waste, and his Christmas 1990 film *Alice* was a light, sprightly comic riff on the earlier drama. Both are the stories of ostensibly happy and successful women whose eyes are opened to the true nature of the people in their lives, and ultimately of their own personalities; both come to those conclusions via heavy doses of magic realism and theatrical effects. The name Woody gives his protagonist is not accidental—this Alice falls into a wonderland of hypnotism, invisibility, confidence, and even flight.

The opening scenes establish the luxury of Alice Tate's (Mia Farrow) existence: a ridiculously posh Upper East Side apartment; days of shopping and pampering; her every need met by her cook, nanny, trainer, masseuse, and decorator; her children an afterthought, almost an accessory. Her husband, Doug (William Hurt), is an inattentive and seemingly unaware heel. But the smoke-and-mirrors transience of her happiness is immediately apparent. She despairs that "I want to do something with my life before it's too late," and the film's first images are a daydream of adultery.

The object of her affection is Joe (Joe Mantegna), and the tender clumsiness of their assignation provides most of the movie's comic highlights. She finally makes her move with a dose of Dr. Yang's herbs, and Allen plays out the entire duet in a two-shot, shifting subtly from medium to closeup, loathe to break away from the charged eroticism of the moment. Once she's out of that trance, her panicked realization of what she's done is sweetly funny ("I was talking about reeds and Coltrane! Who's Coltrane?"), and a later scene, where the ghost of her former lover Ed (played with considerable allure by Alec Baldwin) coaches her through another jittery conversation with her beau, is reminiscent of Bogie prompting Woody in *Play It Again, Sam.*

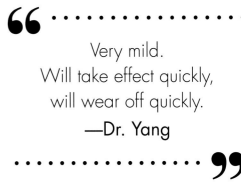

Very mild.
Will take effect quickly,
will wear off quickly.
—Dr. Yang

Both of those scenes make clear that in *Alice*, for the first and only time, Allen wrote Farrow the kind of "Woody role" that he would later hand off to surrogates like John Cusack and Kenneth Branagh. The dialogue rhythms, neurosis, and self-doubt; her nonstop chattering and stammering in Joe's apartment before their first encounter; her fumbling refusal of the opium pipe, which soon degenerates into a cool, "Would you mind holding that a little closer, please"—all are prototypical Woody, and they result in one of Farrow's most charming performances in their entire collaboration.

"I just intended it to be a fable," Allen later said, and in that modest goal, it is a swoony success. It's full of lovely scenes—Alice and Ed enjoying one last dance, her and Joe's sweet flight over the city, the neon-infused flashback to her courtship with her husband—and the special effects are simple, with an almost homemade feel that keeps them from taking over the picture (as these things so often do). The closing scenes are quietly subversive; when she puts the love herbs down the drain, choosing not to find happiness in the love of a man but within herself, Allen is choosing a decidedly feminist outcome for what is, in many ways, a fairy tale.

If *Alice* is light on big laughs, it's full of charm and smiles, and that's quite enough. Its pleasantry was left on screen, though; shortly after the shoot was complete, Allen went into the hospital. The official explanation was over-exhaustion (and considering the six films he'd put out in the last four years, it was a credible one), but it was in fact an acute bout of depression. Little did he know what kind of trouble was on the horizon.

WATCH OUT FOR

Supermodel Elle Macpherson as the supermodel in the dressing room; writer/director James Toback (*Fingers, Two Girls and a Guy*) as Alice's writing professor.

Woody on Woody

"There might have been an amusing sequence here and there—like when she was invisible—but that's all. . . . I have no particular regard for *Alice*. I don't *hate* it. I never think of it."

Mia Farrow's performance as bored Upper East Side housewife Alice Tate is one of her most inspired—and one that occasionally echoes the tics and mannerisms of her writer/director. *Brian Hamill/Getty Images*

Shadows and Fog

RELEASE DATE: December 5, 1991

WRITER: Woody Allen

CAST: Allen, Mia Farrow, John Malkovich, John Cusack, Lily Tomlin, Jodie Foster, Kathy Bates, Madonna, Donald Pleasence

IN A NUTSHELL: A nervous bookkeeper is enlisted in a vigilante mob's search for a serial killer but soon finds himself accused of the crimes.

RECURRING THEMES: Magic; Judaism (implicit); infidelity; fear of fatherhood; prostitution ("A sword swallower? That's my specialty too!")

Though the 1980s found Woody Allen turning out one masterpiece after another, his output late in the decade was increasingly insular. While their styles varied, films such as *Hannah and Her Sisters*, *Another Woman*, *Crimes and Misdemeanors*, and *Alice* were primarily preoccupied with rich Upper East Siders, and Allen's continued fascination with their foibles threatened to drive him into a rut. That neighborhood would remain his base of operations, logistically and narratively, in the 1980s, but his restless nature and curiosity as a filmmaker would lead him to try some rather bold experiments in the 1990s.

The boldest of them is *Shadows and Fog*, deemed "a true curiosity" by Allen admirer Charles Champlin, and for good reason—it seems to be the result of a desire (maybe a dare?) to turn Fritz Lang's M into a comedy. "It's very hard to strike a balance in a story so that it's amusing and also . . . tragic or pathetic," Allen said of the film. The photography (featuring copious amounts of both titular elements) and subject matter are straight out of German Expressionism, a black-and-white nightmare vision of paranoia and terror. It's about the bleakest environment imaginable for comedy, and yet there's Woody, wisecracking his way through the vaporous village, doing his Bob Hope–inspired fast-talking coward act. But this is a tougher room than that of *Love and Death*, with a much higher body count. Critics and viewers found the inherent incongruity of the enterprise too off-putting, which is a shame, as this is one of Allen's most fascinatingly atypical films.

The script was based on *Death*, a one-act play written a good twenty years earlier and included in Allen's 1976 prose collection *Without Feathers*. That play was only concerned with Kleinman; the atmospheric circus and brothel sections were new for the screenplay (as were most of the jokes). But in both works,

> **"**
> I can be very brave! It's just that I can't think about it first.
> —Kleinman
> **"**

On the set of *Shadows and Fog* with cinematographer Carlo Di Palma. *Brian Hamill/Getty Images*

as Champlin notes, anti-Semitism is "an implicit theme," as are mob psychology and mob violence as its volatile ingredients. Richard Schickel goes further, branding the film "a metaphor for the Holocaust. That is to say, we are being presented with an evil unprecedented in the experience of a rationally organized community." Kleinman (one of Allen's most Jewish names) is a bookkeeper (again, filling a type) who is first asked for assistance, separated from "social undesirables" but then put on a mysterious list, subjected to the sniffing of a clairvoyant, branded a "cringing, slimy vermin" pinpointed for "extermination," and chased through the streets by the angry mob.

Those chases and the atmospheric sequences of genuine suspense before the murders showcase Santo Loquasto's smashing, 26,000-square-foot set (the largest ever built in New York) and Carlo Di Palma's vivid photography. This was perhaps the cinematographer's finest hour with Allen, who in this film eschews his customary medium-wide shots to shoot in tight, letting the camera study the shadowy facial landscapes of his actors. In the interest of preserving the conversational rhythms, the camera frequently pans between closeups, as it does in Mia Farrow and Lily Tomlin's first meeting, or when rotating the camera around the brothel table from its center. This is a risky shot (we're looking at passing walls for much of it), but it plays, an arresting moment of visual experimentation in one of Allen's most aesthetically daring pictures.

Alas, it was widely unseen. *Shadows and Fog* was one of the final releases of Orion Pictures, which filed for Chapter 11 bankruptcy protection less than a week after the film's New York premiere. As a result, its release was patchy and promotion was vacant. But even more distressingly, the studio that Allen had called home for a decade, where all of his whims and needs were met, was no more. From now on, he would have to rough it as a free agent.

WATCH OUT FOR

John C. Reilly and William H. Macy as village policemen.

Woody on Woody

"I think I did a good job directing it, and Santo's sets are beautiful. But the picture is in the writing, and people weren't interested in the story. You know when you're doing a black-and-white picture that takes place in a European city at night in the twenties, you're not going to make big bucks."

Husbands and Wives

RELEASE DATE: September 18, 1992

WRITER: Woody Allen

CAST: Allen, Mia Farrow, Judy Davis, Sydney Pollack, Juliette Lewis, Liam Neeson

IN A NUTSHELL: A married couple's unexpected and casual breakup causes their best friends to re-examine their own seemingly healthy relationship.

RECURRING THEMES: Infidelity; younger women ("Why do I hear $50,000 worth of psychotherapy dialing 911?"); frustrated novelists; kamikaze women; prostitution; art vs. life ("Like all of us, he grew up on movies and novels where doomed love was romantic")

F ew films in all of modern cinema are as colored by the viewer's knowledge of what occurred outside of the frame as Allen's 1992 comedy/drama *Husbands and Wives*. On January 13, 1992, shortly after the completion of principal photography, Mia Farrow discovered, in Allen's apartment (they had maintained separate residences across Central Park for the duration of their relationship), a series of explicit Polaroid photos of her adopted daughter, Soon-Yi Previn, then twenty-one years old. The couple split, and when the story broke in August, it became the tabloid sensation of 1992. "I didn't think I was that famous, to warrant such coverage!" Allen says (unconvincingly) in Robert Weide's *Woody Allen: A Documentary*.

The breadth of that coverage, combined with the handheld, documentary style that Allen unexpectedly chose for his film, conspire to make *Husbands and Wives* feel like nothing less than a chronicle of Woody and Mia's breakup. "We've been married about ten years," Mia's character, Judy, says in her first doc-style interview. (At that point, she and Woody had been together, although not married, for about ten years.) When she and Woody's Gabe discuss the breakup of Sally (Judy Davis) and Jack (Sydney Pollack), she asks several pointed questions: "Do you think we'd ever break up?" "Are you still attracted to me?" "Are you ever attracted to other women?" And, most tellingly, "Do you ever hide things from me?" (Like Polaroids?) Gabe's character gives a long discourse to the camera about his unavoidable attraction to "kamikaze women"— "they crash their plane, they're self-destructive. But they crash it into you, and you die along with them"—which is in sharp contrast to

> Was the notion of ever-deepening romance a myth, along with simultaneous orgasm? The only time Rifkin and his wife experienced one was when they were granted their divorce.
>
> —Gabe's story

MARIS ET
FEMMES
Un film de Woody Allen

Judy and Gabe's emotional breakup scene was a reshoot, filmed after Allen and Farrow broke up, dramatically, off-screen. *Lobby card from the Voyageur Press Collection*

Sally/Farrow, whom he was attracted to "because you were solid and stable and not crazy." (Harriet, the woman he's fondly remembering and played by the appropriately named Galaxy Craze, bears an uncanny resemblance to Louise Lasser.) Gabe dismisses an attraction to young women like Rain (Juliette Lewis) as "some kind of symbol of lost youth or faded dreams," but asks, "What am I gonna say, that I feel myself becoming infatuated with a twenty-year-old girl?" And, simplest but most tellingly, Woody Allen and Mia Farrow's last scene together onscreen includes her coming to this unavoidable conclusion: "It's over and we both know it."

Remarkably, that was also the final scene they ever shot together—a reshoot, done after her discovery and their split. "It took me two or three days to convince Mia to come back to work and finish the film," producer Robert Greenhut said, but she did, and it's a devastating scene, particularly if the viewer is aware of where its production fell in the chronology of events. Farrow's emotional exhaustion is apparent on screen (and appropriate to the narrative); the already melancholy writing lent extra power by the voyeuristic nature of the direction.

Allen, as usual, dismissed all readings of the film as autobiographical. "*Husbands and Wives* was written two years before things happened with Mia," he told Eric Lax. "There's no correlation." Of course, this objection entirely ignores the premise of subconscious desire, of wish fulfillment in one's life through their fiction—and it's worth noting that, contrary to real life, Woody's Gabe character resists his attraction to a younger woman ("I don't really think that we should follow up on it," he insists after their first kiss), while Farrow's Judy falls for another man and pushes for their breakup. But she does so passive-aggressively. Judy's first husband tells the camera that "she gets what she wants," a phrase that Farrow's own mother, Maureen O'Sullivan, used to describe her in 1967. Allen

Woody on Woody

"*Husbands and Wives* was one of the more satisfying movies to me. There are still things that I would have written differently, if I could change it. But I can't go back and do anything about it now. But basically, this is one of the most satisfying ones."

WATCH OUT FOR

Nora Ephron, writer of the Allen-inspired *When Harry Met Sally*, as the woman arguing about astrology with Sam at the party; Allen's longtime costume designer Jeffrey Kurland, providing the voice of the narrator/interviewer.

insisted that Mia was originally to play Sally, as if that somehow meant the Judy character couldn't have been inspired by her. Either way, that's who she played, and even Allen's champion, *New York Times* film critic Vincent Canby, had to admit, "The performance is superb. Yet the role now seems mean-spirited. This Judy is a waif with claws. A year ago, no one would have seen anything except the fiction. Today, that's not possible."

And while one can't help but view *Husbands and Wives* through anything other than the filter of *l'affaire* Farrow, this is one of Allen's most daring, complicated, bracing, and successful pictures—in spite of that scandal (or perhaps, in some perverse way, partially because of it). Working in this jagged, handheld style—"herky-jerky and unmatched and unrefined in every way," he explained—had been on his mind for a while; in 1987, he told Lax, "there are some things to do with *cinéma vérité*, where you just put a camera in the room. I'd like to fool around with some of these techniques and not be tied into conventional shooting."

By the time of *Husbands'* production, Allen's long takes and eschewing of traditional coverage already placed him outside the realm of "conventional shooting," and it made the leap to extended, imperfect, on-the-fly scenes a short one. "I said to myself, why not just start to make some films where only the content is important," he told Stig Björkman shortly after the film's completion. He certainly doesn't ease us into the style. Most of the first scene, in which Jack and Sally announce their breakup and Judy reacts badly, is done in one long, excruciating take, the camera breathlessly veering from the affable couple to the "shattered" Judy, giving the emotional parties—and the eavesdropping viewer—little breathing room.

The camera doesn't keep its distance, as is Allen's usual wont; it's right up in their faces, hovering between Sally and Judy as they discuss their marriages or between Rain and Gabe as they chat and flirt in the classroom. Edits are jagged, often coming in midsentence, sometimes in mid-word. Scenes like Gabe and Judy's breakup are chopped to their essence, dispensing with transitions, jumping from one emotional climax to the next. Allen stays entirely off-screen in the extraordinary scene with Rain in the cab, because Lewis's reactions are so interesting that they're worth staying on, cinematic etiquette be damned. "I cut when I wanted to cut and stuck on anything I wanted," Allen said. "I didn't care about the niceties of it."

Tri-Star Pictures hurried *Husbands and Wives* into a wide release to capitalize on the Woody/Mia scandal. *Poster from the Voyageur Press Collection*

He would claim the style was partially chosen out of convenience: "I wanted to do a film where we didn't have to wait." But the roughness of the aesthetic is matched by both the dialogue—it was his first R-rated film since *Manhattan*, and contains more profanity than any of his films to that point, along with a rare bit of nudity—and the subject matter, most sharply in the nasty, nearly unwatchable scene of Jack manhandling Sam, his new girlfriend, out to his car ("Get in the car, you infant! Get in the fucking car!"). Allen wasn't necessarily altering the kind of people he was interested in, but his point of view about them was changing, becoming more jaded and less forgiving.

Fellow filmmaker Sydney Pollack found something of a second career as a character actor, appearing in his own *Tootsie*, Stanley Kubrick's *Eyes Wide Shut*, Tony Gilroy's *Michael Clayton*, and *Husbands and Wives*. Lobby card from the Voyageur Press Collection

His comic approach was changing as well. *Husbands* is a funny film but also his most serious comedy this side of *Crimes and Misdemeanors*, and without the easy delineation between comic and dramatic material. The laughs are borne out of behavior and observation rather than "jokes." Even the Woody character doesn't engage in the kind of setup/punch-line dialogue that Allen can write in his sleep (and tends to fall back on, even in his best comedies). Here the laughs are generated from honest reactions, or from our nervous discomfort over the throttling of good manners such characters would normally insist on (as in Judy's torpedoing of her dinner date with endless angry phone calls to Jack, or the scene in which both Sally and Jack end up at their former home late at night, each with their new lover in tow). Allen's filmmaking is so clever that he occasionally gets laughs with a simple edit, like when he cuts back to Judy's "So he never called her" after the description of Jack's encounters with multiple hookers, or when he cuts from Judy's wandering thoughts on hedgehogs and foxes to Michael's "I got the impression at times that you weren't quite into it."

Husbands and Wives is one of Allen's bleakest films; the closing scenes make a case for the impossibility of long-term relationships without either chilling compromise or total subservience, and in doing so, as Florence Colombani wrote in her *Masters of Cinema* volume on Allen, he "attacks the cowardice and hypocrisy of lovers with unusual violence." The character of Rain may sum the film up best—although she's talking about his novel, she praises the work for "all the suffering, and how you made it so funny." But it is Allen who utters the film's most prophetic line, both about his character and, it would seem, himself: "You know, I don't know. My heart does not know from logic."

• Woody the Romantic •

*"It's very hard to get your head and heart to work together in life.
In my case, they're not even friendly."*
—Cliff (Woody Allen), *Crimes and Misdemeanors*

In the summer of 1989, as Woody was putting the finishing touches on *Crimes and Misdemeanors*, director Rob Reiner and screenwriter Nora Ephron had a surprise box office success with a sophisticated romantic comedy called *When Harry Met Sally*. It told the story of a wry, death-obsessed Jewish New Yorker and his relationship with a sunny shiksa, dramatized with urbane, witty dialogue exchanges in iconic New York locales such as Central Park and Katz's Delicatessen. The soundtrack twitters with pop standards; the opening credits are rendered in white text on a black background. It was, in other words, Woody Allen Lite. But its grosses weren't. The $92 million domestic take (unadjusted for inflation) was far higher than that of even Allen's eventual top earner, *Midnight in Paris*.

The romantic comedy had been around long before either *Harry* or Woody, but Ephron's approach redefined the genre for decades to come. Countless imitations followed suit, from her own *Sleepless in Seattle* and *You've Got Mail* to Nancy Meyers's *Something's Gotta Give* and *What Women Want* to the various vehicles of Meg Ryan, Julia Roberts, Sandra Bullock, and Katherine Heigl. And thus the conventional wisdom has taken hold that Woody Allen is a maker of romantic comedies, his *Annie Hall* and *Manhattan* setting the template for the tortured bastardizations that would later fill the multiplex.

But is this assessment accurate? The primary difference between *Annie Hall* and, at risk of overstating it, every single romantic comedy that has followed is that it's not the story of a boy and girl who fall in love and live happily ever after; Annie and Alvy break up before the picture's end, as do *Manhattan*'s Ike and Mary (and, it's probably safe to

assume, Tracy), and *Anything Else*'s Jerry and Amanda, and *The Purple Rose of Cairo*'s Cecilia and either Tom or Gil.

Though romances are frequently at the center of his stories, the Allen filmography is littered with failed relationships. The couples that meet in his movies, fall in love, and stay that way (presumably) beyond the end credits are few and far between. *Zelig*'s Eudora and Leonard and *Broadway Danny Rose*'s Danny and Tina come to mind (notably, both of these scripts were written during the initial stages of Allen's romance with Mia Farrow), as do *Hannah and Her Sisters*' Holly and Mickey, *Oedipus Wrecks*' Sheldon and Treva, *Curse of the Jade Scorpion*'s C. W. and Betty Ann, and *Melinda and Melinda*'s Melinda and Hobie.

But that's about it, and in a filmography that's closing in on fifty films, that ain't many. "What we had grown up being taught in Hollywood movies," Allen told Richard Schickel, "was that at the end you'd live happily ever after. But that didn't seem to be the case. Almost everywhere I looked, it just wasn't the case." And it's not the case in his work, either, which is littered with the corpses of failed relationships, ended by boredom (*Annie Hall*, *Husbands and Wives*), ego (*Sweet and Lowdown*), the pull of a past lover (*Alice*), the betrayal of a friend (*Manhattan*, *Melinda*), the irresistibility of outside attraction (*Celebrity*, *Anything Else*, *Everyone Says I Love You*), and even death itself (*Love and Death*, *Match Point*, *Crimes and Misdemeanors*).

Most of all, the serial killer of relationships in Allen's work is infidelity. With astonishingly few exceptions, every film from *Manhattan* forward features at least one important character who cheats on a spouse or relationship partner—by my count, only *Cassandra's Dream*, *Scoop*, *Small Time*

Crooks, and *Oedipus Wrecks* don't qualify. This seemingly fundamental and inescapable element of modern romance falls within Allen's admittedly cynical view of relationships "that started with all good faith, and everybody swore allegiance and great love and fealty and then you looked up in six days, or six months, or six years, or whatever, and everything had somehow come to nothing, or something had gone wrong somewhere. It was more frequent than two people who would meet with good intentions and form a relationship and things would last. That was the rarity."

And so it is in his work. Early on, he was a clumsy, comically terrible lover, but as his star rose and his romantic prospects improved ("He could always get the girls, you know," according to Diane Keaton, who *would* know), he moved into the role of romantic leading man. But he wasn't a conventional one. *Annie Hall* was advertised as a "nervous romance," and Allen was a romantic lead for nervous times. Although he's capable of amorous pronouncements (*Zelig* is, ultimately, the story of "the love of one woman that changed his life"), his view of love and romance is perhaps best encapsulated by *A Midsummer Night's Sex Comedy*: as an ephemeral, elusive thing, fleeting and interchangeable.

Allen's characters are, in his words, "high-strung, complex, intellectual people who find it very, very hard—impossible—to have good relationships with the other sex because they're so finely tuned, and have so much difficulty getting pleasure out of life, and are so critical of everything." His are not the stories of career-first bridesmaids who meet handsome, devilish rogues, with whom they spar and battle before falling into bed and love. Allen writes about narcissistic, death-obsessed intellectuals who meet neurotic actresses with whom they know it won't work out—and "he really doesn't want it to work," Allen explains, so when it doesn't, "he'll be able to say, 'My God, this girl was great.

Love and Death's Sonja on love: "To love is to suffer. To avoid suffering one must not love. But then one suffers from not loving. Therefore, to love is to suffer; not to love is to suffer; to suffer is to suffer." *Ernst Haas/Getty Images*

I gave her everything I had, and she, she just screwed it up'—when in fact he picked her for exactly that reason." His characters treat love as a selfish indulgence. They lie to each other, and lie to themselves. And they're always wondering if there's something and someone a little better, just around the corner.

There's no doubt that Woody is capable of moments of lush, romantic sentimentality: the sunrise over the Brooklyn Bridge in *Manhattan*, the first kiss in *The Purple Rose of Cairo*, the title event of *Stardust Memories*. These are, to borrow the closing analogy of *Annie Hall*, "the eggs" his characters need. But his romances aren't fairy tales, which is why they've inspired so many books, appreciations, and discussions, while his imitators—who know the words but not the music—are forgotten by the time you push through the theater's exit doors. Allen's relationships are honest accounts of the pitfalls of modern love, full of deception and illusion and dissatisfaction and frustration, which is why they stick with us: because we see in them something of ourselves.

Manhattan Murder Mystery

RELEASE DATE: August 18, 1993

WRITERS: Woody Allen, Marshall Brickman

CAST: Allen, Diane Keaton, Alan Alda, Anjelica Huston, Jerry Adler, Ron Rifkin, Joy Behar

IN A NUTSHELL: A married couple becomes convinced that their kindly neighbor murdered his wife, and they investigate with the help of their friends—who also offer romantic complications.

RECURRING THEMES: Murder ("I think it's a reasonable assumption that if you're dead, you don't suddenly turn up on the New York City transit system"); infidelity; jealousy; art vs. life ("I'll never say that life doesn't imitate art again")

Woody Allen had been itching to do a murder mystery for years. He and Mickey Rose's early attempt (titled *The Couple Next Door*) had given way to what became *Annie Hall*, though the mystery element was eliminated at the script stage. There was talk afterward of reviving the idea with Allen starring and Marshall Brickman directing, but nothing came of it. Yet Allen still said he would "love more than anything in this world to do a murder mystery. That would be my gift to myself." In 1992, with the Mia affair playing out in the tabloids, Allen apparently decided he needed that gift.

He had originally imagined Farrow playing the female lead of Carol Lipton, but when it became clear that this (to put it mildly) wasn't going to happen, he called on an old friend: Diane Keaton. The circularity of making the film that *Annie Hall* was intended to be with Annie herself back in the lead couldn't have been neater, and though the names and professions are different, *Manhattan Murder Mystery* feels very much like a return to those two beloved characters—older, wiser, experiencing a bit of empty-nest syndrome ("Now that Nick's grown up, we're left facing each other"), and feeling the strain of a long-term marriage that might be losing its spark.

In that last regard, the picture feels like a sunnier pass at *Husbands and Wives* territory. Early on, our protagonists have a slightly tense conversation about whether they've become just another "dull, old aging couple," wearing their dead-shark union like "a comfortable old pair of shoes." Keaton's Carol even asks Woody's Larry the same question that Farrow's Judy asked Gabe in *Husbands*: "Do you still find me attractive?" But this time around, the temptations presented by Ted (Alan Alda) and Marcia (Anjelica Huston) are discounted,

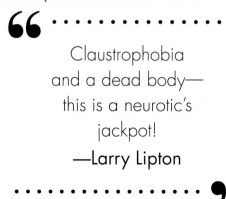

> Claustrophobia and a dead body—this is a neurotic's jackpot!
> —Larry Lipton

and the longtime couple's love is reinvigorated rather than ruined by the events of the film.

"For me it was pure pleasure," Allen said, and that joy shows in the film—in no small part due to the presence of Keaton, who is an utter delight. Her and Woody's well-worn chemistry (they'd been collaborators, friends, or lovers for over twenty years by this point) makes the on-screen relationship entirely credible, and their chemistry and comic timing is dynamite. In some scenes, such as the late-night conversations about Mr. House's mysterious comings and goings, you can actually see them making each other laugh, and Allen's amusement at her closing line seems utterly spontaneous and genuine. He did some rewriting when Keaton came on, to make the role a bit more active and his more reactive, and that was the right call; the dynamic, with Keaton snooping and Allen kvetching ("For God's sake, save a little crazy for menopause!"), plays beautifully.

The film's inspirations are obvious and sometimes even explicitly quoted by the films at Mr. House's revival house: *Double Indemnity, The Lady from Shanghai,* the crime-solving New York sophisticates of the *Thin Man* movies, the murderous neighbor of Hitchcock's *Rear Window.* It's a comedy, but also a pretty good little mystery. Allen is doing less a send-up than a reworking of the genre, sifting in his own idiosyncrasies as an actor (a bundle of klutzy nerves while sneaking around in Mr. House's apartment, hilariously bluffing his way into the hotel by pretending to be a cop) and a director (only Allen would score a car chase in 1993 with Benny Goodman's "Sing, Sing, Sing"). The writing crackles, with one good line after another. The film is entertainment, pure and simple, which was exactly what Woody and his fans needed at that moment.

WATCH OUT FOR

Zach Braff, in his film debut, as the Liptons' son, Nick; *The Wire* star Wendell Pierce as a cop responding to the call at the Hotel Waldon.

Woody on Woody

"It's one of those films that came out just as I envisioned it. I consider it a success. Great fun to make, just the kind of picture I loved to get lost in as a kid."

Manhattan Murder Mystery, Woody reunited onscreen with Diane Keaton, for the first time since *Manhattan. Lobby card from the Voyageur Press Collection*

Bullets Over Broadway

RELEASE DATE: October 14, 1994

WRITERS: Woody Allen, Douglas McGrath

CAST: John Cusack, Dianne Wiest, Chazz Palminteri, Jennifer Tilly, Jack Warden, Mary-Louise Parker, Joe Viterelli, Tracey Ullman, Jim Broadbent

IN A NUTSHELL: David Shayne, a "budding Chekhov," must cast a gangster's chorus girl moll to secure financing for his Broadway play, but he discovers that her bodyguard has an unexpected gift for drama.

RECURRING THEMES: Art vs. artist; show business; organized crime; infidelity; class; ghostwriting; actors and acting

TriStar Pictures had managed to translate the Soon-Yi scandal into decent curiosity box office results for *Husbands and Wives*. But Orion's bankruptcy couldn't have come at a worse time for Woody Allen. Though he disputed the notion that the bitter breakup with Mia Farrow had affected his box office ("The films I made at the high point of the conflict did exactly as well as my other films had done, which is not saying much"), his independence was, for the first time, in jeopardy. "One of the reasons studios loved being in business with Woody," said an anonymous insider, "and were happy to break even, was that surely he was one of the world's great directors, and there was a public relations value in being in business with him." But after the scandal, "that value was diluted." If Allen wanted to keep working in the manner he was accustomed to, he was going to have to come up with something special. And that's exactly what he did.

He made a new production deal, with an old friend. He had met Jean and John Doumanian back in the standup days, and they'd been close ever since. Even after the couple split, Woody cast John as an extra in several of his films, and he was said to be closer to Jean than anyone, sharing meals and phone calls on a daily basis. Her primary claim to fame was as the ill-fated successor to Lorne Michaels as producer on *Saturday Night Live*, but she'd set up a production company, Sweetland Films, with her wealthy companion Jacqui Safra and other foreign investors. Sweetland would retain international rights to Allen's films; Jean would produce and find domestic distribution. And

> " No, no, don't speak. Don't speak! Please don't speak. Please don't speak. No. No. No. Go. Go, gentle Scorpio, go. Your Pisces wishes you every happy return.
> —Helen Sinclair "

just to keep things in the family, Woody's sister Letty Aronson came on as executive producer.

The smooth new business arrangement was a sharp contrast to the turmoil in Woody's personal life. As he started writing his first picture for Sweetland, he and Mia were in the midst of an ugly custody battle for their biological child, Satchel, and the two they had adopted together, Dylan and Moshe. Farrow had accused Allen of molesting Dylan. The hunger for the story among entertainment and tabloid press was insatiable.

Allen, as usual, kept working. As with *Manhattan Murder Mystery*, he found that writing with a collaborator would help keep him focused. He brought on Douglas McGrath, who'd worked with Jean on *SNL* and had just finished a new screen adaptation of *Born Yesterday*, one of Woody's favorite plays. The young writer was duly impressed with Allen's ability to be creative while in the midst of such private drama. In *New York* magazine, he described their brainstorming sessions and how they were frequently interrupted by phone calls in hushed but intense tones. After several of these interruptions, McGrath wrote, Allen "just smiled sheepishly and said, 'Okay, let's get back to our little comic bauble.'"

The bauble they came up with was no mere backstage farce, although it is that, and a great one. In spite of the film's period setting and comic spirit, little bits of Allen's post-scandal angst are all over *Bullets Over Broadway*—most noticeably in the film's preoccupation with the separation between art and the artist. Flender (Rob Reiner), the unproduced playwright and Greenwich Village intellectual, insists that they are one and the same. "An artist creates his own moral universe!" Flender insists, though as Charles Champlin points out, Allen mildly mocks the sentiment by putting it in the mouth of "a ridiculous figure in a nightshirt." Yet these questions have subtly underscored much of the discussion of Allen in the years since the Soon-Yi scandal broke. For casual moviegoers and even some admirers, the two notions had become too intertwined, and particularly in the immediate aftermath of the story, the movie-going public was interested in neither the art nor the artist.

However, it must also be said that Allen insists that he does not think of himself in such terms. "I'm telling the truth," he said in 2000. "I don't see myself as an artist." It's the same point David Shayne—played by John Cusack, with Allen-esque stammers and spectacles—arrives at by the end of the film. Above all else, it is the story of his realization and acceptance of his limitations, a progression from the stubborn pronouncement "I'm an artist!" that opens the film. Just as Allen did after *What's New Pussycat?* and *What's Up, Tiger Lily?*, Shayne insists on directing his writing to protect it: "I won't see my work mangled again! I've been through this twice before!"

WATCH OUT FOR
The Sopranos costars Tony Sirico and Edie Falco as Rocco and Lorna, respectively; Stacey Nelkin, widely considered the inspiration for *Manhattan*'s Tracy, as Rita.

John Cusack, who previously costarred in *Shadows and Fog*, took the "Woody role" of playwright David Shayne in *Bullets Over Broadway*. When Allen adapted the film into a Broadway musical, the role was played by Zach Braff. *Brian Hamill/Getty Images*

But as we hear his dialogue in the early rehearsal scenes, it is stilted and overly stylized and jarringly on the nose, a criticism leveled by skeptics at Allen's dramas. Cheech (Chazz Palminteri) has no patience for it. "It's a stupid way of talking and nobody talks like that," he tells the playwright, and when he makes a suggestion, it's to make the stuffy, stagey text into "the way it would happen in real life." The mediocre artist's clumsy world is punctured by a poet of reality, and the more Cheech helps, first with plotting suggestions and then with on-the-sly dialogue rewrites ("Where I come from, nobody squeals," the thug assures him), the more David realizes what a fraud he is. The praise he receives for Cheech's work rings hollow, because he knows the truth—and getting that close to real talent confirms he doesn't have it.

At times, it seems Allen feels the same way, pointing to the works of Bergman or Kurosawa or Welles as proof of his inadequacies. "Some people think it's too much or even fake humility when I say I haven't made a great movie," he said. But, as Eric Lax points out, the key difference between David Shayne and Woody Allen is that Shayne is certain enough of his inadequacies to throw in the towel and cease being an artist so he can be a functional, normal guy. Allen—as well as *Deconstructing Harry*'s Harry Block and *Sweet and Lowdown*'s Emmet Ray—does the opposite. Cheech is the true unbending artist, who will stop at nothing, even murder, to ensure that his work is not compromised.

All this is rather high-minded deconstruction of what is, when you come down to it, a sparkling, frisky entertainment. It pulses with love for the theater (the Belasco, where Shayne's play is rehearsed and staged, was where Allen's own *Don't Drink the Water* finished its run), and the formalities of the process are lovingly staged. Every supporting role is jazzily written and cleverly cast, particularly Jennifer Tilly as the screeching Olive (a close inspection of her chorus line reveals that she can't even do *that* well, working a half-beat behind the rest of the ensemble); Tracey Ullman as the perky, canine-toting Eden; and Chazz Palminteri, who comes on like an electrical current as Cheech. He kills Olive not out of venom but out of love for his words; he gives philandering leading man Warner (Jim Broadbent) a warning he would normally eschew "because you're a good actor."

And then there is Dianne Wiest's sublime performance as Helen Sinclair, the Broadway diva who makes Norma Desmond look like a shrinking violet. McGrath was shocked by Allen's decision to cast the naturalistic actress in the brassy role, and Wiest was even more skeptical. It took a few difficult days for her to find the role, and it ultimately took Allen giving Wiest line readings for her to realize exactly how broad he wanted her to go. But once she went, there was no turning back. Her Helen is a work of comic brilliance, a woman whose every word, gesture, and vocal inflection is a calculated performance. "You MUST be JOKING!" she exclaims, entering her first scene, and Wiest takes no prisoners from that point on. Every scene is a gas, from her big, over-rehearsed opening speech characterizing the theater as "this church . . . each performance a birth, each curtain a death" to her constant insistence that David "Don't speak!" as he professes her love to her.

As producer Julian Marx (Jack Warden, who's excellent) reads the reviews of *God of Our Fathers* after opening night, Allen gets in a little dig at critics by having them misread the backstage gunfire that precipitates Cheech's death. But the notices for *Bullets Over Broadway* were equally rapturous, and—thanks in no small part to the keen campaign skills of Miramax Films, its eventual distributor—the film racked up an astonishing seven Oscar nominations. Wiest won the statue for Best Supporting Actress. Woody Allen was back.

Woody on Woody

"*Bullets* gives me a fond memory."

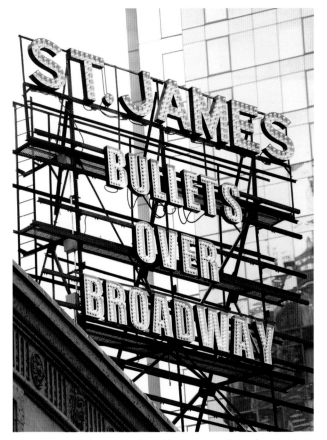

Bullets Over Broadway was adapted for the musical stage by Allen and debuted at New York's St. James Theater in April 2014. It received six Tony Award nominations. *Walter McBride/Getty Images*

Don't Drink the Water

RELEASE DATE: December 18, 1994

WRITER: Woody Allen (based on his play)

CAST: Allen, Michael J. Fox, Julie Kavner, Mayim Bialik, Dom DeLuise, Edward Herrmann, Austin Pendleton

IN A NUTSHELL: The members of New Jersey's Hollander family, vacationing behind the Iron Curtain, are mistaken for spies and find themselves marooned in the American embassy.

RECURRING THEMES: Jewish mothers ("This is my daughter Susan. She was a Caesarean"); magic

Don't Drink the Water, which Woody Allen wrote during his downtime in Paris while shooting *What's New Pussycat?*, opened on Broadway on November 17, 1966, and closed after 598 performances—an impressive run for a non-musical comedy from a first-time playwright. Allen never had much regard for it: "It's not a great play," he told Eric Lax. "Not even a good play. But it's an easy laugh vehicle." Yet his memories of its warm reception prompted an offhand comment to Jean Doumanian, shortly after they'd finished *Bullets Over Broadway*, that an adaptation might make for a funny movie, even if he wasn't all that interested in spending a year reworking a nearly thirty-year-old play. Doumanian proposed a quickie made-for-TV movie—his first—and set up the deal at ABC (owned by Disney, which also housed Miramax, distributor of *Bullets*).

Of course, there already *had* been a film version of *Don't Drink the Water*, shot while Woody was busy with *Take the Money and Run*. Since he wasn't directly involved, he had never bothered to view it until he was preparing his own version. He was horrified by what he saw. "The movie was ghastly," he later said. "As bad as anything ever committed to celluloid." In contrast to that picture, he didn't do much "adaptation," per se; his teleplay is basically the play, with the addition of a scene-setting opening narration and archival footage (he maintained the play's Cold War–era timeframe). It is very much filmed theater, all in the single location of the American embassy, with Carlo Di Palma's medium-wide shots occasionally framed as if through a stage proscenium.

To play the role of Axel Magee (which his friend Tony Roberts had originated on Broadway), Allen cast Michael J. Fox—who, according to his autobiography *Lucky Man*, had just decided to take a break from acting due to

> 66 He's insane.
> Years of insanity have
> made this guy crazy.
> —Walter Hollander 99

his still-secret Parkinson's diagnosis. In doing so, Fox jokingly told his agents, "Just let me know if Woody Allen calls." Reliable Julie Kavner was brought in to play Marion, matriarch of the Hollander family (her worried-mother line readings recall her most famous role, Marge Simpson). And Woody, who had flirted with the idea of playing Axel all those years earlier, had by then aged into the role of the father, Walter.

The film marks the return of the rough handheld style from *Husbands and Wives* and *Manhattan Murder Mystery*, which Allen and Di Palma had eschewed for *Bullets* because it was a period piece. "You want the thing to have an old-fashioned quality," he explained to Douglas McGrath. "To do it hand-held would give it too modern a feeling." But when time came to shoot *Water*, set in 1961, those concerns went out the window. Shooting handheld was faster and easier, and they had only four weeks to make the picture (he typically had more than twice that for a theatrical release), so quick and dirty it was. (Sometimes distractingly so; in Fox and Mayim Bialik's first scene, there's a moment when the cameraman clearly bumps into Fox's desk chair.)

Woody is right about the script—it is very much a joke machine, stopping only for a modestly dull romantic subplot (shades of the Marx Brothers), lacking the depth and nuance of the work he was doing by this time. Some of the jokes ("How many wives does this guy have? I count fourteen wives! How does he ever get in the bathroom?") cross the line from old-fashioned to just plain musty. But it is, for the most part, a funny little diversion—a lively revival of a well-worn but beloved old chestnut.

Woody on Woody

"What I did for TV was fine for what it was. The people were great. Julie Kavner was wonderful. Michael J. Fox was wonderful, and Dom DeLuise, I couldn't keep a straight face. I can hardly work with him, he makes me laugh so hard."

Allen directs Michael J. Fox as Mayim Bialik looks on. Fox's role of Axel Magee was originated on Broadway by Allen's friend and frequent costar Tony Roberts. *Brian Hamill/Getty Images*

• Starring Woody Allen •

When it comes to the films that bear his directorial imprimatur, Woody Allen insists on absolute control: Casting, shooting, editing, even promotion must meet his perfectionist standards. But as an actor-for-hire, he is a good deal less concerned. "I'd love to be extremely wealthy, but I would never do anything to obtain wealth. I mean, I would never make a movie or write a script to do that," he explained in the early 1990s. But, he carefully noted, "If somebody comes along and asks me to act in a movie and offers me a lot of money and it's a silly movie, I will act in it. I don't care about that." And we can thus explain some of the more peculiar blips in the Allen filmography.

The Front (1976)

Woody's best performance for another director is found in this seriocomic drama from Martin Ritt, who was a victim (along with writer Walter Bernstein, co-star Zero Mostel, and several other key personnel) of the Hollywood blacklist that is its subject. Allen plays Howard Prince, a cashier and part-time bookmaker who acts as a "front" for his blacklisted writer friend (Michael Murphy, later to play Yale in *Manhattan*). For his part, Woody turns off most of his usual mannerisms and plays a variation on his standard type; he's not a bundle of tics and insecurities this time, but a smooth, confident con artist. It's a solid, inspired performance in a rich and effective film.

King Lear (1987)

Woody doesn't appear until the last five minutes of Jean-Luc Godard's barely-seen catastrophe—as with *Casino Royale*, almost as a reward for those passing a cinematic endurance test. Godard's nonadaptation is a strange and incomprehensible work that ultimately lapses into

Allen opposite Zero Mostel in *The Front*, his best performance for another director. *Columbia Pictures/Getty Images*

Paul Mazursky's *Scenes from a Mall* paired Woody with Bette Midler as a ponytailed, surfing Californian. Audiences weren't buying it. *Poster from the Voyageur Press Collection*

self-parody. Allen plays "Mr. Alien, the man in charge," sipping from a disposable coffee cup in the film's editing room, reciting a Shakespearean sonnet, and assembling the footage with needle and thread (which might explain the picture's otherwise inexplicable style).

Scenes from a Mall (1991)

"If Phillip starts in on me one more time," Woody says early in this comedy, "about how New York is the cultural center of the world and Los Angeles is a barren desert, I'm gonna stick my fingers in his eyes." It's a nice little self-aware line about the very different role he's playing for writer/director Paul Mazursky, but it also underlines how miscast he is as a surfboard-toting, Saab-driving, Springsteen-concert-going Los Angelino with an unfortunate early-'90s ponytail; it's like casting Bob Hope in a role written for Bing Crosby. The film is marginally better than its terrible reputation, with Woody's impeccable timing wringing a few laughs out of the tired material, and the easy, comfortable chemistry between him and Bette Midler going a long way (as long as you're willing to pretend the movie theater cunnilingus scene never happened).

The Sunshine Boys (1996)

Woody and Peter Falk costarred in this TV movie adaptation of Neil Simon's play (previously filmed in 1975, with George Burns winning an Oscar in Woody's role of Al Lewis). Since both he and Simon are products of the Sid Caesar writers' room, Allen proves adept at delivering Simon's dialogue. It's a delightful performance—his slow build from friendliness to total frustration in their first extended two-scene is comic perfection—in a mixed bag of a film. Simon's updating isn't quite logical or successful, and Falk overplays his age so broadly that he seems old enough to be Allen's father rather than his contemporary. But it's homey and enjoyable enough, and one of Woody's better acting-only appearances.

Wild Man Blues (1997)

Jean Doumanian suggested Allen raise his public profile—and help shine a light of normalcy on his scandalous relationship with Soon-Yi—by inviting documentary cameras along during his jazz band's European tour ("Theoretically, this should be fun for us," he tells them as it kicks off). His skill as a musician, while impressive in spots, isn't white-washed (he eats it, rather spectacularly, in one torturous solo, yet soldiers on), and there are some off-the-cuff laughs ("There's the band; they're eating like they're going to the chair"). "It's like a home movie about the trip," he would later say of the film, which captures, in his interactions with "the notorious Soon-Yi Previn," a portrait of what seems an average or even dull companionship (Her: "The shower was excellent, wasn't it?" Him: "Yes, great pressure").

Antz (1998)

It seems strange to suggest that a computer-animated family movie would be the acting-only appearance that best captured Woody's personality, but here you have it. This kids' comedy plays less like a cartoon and more like an animated Allen film, complete with a supporting cast of actors from his earlier pictures (Gene Hackman, Christopher Walken, Sylvester Stallone, Sharon Stone). Woody is hilarious as a worker ant named Z-4195, beginning the story on his analyst's couch ("I had a very anxious childhood. When you're the middle child in a family of five million, you don't get a lot of attention") and ending up trying to squirm his way out of a war he got into merely to impress a girl, a la *Love and Death* and *Bananas*.

The Impostors (1998)

Shortly after actor and sometimes director Stanley Tucci appeared in *Deconstructing Harry*, Woody made an unbilled cameo appearance in this delightful, Tucci-directed throwback comedy, which riffs Laurel and Hardy by way of the ocean liner scenes in *A Night at the Opera*. Allen's appearance is brief and early, as a playwright/director auditioning our two heroes, but his intricate and verbose directions to them are a nice little in-joke for anyone familiar with his own audition process.

Fading Gigolo was Allen's first acting appearance for another director in thirteen years. *Poster from the Voyageur Press Collection*

Company Man (2000)

Another unbilled appearance for a former collaborator, this time for writer/director/star Douglas McGrath, Allen's co-writer on *Bullets Over Broadway*. McGrath's attempt to make a Woody-style crossover to acting in this "*Bananas Lite*" farce doesn't work at all (he's just not an engaging onscreen presence), but Allen gets some hearty laughs in a handful of scenes as the CIA's clueless Cuban bureau chief.

Picking Up the Pieces (2000)

This oddball black comedy with a healthy dose of mysticism from director Alfonso Arau finds a woefully out of place Woody playing a cowboy hat-sporting butcher in a New Mexico border town who murders his wife. It is easily the weirdest film to bear Allen's name, and probably the only time we'll ever see him costarring with Fran Drescher, Andy Dick, and Eddie Griffin.

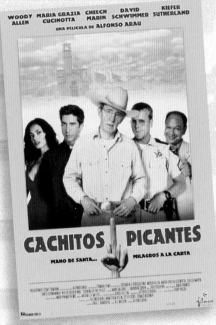

Spanish-language poster for Alfonso Arau's oddball *Picking Up the Pieces*. *Poster from the Voyageur Press Collection*

Fading Gigolo (2013)

Allen barely even acts in his own films anymore, much less for other directors, but he apparently couldn't resist the opportunity to play the "manager" (read: pimp) for writer/director/star John Turturro's title character. To his credit, Turturro plays straight man and gives Allen most of the good lines, letting his one-time director (in *Hannah and Her Sisters*) do the heavy comic lifting and basically steal the low-key picture out from under him.

• The Imitators •

"You can see every third director is imitating Martin Scorsese, and he deserves to be emulated. But young directors are not running out imitating me and shooting films the way I shoot them."

—Woody Allen

All anecdotal evidence indicates that Allen's famously low opinion of his own gifts as a filmmaker is not a case of false modesty—he genuinely feels that his are not major works. But when he insists, "I haven't been any kind of an influence, and maybe it's just as well," sorry, that just sounds crazy. Directors of comedy, romance, and drama have been turning out Woody-influenced pictures for years. These are but a few of the most obvious examples.

FILM	DIRECTOR	ALLEN-ESQUE ELEMENTS
Modern Romance (1981)	Albert Brooks	Writer/director in leading role; comedian-turned-filmmaker as primary creative force; neurotic protagonist; nervous romance
She's Gotta Have It (1986)	Spike Lee	New York setting; writer/director in supporting role; black-and-white photography
When Harry Met Sally (1989)	Rob Reiner	New York setting; Jewish male—gentile female relationship; witty, urbane dialogue; soundtrack of jazz and pop standards; white credits on black screen
Metropolitan (1990)	Whit Stillman	New York setting; witty, urbane dialogue; upper-class intellectual characters
L.A. Story (1991)	Mick Jackson	Writer in leading role; comedian-turned-screenwriter (Steve Martin) as primary creative force; magic realism; nervous romance described in many reviews as an "L.A. *Annie Hall*"
Miami Rhapsody (1995)	David Frankel	Neurotic protagonist; soundtrack of jazz and pop standards; white credits on black screen; breaking the fourth wall; Mia Farrow in key role
Walking and Talking (1996)	Nicole Holofcener	New York setting; witty, urbane dialogue; neurotic protagonist
High Fidelity (2000)	Stephen Frears	Breaking the fourth wall; neurotic protagonist; nervous romance
Kissing Jessica Stein (2001)	Charles Herman-Wurmfeld	New York setting; writers in leading roles; witty, urbane dialogue; neurotic protagonist; nervous romance
Sidewalks of New York (2002)	Edward Burns	Writer/director in leading role; New York setting; neurotic protagonist; faux-documentary format
(500) Days of Summer (2009)	Marc Webb	Neurotic protagonist; nervous romance; Ingmar Bergman homage; *Annie Hall*–style photographic trickery; kamikaze women
Tiny Furniture (2010)	Lena Dunham	Writer/director in leading role; New York setting; witty, urbane dialogue; upper-class intellectual characters
Sleepwalk with Me (2012)	Mike Birbiglia	Writer/director in leading role; comedian-turned-filmmaker as primary creative force; neurotic protagonist; nervous romance; New York setting; breaking the fourth wall
Frances Ha (2013)	Noah Baumbach	New York setting; co-writer in leading role; neurotic protagonist; black-and-white photography; witty, urbane dialogue

Mighty Aphrodite

RELEASE DATE: October 27, 1995

WRITER: Woody Allen

CAST: Allen, Mira Sorvino, Helena Bonham Carter, Michael Rapaport, F. Murray Abraham, Peter Weller, Jack Warden, David Ogden Stiers

IN A NUTSHELL: A sportswriter whose marriage is faltering seeks out the birth mother of his adopted son, and he is shocked to discover she is a porn star and prostitute.

RECURRING THEMES: Infidelity; fear of fatherhood; Jewish mothers (Abraham's Greek Chorus leader laments, "You'd think they'd pick up a phone once in a while"); actors and acting; prostitution ("I feel like I owe you a great fuck!"); Groucho idolatry (Allen proposes not just Groucho, but Harpo as potential names for their adopted son)

On December 18, 1991, Woody Allen and Mia Farrow became joint parents of two of her adopted children, Moses and Dylan. It was an unprecedented case; never before had the New York courts granted joint adoptive status to an unmarried couple. It was, alas, a short-term ruling as well—barely a month later, Farrow discovered Allen's affair with Soon-Yi. But if the breakup with Farrow took those adopted children away from Woody, they continued to inspire him.

It's also not a stretch to assume that there was some of Mia in the character of Amanda, wife to Lennie Weinrib (Allen). It is, after all, the story of a couple who looks to parenthood to revive their stagnant relationship. And it's not just her full-court press for adoption or his response—"I don't want to adopt for the same reason we don't lease the co-op: pride of ownership"—that feel inspired by real conversations. In fact, Woody told *Vanity Fair* in 2005 that when they were casting the movie, fresh off the ugly custody battle, he had suggested to casting director Juliet Taylor that Mia play the role. (Taylor's sensible reply: "You must be kidding.")

The more difficult casting challenge was finding the right actress to play Linda Ash, a.k.a. "Judy Cum," the cheery hooker and mother of his adopted son, whom Lenny tries to help. Mira Sorvino had done a handful of film roles, but nothing anywhere near the ballpark of this character, and Allen was initially resistant. She had to show up for an audition in costume and in character to convince him.

He made the right choice. Her helium-voiced, cheerfully vulgar Linda is a rich and delightful comic creation, the character's genuine sweetness and giddy enthusiasm taking the raw edge off lines like "You didn't want a blow-job, so the least I could do is get you a tie!" Yet somehow, in spite of the fact that she's basically

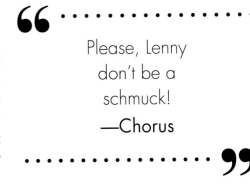

> Please, Lenny don't be a schmuck!
> —Chorus

playing a cartoon character, Sorvino discovers the character's genuine pain when she confesses her regret about giving up her child. She plays the beat seriously without ever dropping the character, and that she can do both simultaneously is impressive indeed. "She was able to bring it off," Woody said. "I'd look at dailies and think to myself, Looks good to me. I hope I'm not going to get killed with this, but it looks good." He didn't "get killed"—Sorvino swept the critics' awards and won the Oscar for Best Supporting Actress. It was the second straight year in which that prize went to a Woody Allen film.

Allen's other comic masterstroke was to intermingle this very contemporary story with the tropes and types of Greek tragedy, underlining the notion that, in his words, "the more he progressed, the more he learned, like Oedipus, the worse off he became." The film opens in the ruins, and the first few lines recited by the traditional Greek chorus are done straight, before taking a sharp colloquial turn with "Take, for instance, the tale of Lennie Weinrib."

Later, they plead to Zeus, who is out and leaves only an outgoing answering machine message. Cassandra appears, warning of "big trouble," to which Lenny snaps, "You're such a Cassandra!" ("I'm not 'such a Cassandra,'" she replies, "I *am* Cassandra!") And, in the film's cleverest leap, his Greek chorus becomes a traditional musical/comedy one, serenading Linda and her young beau in Central Park and closing the film with a rousing rendition of "When You're Smiling." It's appropriate that *Mighty Aphrodite* ends with a big musical production number; it's perhaps the clearest example of one Allen film pointing the way toward the next.

WATCH OUT FOR

Paul Giamatti as the "Extras Guild Researcher."

"The movie came off. Mira helped because she is a very smart girl and a very good actress."

French lobby card for *Mighty Aphrodite. Lobby card from the Voyageur Press Collection*

Everyone Says I Love You

RELEASE DATE: December 6, 1996

WRITER: Woody Allen

CAST: Allen, Goldie Hawn, Julia Roberts, Alan Alda, Edward Norton, Drew Barrymore, Tim Roth, Natalie Portman, Natasha Lyonne, Gaby Hoffman

IN A NUTSHELL: The lives and loves of a rich Upper East Side family are traced over the course of a year in dialogue and song.

RECURRING THEMES: Divorce; infidelity; organized crime ("I've never been kissed by a sociopath before!"); obsession with death ("We're rushing, we're rushing, where are we going? . . . Into the void!"); eavesdropping (Joe's romance with Von is basically a comic remake of *Another Woman*); suicide ("With the time change, I could be alive for six hours in New York but dead three hours in Paris. I could get things done and I could also be dead"); Groucho idolatry

The Manhattan that Woody Allen fell in love with wasn't the island a train ride away from his home in Brooklyn—not really. He was enamored with the Manhattan that he saw in the movies of his youth at his neighborhood theater, "where no one's ever at a loss for the right phase and everything comes out right at the end." He'd go to those movies and find himself transported into their sparkling world, and as a result, "I wanted to grow up, move into Manhattan, and live like that. I wanted to pop champagne corks and have a white telephone and trade ever-ready quips." He would grow up and move into Manhattan, but the life he lived there was not quite as light and airy as he'd imagined. So for his 1996 film, he re-created the spirit of those movies—right down to the period songs.

This meant his actors would have to sing, although they didn't know this until after they'd been cast. "It never occurred to me to tell anyone," he explained, "because I wanted to do a musical paying no regard to whether people could sing or not." The point of the musical numbers wasn't the beauty of the execution—it was the tender, honest emotion of the character and the performance, a bare directness that dialogue often can't put across. "What is more ridiculous than a man singing or dancing, in a certain sense?" he asked. "It's the aspiration of your most intense feelings, musicalized. If you took the music away, it would look so silly. It's so vulnerable and open." The idea, similarly explored in the miniseries and film of Dennis Potter's *Pennies from Heaven*, was that there are some emotions simply bigger than words. This idea is most successfully put across in the sweet love song that Bob (Alan Alda)

> I've been trying, since we got divorced, to find the right woman for him, somebody to match up with his personality. I'm beginning to wonder if the world population isn't too limited.
>
> —Steffi Dandridge

Alan Alda made his third appearance in an Allen film as Bob, the current husband of Woody's ex-wife Steffi (Goldie Hawn). This harmonious portrait of a post-divorce family was a sharp contrast to Allen's own experience. *Mondadori Portfolio by Getty Images*

sings to Steffi (Goldie Hawn), or the quiet, faltering laments of Skylar (Drew Barrymore) and Von (Julia Roberts), and especially in Woody's own melancholy performance of "I'm Through with Love," his voice thin yet disarming.

"When I was making it," Allen recalled, "the people in the music department were saying, 'They can't sing!' And the distributors were saying, 'They can't sing!' And I kept saying, 'Yes, I know that's the *point*. If they sing like they do in the shower, like regular people, that's the idea . . . unless it's like caterwauling and becomes punishment.'" (For the record, Barrymore's voice fell into the latter category; she was dubbed by Olivia Hayman.)

But Woody's musical extravaganza couldn't just be all-talking and all-singing—it had to be all-dancing as well. The big musical numbers (which unfold in such unlikely locations as a hospital, a funeral home, and Harry Winston's) are joyful, high-spirited, and unabashedly goofy. They also mostly play out in Allen's signature unbroken takes, made all the more difficult by the addition of choreography, musical playback, complicated camera blocking, and even (in the Venetian climax) wire work. But the seamless nature of those scenes gives the film the theatricality of a stage musical. "When I see a movie," Allen said, "I want to see the dancers in front of me full length. I hate it when they cut to their feet. I hate it when they cut to their faces. I don't like angle shots. I want to see it the way I see it if I pay $10 and I go to City Center and the dancers are in front of me. You know, straight on."

In addition to paying tribute to the New York of his boyhood moviegoing, *Everyone* was also a loving tribute to his beloved Marx Brothers. The title song was written for their 1932 picture *Horse Feathers*; the story culminates at the ornate "Groucho ball," which includes Woody's credible Groucho impression; he even uses "You Brought a New Kind of Love to Me," which the Marxes sang in *Monkey Business*, as incidental music.

"That film has got its fans, but it was not a huge success. I did it, like all my films, for the few people who like it."

115

Drew Barrymore (l) and Edward Norton (r) in Woody Allen's EVERYONE SAYS I LOVE YOU.

MIRAMAX
A Miramax Films Release © 1996
Photo: John Clifford

Edward Norton was still an unknown when he shot *Everyone Says I Love You.* By the time it was released, he'd become a star thanks to supporting roles in *Primal Fear* and *The People vs. Larry Flynt* earlier that year. Drew Barrymore also appeared in *Scream,* another Christmas 1996 release that received far more attention from *Everyone's* distributor Miramax. *Promotional photo from the Voyageur Press Collection*

If *Everyone Says I Love You* is one of his most glamorously romantic films (its presentation of Manhattan is the lushest in Woody's filmography since, well, *Manhattan*), there is a sense of sadness and despair just under its surface. His ugly real-life custody battle with Mia Farrow had resulted in the loss of visitation rights with their two adopted children, and his visits with their biological son had to be supervised. By the time he was making this film, even those escorted visits had ceased. Yet here is another portrait, similar to *Hannah and Her Sisters*, of a large, extended family (as Farrow's was) in which Allen's departed husband character is not just welcomed but beloved. ("I wonder what would've happened if we'd have stayed together," asks his ex-wife, after they share a romantic dance.) At risk of over-quoting the line, the whole scenario recalls Woody's straight-to-camera confession at the end of *Annie Hall*: "You know how you're always trying to get things to come out perfect in art, because, uh, it's real difficult in life."

And on top of all of that, his work family was breaking up, too. "I can see myself working with Greenhut forever," Allen said in 1978 of producer Robert Greenhut, but *Everyone* would be their last film together, the conclusion of a twenty-year partnership. Ditto for costume designer Jeffrey Kurland, who had been with him since *Stardust Memories*. His next film would be his last with director of photography Carlo Di Palma; still photographer Brian Hamill, who'd shot every Allen film since *Annie Hall*, had been dismissed after *Mighty Aphrodite*; Susan E. Morse, who'd been his chief film editor since *Manhattan*, would only cut two more of his pictures. The culprit: cost-cutting measures within Sweetland Films, which was continuing to fund his projects but at no great profit. There would be a slow changing of the guard behind the scenes, with only casting director Juliet Taylor and production designer Santo Loquasto surviving the slashing. But before they were all gone, Allen would make his most provocative (and, arguably, most autobiographical) film to date.

WATCH OUT FOR

Billy Crudup as one of D. J.'s loves; *The Wire's* Isiah Whitlock Jr. as the cop bringing grandpa home.

• The Black Reels •

When Woody Allen and his editors discard scenes and sequences from his films (see "Buried Treasures"), they are kept, at least for a time, in his editing room. Those spools, dubbed "The Black Reels," are often revisited when he is between productions, as an earlier idea, poorly executed (according to Allen, anyway), may be repurposed for a new project. Those reels are a tangible illustration of Allen's inclination toward recycling, whether the ideas come from earlier films, his nightclub act, or his prose. "I only throw ideas out once I've done them," Allen says, and throughout his career, certain ideas and premises are reworked and adapted for new films or even new media.

ORIGINAL MATERIAL	ADAPTED INTO
The one-act play "Death," published in *Without Feathers*, concerns a man named Kleinmann who is awakened by a mob seeking a killer.	Allen did a full rewrite, expanding the play by adding in the circus subplot and several additional characters, to create *Shadows and Fog*.
"The Kugelmass Episode," which won the O. Henry Award for Best Short Story in 1978 and later appeared in the collection *Side Effects*, concerns CCNY professor Sidney Kugelmass, who is projected into *Madame Bovary* and alters the long-cemented narrative, to the confusion of readers around the world.	*The Purple Rose of Cairo* is something of a reverse "Kugelmass," with a fictional character projected out of a work of art, to the consternation of those in both the fictional and real world. On a smaller scale, Gil's interactions with Adriana in *Midnight in Paris* seem to alter the already-written diary he discovers in the present day.
The nightclub routine "Lost Generation," first heard on the album *Woody Allen Volume 2*, finds our hero gallivanting through Europe with F. Scott and Zelda Fitzgerald, Gertrude Stein, Picasso, and Ernest Hemingway, who frequently punches him in the mouth.	*Midnight in Paris* finds modern-day writer Gil Pender magically transported to the same era and interacting with many of the same figures, and though neither Hemingway nor Stein punch him in the mouth, he helps save Zelda Fitzgerald from suicide.
An unpublished story, later read by Woody at a PEN fundraiser in November 1985, concerns Phil Feldman, a regular guy whose hostility escapes while he is sleeping and goes on a rampage.	An "escaped hostility" sequence pops up in *Stardust Memories*, as a scene from one of Sandy Bates earlier pictures.
During the writing of *Annie Hall*, Allen asked co-writer Marshall Brickman, "What if the characters just sang at that point?" Brickman didn't think it would work.	Twenty years later, Allen made *Everyone Says I Love You*, a romantic comedy where, at certain points, the characters just sing.
In a cut sequence from *Annie Hall*, the Devil takes Alvy, Annie, and Rob on a guided tour of Hell. According to the *New York Times*, "The four enter an elevator, which goes down. At each level, some of Mr. Allen's favorite enemies get on: C.I.A. assassins, F.B.I. informers, fast-food servers."	Allen repurposed the cut scene for *Deconstructing Harry*, with Hell's inhabitants updated to include book critics, aggressive panhandlers, right-wing extremists, TV evangelists, the NRA, lawyers who appear on television, and, of course, the media.
The flashbacks to Alvy's childhood, cut heavily in the transition from *Anhedonia* to *Annie Hall*.	Biographer John Baxter says that "fully a third" of *Radio Days* was pulled from themes and actions in early drafts of *Annie Hall*, which also provided some material for *Manhattan*.
The original plot of *Annie Hall* had Annie and Alvy involved in a murder mystery concerning a neighbor down the hall.	Woody and co-writer Marshall Brickman reworked this premise (and brought back Diane Keaton to play it) for *Manhattan Murder Mystery*.
An unfinished short story from the early 1980s was about a nebbish who "loses" his overbearing mother.	Allen revised this story draft to create his short film *Oedipus Wrecks* for the compilation *New York Stories*.

Deconstructing Harry

RELEASE DATE: December 12, 1997

WRITER: Woody Allen

CAST: Allen, Billy Crystal, Judy Davis, Elisabeth Shue, Bob Balaban, Hazelle Goodman, Kirstie Alley, Julia Louis-Dreyfus, Richard Benjamin, Stanley Tucci, Demi Moore, Robin Williams, Tobey Maguire

IN A NUTSHELL: Novelist Harry Block deals with the fallout of his autobiographical works, battles writer's block, and travels to his alma matter to be honored.

RECURRING THEMES: Art vs. life ("I'm not gonna stand out here and get lectured by my own creation"); art vs. artist; writers; infidelity ("You think getting a blowjob from a big-bosomed twenty-six-year-old is *pleasurable* for me?"); prostitution; Judaism ("I may hate myself, but not because I'm Jewish"); familial attraction; obsession with death; the afterlife as farce

I'm going right into the teeth of it," Woody Allen told *The New Yorker*'s John Lahr in 1996, about his next picture. "It's about a nasty, shallow, superficial, sexually obsessed guy. I'm sure everybody will think—I know this going in—they'll think it's me." He would later explain, "I tried to get someone else to play it—I tried to get everybody else to play it." Robert De Niro, Dustin Hoffman, Elliott Gould, Albert Brooks, Dennis Hopper; they all turned him down, he insisted, until finally, "maybe less than two weeks before shooting, I said I'd play it." His story is, to say the least, suspect. It stretches credibility to believe that a) a director known for having his pick of Hollywood's hottest actors was simply unable to find *anyone* to play the lead in his new film, or that b) he would let such a thing go until the eleventh hour.

But making such a claim—insisting yet again that an intensely personal work wasn't even about him and that he'd only taken the leading role under duress—is somehow perfect for the set of meta-textual funhouse mirrors (that Welles-inspired area behind the screen in *Manhattan Murder Mystery*'s climax, if you need a visual) he had not only set up by this point in his career, but is commenting on, prodding, and poking at in *Deconstructing Harry*. This is a film whose very subject is the idea of an artist mining his own life for material, a film that ends with no less a self-conscious gesture than the dramatization of its own conception ("I like it! A character who's too neurotic to function in life, but can only function in art!"). And as per usual, Allen shakes his head and tsks to himself and notes that no, we're dead wrong, it's not autobiographical at all.

Yet the film is full of head-on confrontations with not only the close readings of autobiography that have haunted him for years, but of the surrogate characters that were beginning to appear in his work, and of the idea that he is a "self-hating Jew." He addresses all with

> " He has no spiritual center. He's betting everything on physics and pussy.
> —Doris "

uncharacteristic viciousness; Richard Schickel notes the sharp contrast between his earlier characters and the "essentially unlovable" Harry, surmising that Allen was consciously "flinging this figure into the face of his bad publicity." As Ian Jarvie wrote in *Woody Allen and Philosophy*, "Harry is an unpleasant character, one of the most unpleasant Allen has created, and certainly the most unpleasant he has ever decided to play himself."

To be sure, it is a shock to hear our Woody unflinchingly unleash phrases like "world-class meshugana cunt" or demand that his hooker for the evening "tie me up, hit me, and then give me a blowjob." But the film is as intent on jarring its audience as it is on entertaining it. This is his most formally experimental work since *Stardust Memories*, utilizing a fractured (or deconstructed) timeline alternating Harry's own story, dramatizations of his stories, and scenes in which he interacts with his fictional characters and is privy to the private conversations of those close to him. Most controversially, he and editor Susan E. Morse return to the jump cuts of *Husbands and Wives* and crank up their jaggedness, often stacking pieces of film atop one other and holding shots for only a few frames.

This isn't just a stylistic trick or an editing shortcut, however. In nearly every instance, the jump cuts indicate some sort of alteration of Harry's mental state, from the contact high of Cookie's joint, the ingestion of too many pills and booze before phoning Fay, or the anxiety and fear of Lucy's pistol-waving appearance in the first scene. But as Allen notes, though he used the stylistic flourish to give the picture "a nervous, jerky, and

Woody on Woody

"I didn't dislike it."

Allen would distance himself from Harry Block but admitted that, like the character, "for me, artistic creation was a savior. If I didn't have it, I don't see what else I could have done." *Fine Line Features/Getty Images*

WATCH OUT FOR

Jennifer Garner as the girl on
the elevator; Paul Giamatti as one
of the writing students.

disjointed rhythm," he chose to forgo them during the sequences that showcase Harry's stories. Those stories-within-the-story "had to be edited in a very linear manner, and I didn't want anything to disrupt them, so you could appreciate the shift between a neurotic existence and an existence entirely controlled by art."

That contrast is best conveyed in a sequence that deftly intercuts Harry lying to Jane (so he can sneak off with Lucy) with Ken lying to Janet (so he can sneak off with Leslie), a sequence in which the lines are so fuzzy that fictional characters ask questions that real people answer (or, more precisely, the still-fictional characters that are one level closer to our reality). The elevator gets stuck in Harry's story, and Allen hard-cuts to Harry telling Fay, "If this was one of my stories, the elevator would get stuck between floors." But such contrivances aren't necessary. "This is not a book. We're not characters in a fictional thing," insists Woody's character in a fictional thing.

This jaded and often cynical film closes with a surprisingly warm and fanciful scene. Harry's arrest for kidnapping his son (and it's worth noting again that by this point, Allen no longer had any contact with his biological son) has prevented him from attending the ceremony honoring him at his old school. Yet back in his apartment, he imagines such a gala, attended not by blueblood donors and hangers-on but by all the characters he's created, who shower him with the kind of unqualified love he no longer receives from "real" people. And he shares the affection: "I love all of you, really. You've given me some of the happiest moments of my life—you've even saved my life at times." It's a wonderful sequence, and one that seems to encapsulate not just a film, but a career.

Deconstructing Harry reunited Allen with Mariel Hemingway for the first time since *Manhattan*, albeit in a far more confrontational role. *Lobby card from the Voyageur Press Collection*

Woody the Actor, the Character, the Persona

"It's me, thinly disguised. In fact, I don't think I should disguise it anymore. It's me."
—Harry Block (Woody Allen), *Deconstructing Harry*

When Woody Allen started doing his nightclub act, he quickly realized that there was more to being a performer than the joke-machine writing he'd been doing since high school. Strong material wasn't hard to come by, and that's why Catskills comics with socko gags were a dime a dozen. The comics he idolized (Bob Hope, Groucho Marx, W. C. Fields, Jack Benny) were about character first and jokes second. Once the audience knew and understood the character, they would chuckle at even their weakest bits. To maximize your laughs, you had to have a persona.

And from that realization, "Woody Allen" was born. He wore thick-rimmed black glasses, the telltale accessory of a bookish intellectual, a notion furthered by his frequent literary allusions and surrealistic wordplay. Part and parcel for the comic intellectual, then, was the presumption of physical weakness, the image of the meek, bullied nebbish, an image further bolstered by the slight frame and thinning hair that made him a combination of ninety-eight-pound weakling and redheaded stepchild. He would feign braveness, but back off immediately—in both physical altercations with the same sex and romantic entanglements with the opposite, talking the game of a white-hot lover but, in practice, more of a horny bumbler. And then there was the voice—"a nice Jewish boy gasping for air," as writer Foster Hirsch put it—a nasal Brooklynese that danced right up to the edge of a whine.

His onstage and onscreen patter was a tumult of stammers and mumbles, charging and backtracking, pausing and rephrasing, all little tricks that created the impression of nervousness and aimlessness, yet diverting us (his magician's training coming into play) from noticing the clever construction of the setups and punch lines, or how masterfully he deployed those "um"s and "tch"s as part of the musical rhythm of his joke delivery.

Woody, circa 1969. *CBS Photo Archive/Getty Images*

The timing was right for this kind of character. Art goes in cycles, and the aggressive style of Milton Berle, Alan King, and their ilk was on the way out. Allen's approach was quiet, contemplative, thoughtful. He objected to the label "intellectual comedian," insisting, "I'm a one-liner comic like Bob Hope and Henny Youngman. I do the wife jokes. I make faces. I'm a comedian in the classic style." However, his work was peppered with references far beyond the scope of a Hope or Youngman, and while he did "do the wife jokes," much more of his material—and the best of it—looked inward.

Woody's rise coincided not just with a proliferation of a more pronounced ethnicity in nightclub comedy, but—particularly when he migrated from the stage to the screen in the 1970s—a shift in cultural attitudes about masculinity and sexiness. Matinee idols like Redford, Newman, and Beatty had to make way for the likes of Hoffman, Hackman, and Pacino, movie stars who looked like real people. The triple-threat Allen would come to embody, in the words of critic Diane Jacobs, "the struggles of late-twentieth century urban man." Woody himself put it another way: "My character was assigned to me by my

Contrary to his clumsy onscreen persona, Allen was actually an accomplished and multi-talented athlete in his youth.
AP Photo/Bob Schutz

Diane Keaton, pictured with her *Play it Again, Sam* costars, said: "He could always get the girls, you know." *AP Photo*

audience. They laughed more at certain things. Naturally, I used more of those things."

In retrospect, it's somewhat astonishing how quickly that persona took hold. His 1966 film *What's Up, Tiger Lily* already has him caricatured, dominating the opening credits in a *Pink Panther*–style cartoon. The "little redhead kid" avatar (later seen in *Annie Hall* and *Radio Days*) is in place as early as 1969's *Take the Money and Run*. The character was so well-defined that when he appeared on *The Dick Cavett Show* in September 1969 and casually mentioned, "I played all sports well," he got a giant, show-stopping laugh.

Complicating matters, Woody actually *did* play all sports well. Already he was struggling with the conflation of "Woody Allen" the character with Woody Allen (nee Allan Konigsberg) the man. "Woody" was, as biographer Eric Lax writes, "a hilarious creation concocted from a wildly exaggerated personal basis." Allen, as he has frequently protested, was no intellectual; he got lousy grades and only read the great works of literature to keep up with college girls he wanted to bed. Like Leonard Zelig, he "preferred watching baseball to reading *Moby Dick*." And Diane Keaton has said that he had no trouble

getting girls—particularly, we can presume, after he became a stage and screen star.

The two halves of this split personality began to merge in 1977, when he made *Annie Hall*, his first film to draw on personal relationships and recognizable characters rather than broad parody and wild verbal cartoons. Since the romance at its center was mirrored by that of the actors dramatizing it, audiences and critics presumed it was based on their relationship—indeed, this level of voyeurism may have initially contributed to the film's appeal. And from that point on, puzzling out the genealogy of Allen's stories, figuring out what was "real" and what was fiction, became an inextricable component of Allen fandom.

The filmmaker objected—quietly, at first. "My films are only autobiographical in the large, overall sense," he said in 1980. "The details are invented, regardless of whether you're talking about *Annie Hall*, *Interiors*, or *Manhattan*." He said this while promoting *Stardust Memories*, about which he predicted, "This is not me, but it will be perceived as me." Was it ever. That film's portrayal of a harried filmmaker driven crazy by the demands and inanities of his monstrous fans provoked a backlash, under the assumption that this was, in fact, the opinion Allen held of those who admired him. Two years later, he was still trying to explain it: "Not only did those things not happen to me, I do not have those problems. I play a character who's a filmmaker because I'm familiar with the outer trappings of a profession like that. I can write about them. I'm not going to make myself a nuclear physicist who's having a nervous breakdown, because I just don't know what he'd do in the course of a typical day."

But the die was cast, and as the years passed, Allen became less tolerant of all this talk of autobiography. "The public doesn't know me," he told Eric Lax, "only the character I present to create conflict and laughs." In an interview with John Lahr, he insisted, "I'm not that iconic figure at all. I'm very different from that." And in his book-length interview with Stig Björkman, he went even further: "It's infantile. I can understand that certain segments of the population would do that. But I would think differently of the more educated critics and the more sophisticated audience. But people used to go up to Clark Gable and pick fights with him and say, 'Listen, you think you're so tough. . . .' They confuse the character you play with who you are. People tend to think that Humphrey Bogart was so tough, when in fact he was a very educated man."

The comparison is dubious, because Gable and Bogart did not write and direct their own films. And even Charles Chaplin and Jerry Lewis—who did write and direct their own films, and whom Allen also uses as examples—weren't working in anything resembling the realistic style Allen is. When the topic comes up (and it often does), he wants to have it both ways, it seems. He'll admit to Björkman that his characters "all reflect me," yet he'll also announce, "I've never been the character I've played."

To be sure, viewing the entirety of his work through the frame of autobiography is a minimizing approach. There is so much to dig into that running every film through a life-to-art decoder misses what is so valuable and remarkable about his fiction. But Allen himself admits that the "dividing line

Allen's second wife, Louise Lasser, appeared in six of his films.
Arthur Schatz/Time & Life Pictures/Getty Images

between life, my own life and art is so indistinct, so fine that it's an obsessional theme with me." In his book *The Reluctant Film Art of Woody Allen*, Peter J. Bailey writes of *Husbands and Wives*, "for Allen to pretend that a film which insists (as many of his screenplays do) on the autobiographical basis of art should be read completely in isolation from the real-world circumstances that clearly inspired its mood, and certainly influence its plot, reflects an equally oversimplified understanding of the complex transactions between art and life which are his films and which so often comprise the subject of his movies." Moreover, Bailey writes, "Allen is right to object that critics identified him excessively with Sandy Bates in *Stardust Memories* and with Harry Block [in *Deconstructing Harry*] as well, but in doing so he often minimized the inducements those films offered to make them 'think it's me.'"

And those inducements are many. The "kamikaze women," the exciting, chaotic, but unstable romantic partners of *Stardust Memories, Match Point,* and *Anything Else,* share much with the bipolar, self-destructive personality of Allen's second wife (and early costar) Louise Lasser. The dysfunctional family and suicidal mother of *Interiors* were, Lasser believed, "my family right down to the single most specific detail," and she even tells of calling Allen to protest ("I don't think you got my mother right," she told him, to which he reportedly responded, "I thought I was pretty spot-on about her"). In her memoir *What Falls Away*, Mia Farrow wrote that, in *Hannah and Her Sisters*, he "had taken many of the personal circumstances and themes of our lives and, it seemed, had distorted them into cartoonish characterizations. . . . He had taken the ordinary stuff of our lives and lifted it into art. We were honored and outraged." And then there is the matter of *Husbands and Wives*, the only film in which he and Farrow play a longtime couple, albeit one exhausted by each other's peccadillos and where each is tempted by other potential partners—in his case, a much younger woman.

Woody in *Deconstructing Harry*. "I'm sure everybody will think—I know this going in—they'll think it's me." AP Photo/HO

Allen insisted that *Husbands and Wives* was conceived and written before he began his relationship with Soon-Yi Previn, as if that puts the matter to rest; it's like his parsing of details in defending against claims of autobiography in *Manhattan* ("I never had a friend who was married and having an affair, then broke it off, and finally went back to the mistress when I was dating her") or *Annie Hall* ("My father didn't work in bumper cars in Coney Island. I didn't grow up in Coney Island but in Flatbush. I didn't meet Diane Keaton that way and she didn't leave and go with a rock singer"). It's as though he's conflating—deliberately, perhaps—the notions of memoir and autobiography. If specific facts don't jibe on a point-for-point basis, that doesn't necessarily make the work any less autobiographical. *Annie Hall* was clearly inspired, at least to some degree, by the soul-searching and loneliness he experienced after his relationship with Keaton ended, just as *Husbands and Wives* was written in the mindset that had not yet ended a long-term relationship for a far younger woman, but was perhaps capable of doing so.

From there, the line to *Deconstructing Harry*—a film about nothing less than the equally productive and destructive inclinations of merging fact and fiction—is that much clearer. As Foster Hirsch wrote in *Love, Sex, Death, and the Meaning of Life*, "In caricaturing the public perception of him as a sex-addicted workaholic—an image that Allen himself has fostered—he seeks to defuse the prosecution. In giving so much apparent ammunition to his denouncers—see what a prick I am, how I use people for my work, how untrustworthy I am in affairs of the loins and the heart—he enforces a countermove. . . . It's as if Allen decided to paint a portrait so extreme that his detractors might be coaxed into reevaluating their estimate of him." And it is that play with persona and perception, coupled with the film's raw language and attitudes (is this the *real* Woody who's been hiding all this time?) that gives the film its undeniable charge.

"I know it's kind of a fun parlor game to play," documentarian Robert Weide says, "but I think in the long run, it's a little meaningless. In the same way that any author uses their own life experiences, their own thoughts, and then infuses those things into their books and into their work, I think Woody does that—no more and no less than any other writer, or writer/director." He may be right. Way back in 1974, a less-reserved Allen told Eric Lax, "Almost all my work is autobiographical, and yet so exaggerated and distorted it reads to me like fiction." This may be the key to understanding his films in relationship to his life—rooted in his own experiences, loves, thoughts, and fears, yet, for him, turned into fiction once it comes out of the typewriter. Once it's out of his head and out in the world, it is no longer him. But there's also little doubt that the candor and honesty of Allen's work is what makes it so open and relatable to those who view it; the more personal he gets, the more universal it feels.

Celebrity

RELEASE DATE: November 20, 1998

WRITER: Woody Allen

CAST: Kenneth Branagh, Judy Davis, Leonardo DiCaprio, Winona Ryder, Joe Mantegna, Melanie Griffith, Famke Janssen, Charlize Theron

IN A NUTSHELL: A writer and his longtime wife, newly divorced, attempt to restart their lives while poking around on the fringes of fame.

RECURRING THEMES: Celebrity; frustrated novelists; infidelity; divorce; prostitution; filmmaking and filmmakers ("He's in town filming the adaptation of a sequel of a remake"); jealousy; neurotic actresses; kamikaze women ("Every guy I meet thinks he's the one that can make me faithful")

Of his own famously prickly relationship with fame, Woody Allen told Richard Schickel this: "Yes, your private life is no longer private, and you're inundated with paparazzi and things are printed in columns and things are said about you and that's the downside, and it's not pleasant. On the other hand, you know, you get very good seats at the World Series, and reservations at the restaurant, and if you call your doctor on Saturdays or Sundays, he'll see you. There's a lot of perquisites that a celebrity gets that are wonderful. In the end I think they outweigh the downside of it." Still, the downside seems to get much more weight in his 1998 film *Celebrity*—though when that movie was made, his recent stint as a target of celebrity journalism no doubt put him in a more acidic temperament.

There's nothing inherently wrong with Woody letting loose a foul mood and a foul mouth (as *Deconstructing Harry* proved). But alas, after a long string of excellent pictures, *Celebrity* marks the beginning of Woody's sketchiest period. *Celebrity*'s black-and-white photography (the product of Allen's final collaboration with Sven Nykvist) is gorgeous. Some of the show-biz satire lands, particularly the vapid, vacantly sexy dialogue of the celebrity interview ("I used to lay on my bed naked and watch my body develop") and the hilarious mixing of the Klan and skinheads with the Nation of Islam minister and the rabbi in the talk show green room ("The skinheads ate all the bagels!"). And Leonardo DiCaprio, fresh off his phenomenal success in *Titanic*, gives the picture a jolt of real electricity, creating the richest of the film's comic vignettes by magnificently sending up his own station as bad boy heartthrob flavor-of-the-month ("I make the first DiCaprio film after *Titanic*," Allen noted with a laugh, "and it didn't make a dime").

But many other sequences are underdeveloped, petering out before the punch line or failing to ignite at all. Allen fumbles the payoff of the Charlize Theron sequence; we don't even see what causes Lee (Kenneth Branagh) to go off the road and crash his car. His sexual encounter with Nicole (Melanie Griffith) plays like a celebrity

> " I've become the person I always hated, but I'm happier.
> —Robin Simon "

journalist's *Penthouse* letter. The tossing of Lee's manuscript—the only copy, of course—into the East River is an awfully moldy bit of business (echoing when the only copy of Gabe's book is left in the cab by Rain in *Husbands and Wives*). And the less said about Bebe Neuwirth trying to give Judy Davis a lesson in oral sex with a banana, the better.

Then there is the matter of Branagh, who isn't just the Woody surrogate—he's playing Woody, doing an outright impersonation of his director's well-known stammers, tics, and comic timing. In a later interview, Allen would insist, "Kenneth Branagh is very different from me as a natural personality, and even if he was imitating me, which he wasn't, *so what?*" The whole line, particularly the "which he wasn't," is befuddling—has he really convinced himself that it's not an imitation, or is he just messing with us?

Celebrity marks Allen's final collaboration with longtime editor Susan E. Morse, but it almost seems as though she left the job undone. The film runs a staggering (for Allen) 113 minutes, and often plays like an in-progress first assembly with good bits that still need to be dug out. It's not that it's a terrible film, merely one heavy with the flop sweat of a filmmaker spinning his wheels. Maybe the "HELP" skywriting that opens and closes the picture isn't a metaphor after all.

WATCH OUT FOR

Sam Rockwell and Adrian Grenier as members of DiCaprio's entourage; Debra Messing as a TV reporter; Allison Janney as the celebrity realtor; Jeffrey Wright as Nola's director; J. K. Simmons as the Jesus souvenir hawker; *Superbad* director Greg Mottola as the director of the film within the film; *Bullets* co-writer Doug McGrath as Nicole's publicist.

Woody on Woody

"That picture will be judged much more objectively years from now, when people are not so interested in me—not that I'm in their consciousness—when they'll be able to look at that picture and judge it apart from whether Branagh is imitating me. . . . I think that movie came off."

Celebrity

SCHÖN. REICH. BERÜHMT.

Celebrity was the first film Leonardo DiCaprio made after *Titanic*—"and it didn't make a dime," Allen would note. *Lobby card from the Voyageur Press Collection*

Sweet and Lowdown

RELEASE DATE: September 3, 1999

WRITER: Woody Allen

CAST: Sean Penn, Samantha Morton, Uma Thurman, Anthony LaPaglia, James Urbaniak, Denis O'Hare, Allen

IN A NUTSHELL: The story of Emmet Ray, an obscure 1930s jazz guitarist "second only to the great Django Reinhardt."

RECURRING THEMES: Art vs. artist; infidelity; the seductiveness of guitar music; show business; organized crime; writers; prostitution

If it's surprising that a jazz musician and aficionado such as Woody Allen took so long to make a movie about the music, it wasn't for lack of trying. Back in 1970, Allen proposed, as the first film for his initial three-picture deal with United Artists, a drama titled *The Jazz Baby*. "The executives at United Artists read the script and they were stunned," he told Stig Björkman, "because they expected a comedy like *Take the Money and Run* or something like that." He put the script aside and did *Bananas* instead.

Nearly thirty years later, he decided to make another go of it, reworking the script into *Sweet and Lowdown*. "The structure was the same," he said. "Some of the character traits were the same. . . . It was much less amusing—not that this film is a laugh riot." Maybe not, though it does contain some genuinely funny lines, a terrific running gag about Ray's perpetual also-ran status to Reinhardt, and two near-perfect comic sequences: the warring versions of the gas station story, and the unveiling of the elaborate "crescent moon" prop. The latter is like a master class in comic film construction—witness the careful composition of the wide shot during its rickety entrance, the exquisitely timed pause before it crashes back down to the stage, and the cut to Ray hacking the burning moon to pieces after the gig.

But *Sweet* is, at its heart, a serious story about a talented yet self-destructive louse and the limits to which we'll tolerate terrible behavior from those blessed with genius. Ray is a drunk, a part-time pimp, a kleptomaniac, and a raging egotist. But that ego is borne out of real talent. "I can't have my life cluttered!" he insists. "I'm an artist!" That proclamation harks back to the opening lines of *Bullets Over Broadway*. And from its period setting to the Cheech-like bodyguard character (here played by Anthony LaPaglia), *Sweet and Lowdown*

> "Not only are you vain and egotistical, but you have genuine crudeness!"
> —Blanche

128

Allen instructed Samantha Morton to watch Harpo Marx for inspiration to play the mute Hattie. Both she and Penn earned Academy Award nominations for their work in this film. *Hulton Archive/Getty Images*

plays like a more serious riff on that earlier picture's themes of the demands placed on artists and the degree to which the world around them bends to their own morality. The figures at their centers differ—*Bullets'* David Shayne realizes he is not an artist, but Emmet Ray is, and is thus incapable of the escape to Philadelphia that constitutes the former film's happy ending. Ray may cover his heartbreak in hubris and chest-thumping, but in *Sweet's* remarkable final scene, he finally uncorks the pain that makes his playing so sublime.

It's a searing bit of acting from Sean Penn, whose characterization of a fast-talking, odd-walking, self-centered dandy is full of jolting little moments. But he's at his best in his wordless scenes of musical performance. Penn does his own fingering (the result of months of preparation), and a peace comes over his turbulent face as he plays, which seems to be Woody's primary connection to the character; you see Allen take on that same elevated expression when he wails on his clarinet in *Wild Man Blues*.

Samantha Morton, as Ray's mute love Hattie, is every bit his equal; both were nominated for Oscars. Unsurprisingly, Allen instructed her to study Harpo Marx, whose muteness and voracious appetite are all over the character ("Who's Harpo Marx?" responded the young actress), as is his wide-eyed innocence, an essential goodness that contrasts Ray's casual cruelty. But her best acting moment comes in the lovely post-coital two-shot as he plays the guitar for her for the first time. His ethereal playing transports her as well.

Warm, funny, and ultimately heartbreaking, *Sweet and Lowdown* is too often excluded from conversations about Woody's best work. It's an underrated masterpiece, perhaps forgotten in light of the admittedly bumpy stretch of work that was to follow.

Woody on Woody

"I feel good about that picture . . . . The picture looked good, and the relationship between Sean and the mute girl was an interesting one, I thought."

WATCH OUT FOR

Cult director John Waters as the hotel manager.

Wild Man Blues:

Woody's Great American Songbook

by **Jason Gubbels**

Fifty years of filmmaking complicates the attempt to highlight single sequences, but perhaps no episode typifies Woody Allen's philosophy of music quite so handily as the back-to-back nightlife outings dramatized in *Hannah and Her Sisters* (1986). Dianne Wiest's character Holly first drags Mickey Sachs (Woody himself) to the Bowery for a punk rock concert at CBGB's, where she informs the aghast Mickey, "You're witnessing genius." Later, Mickey retreats to the upscale Café Carlyle on East 76th Street to swoon over Bobby Short, a New York jazz legend and the personification of elegance.

While Allen has long cautioned against conflating onscreen characters with himself, it's impossible to overlook how Mickey's horrified scorn for the punks ("After they sing, they're gonna take hostages!") jibes perfectly with Allen's general disdain for post-1950s popular culture. Moreover, Bobby Short's appearance was no fluke: The tasteful throwback had enjoyed a thirty-five-year Carlyle engagement that neatly shadowed Woody's own weekly Dixieland gigs at the same venue. Even the way that Allen's camera considers the different musicians reveals his sympathies. Note how the film continually cuts away from the hapless punk rockers (far more New Wave than punk rock, actually), the better to record Mickey's outraged responses. Then consider how the camera lingers respectfully as Short winds his way through an expert performance, all attention given over to his smooth delivery. Sure, the noisy flailing of pop

culture can continue to make its racket into the night, Allen seems to suggest. But as is explicitly posited near the end of *Manhattan* (1979), respect must be paid to those things that make life truly worth living—the second movement of Mozart's Jupiter Symphony, Louis Armstrong's recording of "Potato Head Blues," and, we may suppose, Bobby Short at the Carlyle.

Despite a voluminous output, Allen's use of music has remained exceptionally consistent; witness how few of his films claim an original score. Early projects handed scoring duties over to Tinseltown wunderkind Marvin Hamlisch, who supplied the whimsical "*Quiero La Noche*" for *Bananas* (1971). This would prove to be a rare future event, although Allen would grant Nick Apollo Forte the honor of crafting lounge singer Lou Canova's purposefully inane single "Agita" ("Some people like their pizza / Some people like-a suffrite") for *Broadway Danny Rose* (1984). Following jazz guitarist Mundell Lowe's scoring of 1972's *Everything You Always Wanted to Know About Sex* (*But Were Afraid to Ask)*, the filmmaker would avoid commissioning an original score for another thirty-five years, a decision Allen himself has noted was determined as much by the financial realities of filmmaking as any greater aesthetic choice, finally breaking the drought with Philip Glass's contribution to *Cassandra's Dream* in 2007.

Equally notable is Allen's avoidance of post-1950s popular music. His feature-length debut *What's Up, Tiger Lily?* (1966) includes performances by Greenwich Village folk-rock band The Lovin' Spoonful, added during post-production without Allen's consent, and it's easy to interpret the event as influencing the filmmaker's future insistence on creative control (and subsequent refusal to capitulate to pop trends). Rock music in Woody Allen films thereafter become scarcer than hen's teeth, although the novelty 1958 instrumental "Tequila" pops up in *Small Time Crooks* (2000), and Ramsey Lewis's funky "The In-Crowd" accompanies *Mighty Aphrodite* (1995). Far more typical is Alvy Singer's eye-rolling at Shelley Duvall's character in *Annie Hall* (1977), after the *Rolling Stone* reporter gushes over Bob Dylan's "Just Like a Woman."

Classical and orchestral music, on the other hand, receive Allen's adulatory respect. Much as Jean Renoir utilized Mozart's Three German Dances to lend highbrow gravitas to 1939's *The Rules of the Game*, Allen routinely employs classical performances to elevate proceedings—such as the persistent presence of Schubert's String Quartet No. 15 in *Crimes and Misdemeanors* (1989). Likewise, *Love and Death*, his 1975 spoof of Russian literature, is saturated with the music of Sergei Prokofiev, including the Cantata from Eisenstein's epic film *Alexander Nevsky*, an allusive set of references dense enough to bedazzle any Russophile. Not that

Allen isn't above using high culture to punctuate a joke: The filmmaker's choice of the march from Prokofiev's satirical opera *The Love for Three Oranges* to accompany Boris Grushenko's execution is one of his wryest gags.

Later in his career, Allen seemed to consider more fully the example of his cinematic idol, Ingmar Bergman, who routinely turned to the music of Chopin, Liszt, and Bach. And just as Bergman's *Saraband* (2003) structurally mimicked the Baroque-era dance from which it derived its name, Allen's 2005 thriller *Match Point* incorporated operatic performances to a notably sophisticated degree. The bulk of the film's musical accompaniment comes courtesy of shellac 78 rpm recordings of arias performed by famed Italian tenor Enrico Caruso. While these operatic selections both mirror the film's plot turns and underscore the opera-loving proclivities of lead character Chris

Woody Allen, both a music lover and a music maker. *Mondadori Portfolio via Getty Images*

Wilton (Jonathan Rhys Meyers), Allen's use of a lengthy selection from Giuseppe Verdi's 1887 *Otello* over the film's climax departs notably from standard practice. Rather than borrow the melodic richness of an aria to convey mood, Allen's use of Otello and Iago's Act II nonmelodic dramatic dialogue complicates the scene's already-dense narrative structure (while also offering knowledgeable opera fans a rare noncanonical treat).

Yet all Woody Allen fans know that his true musical passion lies within the rhythms and improvisation of American jazz, from the Dixieland ensemble he plays clarinet with to the swing-era performances populating nearly all of his films. Although Allen himself characterizes his clarinet abilities as amateurish, Barbara Kopple's 1997 documentary *Wild Man Blues* suggests an able performer as it chronicles his European tour with the defiantly old-fashioned New Orleans Jazz Band. Somewhat surprisingly given his love for the genre, Allen's films rarely feature Dixieland jazz; notable exceptions include the Original Dixieland Jass Band's 1920 recording of "Palesteena" in *Stardust Memories* (1980) and the opening moments of *Sleeper* (1973), which feature Allen himself on clarinet fronting the Preservation Hall Jazz Band on a romp through "Tain't Nobody's Biz-ness If I Do."

But the absence of Dixieland in his soundtracks may not be that surprising, after all—Allen has alluded to swing-era rhythms being more conducive to the pace of his films than those of "Hot Jazz" (and by extension, the post-swing complexities of bebop). Whatever the reasoning, Allen's use of the Great American Songbook claims few rivals in cinema, with individual songs routinely keyed to underline (or undercut) emotional cues. In *Stardust Memories*, Sandy Bates recalls the best moment of his life being when he simultaneously gazed upon the luminous Dorrie (Charlotte Rampling) while Louis Armstrong's 1931 rendition of "Stardust"

played on the stereo. (*Stardust Memories* is named after Armstrong's alternate take of the jazz standard, in which the trumpeter/vocalist ad-libbed "oh, memory" in the studio.) Still, Allen features performers across the spectrum of jazz/pop, from relative featherweights Guy Lombardo (*Zelig*) and Jackie Gleason (*Whatever Works* and *Hollywood Ending*) to such heavy hitters as Coleman Hawkins ("Sweet Georgia Brown" in *Crimes and Misdemeanors*) and Frank Sinatra.

Sinatra caps the remarkable sequence in *Radio Days* (1987) in which the film's narrator, Joe, recalls the glory of 1930s-era Radio City Music Hall. As the camera pans lovingly across the majestic interior, Sinatra's 1944 "If You Are But a Dream" unfolds in its entirety, lushly echoing Joe's observation that Radio City was "like heaven." As befits Allen's most unapologetically working-class film, *Radio Days* boasts perhaps his most wide-ranging use of popular song, from the grand silliness of Carmen Miranda's "The South American Way" to Bing Crosby and the Andrews Sisters injecting urbanity into Al Dexter's honky-tonk classic "Pistol Packin' Mama." And although the film's establishing shot of Rockaway Beach opens to the austere strains of Kurt Weill's "September Song," Allen concludes on a sugar-sweet note with Diane Keaton crooning "You'd Be So Nice to Come Home To" over a New Year's Eve broadcast set against images of a family together in their modest home. (Allen often rewards Keaton with uninterrupted turns at the microphone, such as her renditions of "It Had to Be You" and "Seems Like Old Times" in *Annie Hall*.)

Radio Days might well represent the peak of Woody's love of pop/jazz, even more so than ostensible musical *Everyone Says I Love You* (1996) or fictional jazz bio-pic *Sweet and Lowdown* (1999). The former certainly assembles winning selections from the Great American Songbook (although

Sean Penn as Emmet Ray, the second-best jazz guitarist in the world, in *Sweet and Lowdown*. *Hulton Archive/ Getty Images*

the film's best moments come when Allen tips his hat to the Marx Brothers, whose 1932 film *Horse Feathers* supplies the title number), and the latter's portrayal of fictional troubled jazz guitarist and Django Reinhart–worshipping Emmet Ray (Sean Penn) offers splendid guitar solos from West Coast performer Howard Alden. But neither soundtracks flow as charmingly as the nostalgia-driven *Radio Days*. And nostalgia remains one of Allen's inspirational forces, as is evident in his peerless use of George Gershwin's music in *Manhattan*.

Familiar tricks adorn the film's soundtrack, with an especially delicious joke arising when Allen pairs Gershwin's "Oh, Lady Be Good!"

with Isaac Davis's discovery of his ex-wife's tell-all biography. But far more subtle commentary is at work here, most notably *Manhattan*'s justly praised opening sequence. Consider Allen the lifelong New Yorker and clarinet aficionado; now consider Isaac romanticizing New York "out of all proportion" while perhaps the most famous clarinet glissando in American music emerges out of the darkness with the opening of Gershwin's 1924 "Rhapsody in Blue." A montage of Manhattan landmarks and locales then unfurls over the "jazz concerto," all while Isaac struggles with a suitable opening line for his New York novel. After he strikes upon the mock-heroic "New York was his town, and it always would be," Gershwin's score takes over for nearly two minutes of dialogue-free fast cuts, reaching a crescendo in which fireworks explode across the cityscape as the musical number crashes to conclusion.

"Rhapsody in Blue" serves multiple purposes in *Manhattan*'s opening moments: a bulwark against what Isaac details as "the decay of contemporary culture"; a flush of nostalgia to fight off recent dreadful memories like the '77 blackout; and a deliberate archaism to accompany Gordon Willis's black and white cinematography, thereby ensuring the film would prove no late-1970s period piece. Yet the prologue's concluding lengthy shot of fireworks bursting to Gershwin also resembles similar moments throughout Allen's career in which he insists the viewer pay proper respect to an unfolding musical performance—Louis Armstrong singing "Stardust," Emmet Ray channeling Django Reinhardt, Bobby Short performing at the Carlyle. In each instance, the filmmaker seems to be telling his audience, we're privileged to be privy to those rare events that help make life worth living.

Jason Gubbels is a contributing freelance writer to *SPIN* magazine and *Rhapsody*. He has a master's degree in library science and lives in Lake Bluff, Illinois, with his wife and son.

Small Time Crooks

RELEASE DATE: May 19, 2000

WRITER: Woody Allen

CAST: Allen, Tracey Ullman, Elaine May, Hugh Grant, Jon Lovitz, Michael Rappaport, Elaine Stritch, Tony Darrow

IN A NUTSHELL: A failed criminal and his wife inadvertently become millionaires.

RECURRING THEMES: Crime; class; celebrity

After years without a standing studio arrangement (his previous three pictures had been released by three different distributors), Woody Allen finally made a new and lucrative deal in 2000. It was a three-picture contract with DreamWorks, the upstart outfit for which he'd voiced the leading role in the hit animated movie *Antz*. He had the same creative freedom he'd always demanded, although he may have felt some pressure to deliver an audience, since his first picture for the company was a throwback to the "early, funny movies," a straightforward comedy about a failed bank robber that could just as well have been a sequel to *Take the Money and Run*.

"It was an old idea of mine that was lying around for years," Allen said of the film. Its best quality is its ingenious structure: It starts as a heist film, and was marketed as such, but the source of wealth for Ray (Allen) and Frenchy (Tracey Ullman) turns out not to be the bank robbery scheme but the cookie shop they've set up as a front. The second act finds the couple trying—and failing—to fit in to high society. In the third act, Ray tries to pull off one more job to break his boredom.

Ray was the least intellectual character Woody had played since Danny Rose. He's taking another crack at a blue-collar lowlife type, and there's a pronounced *Honeymooners* vibe to Ray and Frenchy's relationship, in which they trade insults, physical threats, and ultimately affection (the closing line, "Sweetheart, you're the greatest," paraphrases Jackie Gleason's frequent episode closer, "Baby, you're the greatest"). Perhaps due to the sitcom roots of the characters, Allen and Ullman's acting is especially broad, which doesn't exactly work; it makes the schematic setup/punch line nature

> " ....
>
> I was a lousy student and I always hated school. And I don't care about it. If I could find my school principal today, now that I got some dough, I'd put a contract out on her.
>
> —Ray
>
> .... "

Allen re-teamed with *Bullets* costar Tracey Ullman to play the Kramden-esque couple at the center of *Small Time Crooks*. *Getty Images*

of the writing all the more obvious and muddies his attempts to wring pathos from their misfortune and ultimate reconciliation in the film's final, clumsy, rather overwritten scene.

Allen dismissed the movie as "trivial," and that sounds about right. Its pleasures are primarily found in the supporting performances of the great Elaine May—who is, as her character is described, "most amusing"—and *Mighty Aphrodite*'s Michael Rappaport, playing another likable lunkhead. (The disappearance of Ray's crew from the third act is a puzzling loose end from a writer who usually steers clear of such errors.) There are some interesting thematic overtures as well, particularly the *Annie Hall*–era notion of Woody's better half outgrowing him (this time under someone else's tutelage rather than his own) and its examinations of class and social climbing.

"Will you knock it off?" Ray demands of his wife. "You're Frenchy Fox from Jersey; quit puttin' on airs." He finds this salt-of-the-earth pair far more honorable than the rich twits who snicker at them (he gets a few good laughs out of chattering class complaints like "He got custody of the polo ponies"), and it's somewhat telling that the words Frenchy uses to describe Ray ("He likes to watch TV in his underwear, sucking a Bud") are so similar to those Allen has used, in interviews, to separate himself from his screen persona ("I'm the guy that you see in his T-shirt with a beer watching the baseball game at night at home on television"). Yet Mr. Allen is also a connoisseur of European art cinema and classic literature. Is he, too, "puttin' on airs"?

Not that *Small Time Crooks* has such introspection on its mind. It is a light, airy picture, a soufflé, albeit one that falls fairly regularly. It's not an awful picture, but it's an awfully forgettable one.

WATCH OUT FOR
Designer Isaac Mizrahi (who also cameoed in *Celebrity*) as the couple's chef.

Woody on Woody

"That was a trivial picture. A silly little picture. It does have some laughs in it because I was more skillful, the idea was clever, the jokes were clever, and playing a two-bit crook with grandiose ambitions was within my range."

The Curse of the Jade Scorpion

RELEASE DATE: August 24, 2001

WRITER: Woody Allen

CAST: Allen, Helen Hunt, Dan Aykroyd, Charlize Theron, Wallace Shawn, David Ogden Stiers

IN A NUTSHELL: An insurance investigator unwittingly becomes a thief when he's placed under powerful hypnosis by a crooked magician.

RECURRING THEMES: Magic (both Stiers's hypnotist and Shawn's amateur magician); crime; infidelity; suicide; kamikaze women ("She seems a little demented, but hey, in a hotel room that can be a lot of fun")

Woody Allen's run of three straight farces in the early 2000s was less a matter of pressing artistic need than simple housecleaning; all three were old ideas he found in his fabled drawers and decided to dust off. "I wanted to do these films 'cause I thought they were all amusing ideas," he told Richard Schickel, "that I'd have a good time doing them and that people would enjoy the pictures, that they were perfectly respectable pictures." As with the lighter *Manhattan Murder Mystery* in 1993, they also served as a bit of a diversion from off-screen trouble. After *Small Time Crooks*, Allen parted company with his longtime friend and producer Jean Doumanian, suing her and partner Jacqui Safra for defrauding him of $12 million. Doumanian and Safra countersued, prompting a trial that the New York press covered almost as breathlessly as Allen's custody battle the previous decade. From *Curse of the Jade Scorpion* onward, Woody's producer would be his sister, Letty Aronson, of whom he says (perhaps not entirely jokingly), "She's family, so I know she is completely honest."

The partnership did not get off to an illustrious start. At $26 million, *Curse* was Woody's most expensive movie to date; its worldwide gross of $18 million didn't come close to recouping that cost. To be fair, you can see all the money on the screen—Santo Loquasto's 1940s production design is as gorgeous as the photography by Zhao Fei (his third and final collaboration with Allen, after *Sweet* and *Crooks*). True to Woody's word, it is an amusing idea, a fast-talking screwball comedy with a *noir* flavor.

But for such a clever comic premise, *Curse* is strangely light on laughs. The jokey insult banter of *Small Time Crooks* is back, and creakier for wear, though he makes a dependable running gag of Helen Hunt's intricate, detailed descriptions of the injuries and deaths

> " My clergyman, who happens to be wanted for pederasty, will vouch for me.
> —C. W. Briggs "

Celebrity's Charlize Theron was one of the few memorable elements of *Jade Scorpion*. "Charlize Theron has screen humidity," Woody later said. *Lobby card from the Voyageur Press Collection*

she's carefully warning him to avoid. Yet even more than in *Crooks*, the setups and punch lines feel a little wheezy, the sound of an aging jokesmith going through the motions.

Frankly, that's the clearest prism through which to view this bumpy series of pictures: an artist trotting out his old tricks one more time and finding they don't fly as well as they used to. Woody's witty and naturalistic dialogue is, this time, often stilted. His old pop standards are always welcome, but here (as in *Crooks*) he insists on monotonously reusing the same ones over and over again. And the sixty-five-year-old Allen writing himself a role where he's utterly irresistible to Helen Hunt, Elizabeth Berkley, *and* Charlize Theron seems the height of wish fulfillment. He took the blame for that bit of casting. "I went wrong in playing the lead," he told Eric Lax. "I would have been better off if I had less laughs and had a straighter, tougher leading man. . . . And I felt it as I was seeing dailies every day. I didn't know how to get out of it." The complex production and intricacy of the design made the reshoots he'd have normally done to replace a miscast actor an unaffordable luxury.

All that said, the least of Allen's films is still better than most anyone else's best, and scattered elements here and there do work: the mystery plot, Hunt's zippy way with her smart-dame dialogue, Theron vamping it up as the *femme fatale* she was born to play. And the notion of one last kiss "before the ugly curtain of reality drops on both of us" is, in its quiet way, a rather profound statement of not just the power of magic but of cinema itself. But otherwise, *Curse* mostly falls flat.

Woody on Woody

"I, from my personal point of view, feel that maybe—and there are many candidates for this—but it may be the worst film I've made. It kills me to have a cast so gifted and not be able to come through for them."

137

Hollywood Ending

RELEASE DATE: May 3, 2002

WRITER: Woody Allen

CAST: Allen, Téa Leoni, Debra Messing, Mark Rydell, Treat Williams, George Hamilton, Tiffani Thiessen

IN A NUTSHELL: A washed-up Hollywood director gets one last shot to direct a big movie—and goes temporarily blind just as shooting begins.

RECURRING THEMES: Filmmaking and filmmakers; divorce; infidelity; masturbation ("For me, the nicest thing about masturbation is afterward, the cuddling time"); California hatred ("I gotta run, I'm having another skin cancer removed"); hypochondria ("Elm blight? Only trees get elm blight"): estranged children

Curse of the Jade Scorpion was still in theaters on September 11, 2001, when Woody's beloved hometown was crippled by tragedy. He contributed to the healing in two high-profile ways. First, he directed a delightful short film called "Sounds from a Town I Love" for the October 20th "Concert for New York City" benefit. And then, the following February, he shocked the industry by making a surprise appearance at the 2002 Oscar ceremony, introducing a tribute montage to the city and doing a short but uproarious monologue (his first standup in something like thirty years) in the process.

Hollywood was delighted to see Allen turn up, at long last, on their biggest night. They just weren't all that interested in his latest picture, a satire of the movie business—and, to some degree, of himself. Though Woody had never been the kind of filmmaker who helmed $60 million studio pictures (as his character, Val Waxman, does), it's hard not to think of the writer/director's own peccadillos as execs despair of his perfectionist tendencies and his reputation for replacing actors. Other self-reflective moments include his interaction with a Chinese cinematographer who speaks no English (just like Zhao Fei, whom he'd just shot three pictures with) and, perhaps most tellingly, when his girlfriend (Debra Messing) wails, "I'm tired of all the talk about how big you were ten years ago!"

Sadly, on the evidence of *Hollywood Ending*, Allen's portrait of a director past his prime also seemed apt. The picture, while blessed with sporadic laughs and fine performances (particularly from Téa Leoni, who could've ended up in the pantheon of great Allen heroines were she working with stronger material), is oddly listless and rambling. Its biggest issue is pacing. The film runs an interminable 114 minutes, and the primary comic

> 66
>
> A tenth of a point after quadruple break-even! You really are a shark, Al."
>
> —Val Waxman
>
> 99

Téa Leoni with Allen on the set of the movie-within-a-movie. *Lobby card from the Voyageur Press Collection*

complication of Val's blindness doesn't even reveal itself until the forty-minute mark. The cutting simply isn't disciplined; numerous scenes run on well past their sell-by date, repeating the joke instead of expanding it.

The script has more outright groaners than we're used to even in lesser Allen ("I've got two Oscars!" Val fumes, from a snowy Canadian shoot. "Up here you don't need Oscars; you need antlers!"). The gags based on his long-running distaste for California culture are uncharacteristically toothless and out of touch ("Send some flowers to Haley Joel Osment with a card: 'Congratulations on your lifetime achievement award'"). And he oddly miscalculates how to visually convey his character's blindness—even neophyte sightless people at least look in the general direction of the person who's talking; Val *turns away* from people when they move into his line of sight. It's not funny; it's just frustrating. And so it goes for the movie.

Woody, ever the contrarian, insisted audiences had missed the boat: "I just thought it was just such a funny idea and the whole thing came off and I played it and was well done. I think if people had gone to see it they would have enjoyed it. But they didn't go to see it." Maybe they heard critics complaining, again, that Woody was too old to play the romantic lead; as with *Jade Scorpion*, his Val is the object of desire for three gorgeous, much younger women. (This would be his last time in such a role, heretofore confining his limited appearances to older, mentor types.)

However, its ending (aside from the element of the filmmaker's reunion with his estranged son) would prove prophetic. *Hollywood Ending*'s titular moment arrives when Val gets word that European audiences are vaunting his seemingly inscrutable film, and he has been summoned to the continent to make another picture. Woody's own European exodus was still two years away. In the meantime, he would return to the themes and style of two of his most acclaimed films.

Woody on Woody

"The biggest personal shock to me of all the movies that I've done is that *Hollywood Ending* was not thought of as a first-rate, extraordinary comedy. . . . I thought it was a simple, funny idea that worked, and could have been done by Charlie Chaplin or Buster Keaton, Jack Lemmon, Walter Matthau. . . . I generally don't love my own finished product, but this one I did."

Anything Else

RELEASE DATE: August 27, 2003

WRITER: Woody Allen

CAST: Allen, Jason Biggs, Christina Ricci, Stockard Channing, Danny DeVito, Jimmy Fallon

IN A NUTSHELL: A young comedy writer struggles to maintain a relationship with his neurotic girlfriend.

RECURRING THEMES: Infidelity; Judaism; masturbation ("I happen to prefer it!"); show business; standup comedy; neurotic actresses; sexless relationships; psychoanalysis ("You chose psychoanalysis over real life? Are you learning disabled?"); frustrated novelists; jealousy; Bogart idolatry; past vs. present; kamikaze women

A fter a string of wobbly comedies, *Anything Else* finds Allen steadying himself by (consciously or otherwise) reworking his most iconic film, *Annie Hall*. Consider the evidence: It opens with Woody telling old jokes that hold the secrets to life; its protagonist (Jerry Falk, played by Jason Biggs) is a struggling young comedy writer; it is primarily the story of his "nervous romance" with a neurotic actress/singer; that story is told in a winding, nonlinear fashion; it includes an interlude involving cocaine; Allen's character is paranoid about overheard anti-Semitism; and the film is filled with directorial flourishes like split-screen, direct address, and characters appearing twice in the same frame. (For good measure, he also throws in a *Danny Rose*–style manager who fears being left by his client when things get good.)

In spite of all those similarities, *Anything Else* does not feel like a warmed-over *Annie* retread. Woody puts a new spin on the material, revamping the story for younger characters and managing, in the process, to create the kind of compelling boy-meets-girl rom-com that he is often identified with (even though he's done comparatively little of it). Passing off leading-man duties to *American Pie* star Biggs—who's not entirely up to the task—Allen wears his new role of crusty supporting player well, and he seems to enjoy playing this darker variation on his regular character, here envisioned as a wise purveyor of Catskills wisdom but also a paranoid survivalist. (One interesting divergence from his previous films: Jerry's happy ending is an opportunity to write for television in Los Angeles, both long-time objects of ridicule in Allen's work and life.)

Most importantly, the film's central relationship makes for both believable conflict and witty repartee. The flashbacks to Jerry and Amanda's introduction evocatively capture the rush of a new infatuation, while

> " I've had a crush on you since we met. Couldn't you tell, the way I was ignoring you?
> —Amanda Chase "

Jason Biggs and Christina Ricci make like Annie and Alvy Jr. in *Anything Else*. Lobby card from the Voyageur Press Collection

the back-and-forth of their subsequent arguments are sharp and snappy ("Do you love me?" "What a question! Just because I pull away when you touch me?"). Christina Ricci's Amanda is more of a mess than Annie, less fizzy than destructive, but she pulls off the tricky feat of both making you see how she would make her lovers go insane (her dialogue in her first scene, about how she came to eat most of the food in their apartment in advance of their anniversary dinner, is a masterpiece of circular logic) and why they would be willing to go there.

Throughout the film, Biggs's Jerry makes mention of his perpetually unfinished novel; interestingly, Allen had recently finished a novel of his own but was unhappy with it, although he put "a certain amount of it" into the *Anything Else* script. (That's not the only recycled element—the title was one of many considered for what eventually became *Crimes and Misdemeanors*.) However full it was of echoes from works both acclaimed and unseen, *Anything Else* marked a step in the right direction for the filmmaker—though DreamWorks may have considered it too little, too late. The trailers and TV spots didn't just play up the film's younger leads, they left Allen out altogether, seemingly almost ashamed of the picture's auteur. "It's as if they have the treasure of a Woody Allen movie," Roger Ebert wrote, "and they're trying to package it for the *American Pie* crowd." It didn't work; the grosses were right around his usual range, and his contract with the studio came to an end. For his next two films, Woody would revisit another masterpiece, 1989's *Crimes and Misdemeanors*—first returning to its structure and then (most successfully) to its themes.

Woody on Woody

"I thought it was a good movie. I was crazy about Christina, and Jason was adorable, and Stockard Channing is always a really strong actress. . . . I think it came off fairly well."

WATCH OUT FOR
Adrian Grenier as the heartthrob in Amanda's acting class.

• The Allen Style •

"Technique is something you learn. You know what it is? It's like throwing a ball or playing billiards or playing the piano, where all of a sudden you come to a point where you can do it."

—Woody Allen

Early on, Allen admits, crafting a distinctive filmmaking style was not among his primary concerns. "If the movie was funny, it was successful," he later said. "If it was not funny, it wasn't. And I could always be funny. That I had control over. So everything was subjugated *to the joke*. The films were a series of jokes." In that equation, aesthetics were decidedly secondary. "I never had any ulterior motive in terms of style or content or breaking new ground or anything like that," he said in 1976. "The only interest to me was making people laugh." And in straight comedy, the preferred style is no style—to sell the joke, you look right down the barrel of it, instead of dazzling the audience with cinematic curlicues.

That started to change in 1972, with *Everything You Always Wanted to Know About Sex*. At the time, he pinpointed its Italian cinema parody as "the most fun I've had with anything," since, for the first time, "I didn't have to think about anything except what is the best shot I can make with the camera. I didn't have to worry if it was dark or if it was moody, or if someone was half shadowed or half blocked, because it contributes to the joke—I'm satirizing that style of shooting." It wasn't just the Italian sequence; each segment, be it the starkness of the sci-fi scene, the fuzzy game show parody, or the "women's pictures"–inspired warmth of the bestiality vignette, has a look and style that contributes to the gag without undermining it.

From that point on, he would change his thinking. His growth as a filmmaker was borne out of his growth as a writer. If the early pictures were haphazardly filmed dramatizations of his nightclub act and prose pieces ("gags and sketches and

monologues, with bodies attached to the jokes," according to early biographer Myles Palmer), subsequent screenplays that were as interested in character and narrative as laughs-per-minute allowed their director equal latitude.

During rehearsals for *Play It Again, Sam*, Allen told director Herbert Ross that he was handing over the film because "this is a story with plot and character, and I couldn't do that." But he would come to reconsider (perhaps after observing how Ross made the material work on screen), and the turning point came when he made *Annie Hall* five years later. It was his first collaboration with cinematographer Gordon Willis, the key figure in what Allen later called "my maturity in films," and it features our first glimpses of what would become his signature style.

Most obviously, the picture found Allen playing out entire scenes in long "master" shots. The standard Hollywood playbook, particularly in comedies, is to shoot "coverage"—that is, to shoot the scene several times, from several different angles, in mediums and close-ups. "When I worked with the editor of *Take the Money and Run*," Allen recalled, "he said, 'always take a lot of coverage, because then we can do everything we want here, in the editing room.' So, on *Bananas* and *Everything You Always Wanted to Know About Sex* and *Sleeper* I did a lot of coverage all the time—for security. But then I stopped. It seemed silly to me."

That simple explanation makes sense to anyone who's been on a film set; it does seem as though you spend forever doing the same thing, over and over, ad nauseam.

And while, as his editor explained, it does allow limitless options and the capability to shape and reshape a scene after the fact, it also robs scenes of their natural rhythm and fluidity. Those qualities are preserved by Allen's long, unbroken takes, which will often cover an entire scene and go on for several minutes of screen time. It's a touch that has only made the filmmaker seem more idiosyncratic compared to the increasingly frenetic, ADD-inspired rhythms of Hollywood product. Where a film like *Transformers* has an average shot length of three seconds, films like *Bullets Over Broadway* and *Alice* average a cut every forty seconds.

This shooting strategy places considerable pressure on the actors. In a six-page dialogue scene, any fumble means the whole take is blown and must begin anew. But "the actors love them," Allen says. "They get a chance to do five minutes of material, or seven minutes of material, or three minutes of material, instead of one sentence and cut, and then turn the camera around." It also speeds up the process considerably—Allen has said, not entirely in jest, that he shoots this way out of mere laziness ("I don't have the patience or concentration. I can't stand listening to it so much"), though he does grant that the "cover everything and give it to the editor" approach "often lacks personality and doesn't have any individual imprint."

Woody developed another of his "individual imprints" in *Annie Hall*—the surprisingly radical idea of a frame that actors move in and out of freely, rather than one that captures their every move. It occurred accidentally; while shooting one of the Alvy/Annie dialogue scenes, Allen went to Willis with a concern. "I said to Gordie, 'Hey, if we shoot Keaton this way, I'm going to be offstage when I do my

Allen on the set of *Hannah and Her Sisters,* for which he earned his second of seven (to date) Academy Award nominations for Best Director. He did take home the Oscar for Best Original Screenplay for the film. *Brian Hamill/Getty Images*

joke,'" he recalled. "And he said, 'That's okay, they can *hear* you.'" It was a simple realization for Woody, but revolutionary. ("In every movie there's at least one scene

Allen with Gordon Willis, legendary cinematographer of *The Godfather* films and *All the President's Men*. He shot eight films for Allen. *Brian Hamill/Getty Images*

where nobody's on and there's just talking," he's said. "I throw one in always in honor of Gordon.")

Annie Hall also marked the beginning of Woody's exploration of color temperatures and palates. He used three different visual textures for the film: clean, crisp color for the present day; aged yellow for the memories of his childhood; and a sun-bleached starkness for Los Angeles. In subsequent films, whether working with "Prince of Darkness" Willis, Bergman favorite Sven Nykvist, frequent Antonioni collaborator Carlo Di Palma, or versatile Iranian Darius Khondji, Allen has migrated toward a warm, autumnal look. "I just like warm colors. It's a personal taste," he explained. "I like deeply saturated, warm films, in the sense of what Matisse felt, that when you look at a painting, it should be like sitting down in an easy chair; a picture should be a comfortable chair for your eyes."

When he parted ways with Willis after *Purple Rose*, he felt his education was complete—"It's like when you leave your parents' house; now you're grown up and you go out and do your own thing." His confidence as a filmmaker was secure, and during that fertile period of the 1980s that followed, as he turned out masterpiece after masterpiece, his preferences became more firmly entrenched, the filmmaker developing what he would self-effacingly call "certain clichés" that pop up throughout his filmography: "People are walking down the block toward the camera and then they get close to the camera and then the camera begins to dolly. That's one." Another familiar Allen "cliché" is to have the camera on the opposite sidewalk going parallel as people are walking along the other side of the street.

These visual and aural cues help to give Woody Allen movies their recognizable look and feel. "If I was satirizing my movies," he said, "I would do the black-and-white titles and some sort of jazz music, Duke Ellington, say, and then probably have somebody talking to the audience and then do broad stuff about the meaning of life."

He jokes, charmingly, about such crutches, but in doing so, he downplays the degree to which he has continued to experiment with camerawork (the harrowing handheld photography of *Husbands and Wives*) and editing (the jagged jump cuts of *Deconstructing Harry*) well past the point at which his calm, "well made" style seemed established. Yet he maintains in interviews that, all things being equal, his style is relatively unimportant. "What the audience comes away with emotionally, spiritually, is the content of the film," he told Stig Björkman. "The characters, the substance of the film. The form of the film is just a simple, functional thing."

This cavalier attitude and the casualness of his long master shots, combined with the wit and skill of his

dialogue (fostering a perception that he is a writer first and director second), causes Allen's sophisticated filmmaking style to be taken somewhat for granted. "It's funny," *Woody Allen: A Documentary* director Robert Weide told me. "I had already seen *Tall Dark Stranger* two or three times, but then I watched it on an airplane without the sound, and when you watch his movies without the sound, you realize how complex these shots are." Allen may pooh-pooh the notion that he is a stylist, but he'll also grant that "there are certain filmmakers that, no matter what their subject matter, you can tell it's their film. There is some kind of philosophical or emotional sensibility, some kind of thing that permeates the material, and you just *feel* that it's one of their pictures." In *Woody Allen at Work*, Charles Champlin puts a finer point on it: "Allen has matured into an auteur in the truest sense of the term, a writer/director whose films (even those he has co-written with others) carry his unmistakable signature on every frame."

Iranian-born Darius Khondji has been the cinematographer on four of Allen's pictures, including *To Rome with Love* (seen here) and 2014's *Magic in the Moonlight*. Ernesto Ruscio/Getty Images

Melinda and Melinda

RELEASE DATE: March 18, 2005

WRITER: Woody Allen

CAST: Radha Mitchell, Will Ferrell, Chloe Sevigny, Amanda Peet, Jonny Lee Miller, Wallace Shawn, Steve Carell

IN A NUTSHELL: The story of a distraught woman interrupting a dinner party is told in two ways, simultaneously: as a human comedy and a dramatic tragedy.

RECURRING THEMES: Infidelity; kamikaze women ("She was nuts then and she's nuts now!"); actors and acting (Hobie's acting strategy is apparently to play every role with a limp); sexless relationships; filmmaking and filmmakers; murder; psychoanalysis ("He'd just recommend Prozac. I think he has stock in the company, honestly"); magic ("I believe in magic. I think it's the only thing that can save us")

Melinda and Melinda opens with a dinner conversation between four people, but the topic of their talk, and the passion with which they address it, makes it feel more like an argument between the voices in Woody Allen's head. The subject: the intellectual merits of comedy vs. tragedy, and which is the more appropriate method for portraying the human struggle. As an exercise, one of the characters, a writer of drama, spins a simple situation—an uninvited, unstable woman breaks up a dinner party—into a tale of temptation, betrayal, adultery, and attempted suicide. His opposite writes comedies, and he puts a screwball spin on the premise, resulting in a comedy—about temptation, betrayal, adultery, and attempted suicide.

"It's all in the eye of the beholder," remarks one of their dinner companions, and she's right. Melinda and Melinda, which is one of Woody's most formally interesting and slyly experimental pictures, is less about the outcome of either story than it is about the writing process itself, particularly as it pertains to Allen, a writer who had by this point spent more than thirty years weighing the pros and cons of each approach.

In its clean delineation between the two styles, the picture recalls *Crimes and Misdemeanors*, an echo pinpointed by many critics (prompting, in most cases, unfavorable comparisons). But this time around, the premise allows the stories to intertwine far more organically. Allen crafts an inventive back-and-forth structure for the script, with one story picking up where the other leaves off, the two narratives riffing off each other, resulting in a kind of parallel storytelling quite unlike anything he'd yet attempted.

Looking back on it in a conversation with Eric Lax, Allen felt the picture was uneven: "Again, it was a film in which the dramatic story interested me the most. All the heat and passion was in the dramatic story. . . . The comic half

> 66
> I'll give you all the details and you tell me: comedy or tragedy?
> —Al
> 99

never interested me as a writer as much as the other half of it." If he was phoning in the comic half, you certainly can't tell. Will Ferrell makes a fine lead, fusing his own style with the unique rhythms of Allen's comic dialogue to create one of the more satisfying Woody surrogates, and his growing affection for Melinda is subtly, cheerfully sweet (but with a bite, as glimpsed in the hilarious insults he hurls at her potential beau).

The dramatic story, while satisfying, is comparatively dry and stilted, its clunkily expositional dialogue closer to *September* than *Crimes*. But there's much to admire in it: Radha Mitchell, excellent in the title roles, has some of her best moments here (the monologue describing her adultery is exquisite). And Chiwetel Ejiofor's Ellis is something even Woody's diehard apologists had waited too long for: a black character who wasn't a servant or hooker. He had explained away the lack of diversity in his casts by pleading ignorance, telling Stig Björkman, "I don't know the black experience well enough to write about it with any authenticity." For *Melinda*, he seems to have finally figured it out: just write the role like any other, cast a (very good, in this case) black actor, and be done with it.

In his glowing review of the film, Roger Ebert wrote, "I cannot escape the suspicion that if Woody had never made a previous film, if each new one was Woody's Sundance debut, it would get a better reception." He may be on to something there; this is a clever, fast-paced, marvelously executed gem, and too many critics greeted it with a collective yawn. It was starting to look like Allen was going to have to do something genuinely startling to get their attention. And in his next effort, that's exactly what he did.

WATCH OUT FOR
Humorist Andy Borowitz as one of the guests at Hobie and Susan's dinner party.

Woody on Woody

"I had a good time making the picture but in retrospect would like to make a picture just of the serious part. Exactly my feelings after I saw *Crimes and Misdemeanors*."

un film de Woody Allen
MELINDA ET MELINDA
ÊTES-VOUS PLUTÔT COMÉDIE OU TRAGÉDIE ?

Allen cast *SNL* favorite Will Ferrell because "there was something in him that I thought was sweet and vulnerable." Mere months after *Melinda*'s release, Ferrell's cult hit *Anchorman* hit theaters. *Lobby card from the Voyageur Press Collection*

Match Point

RELEASE DATE: December 28, 2005

WRITER: Woody Allen

CAST: Jonathan Rhys Meyers, Scarlett Johansson, Emily Mortimer, Matthew Goode, Brian Cox, Penelope Wilton

IN A NUTSHELL: A social-climbing British tennis instructor embarks on an ill-fated affair with an American actress.

RECURRING THEMES: Murder; infidelity; class; actors and acting; sexless relationships; magic realism; morality; neurotic actresses; kamikaze women; the value of luck and chance

Europe has saved my life in the last 15 years," Woody told Stig Björkman in 1993. "Films that were commercially unsuccessful in this country made their money in Europe, or at least made enough in Europe, so the loss was minimal." European fans weren't just providing a box office lifeline; a European consortium had joined the Safra family in bankrolling Sweetland Films back in the '90s. In the same extended interview, he confessed, "I could consider the idea of going to Europe and make a film. I wouldn't mind that, if the story is right for it."

In 2005, the story was right, though it wasn't meant to take place there. Allen originally wrote *Match Point* as an American film, set in the Hamptons, "and then we raised the money in England. It was very easy to transfer the story to London. It would not have transferred to every place, but London was an easy place to transfer it to." And thus, the filmmaker who had once confessed that he liked to shoot in New York because "I like to eat at my favorite restaurants and sleep in my bed" embarked on a phase in his career where he would seldom do either.

He had shot outside New York before; most of his pre–*Annie Hall* pictures were done elsewhere, and he traveled to Venice and Paris for *Everyone Says I Love You*. But if New York was the city he was most identified with, there was also an argument to be made that a change of scenery might end the creative rut he'd recently found himself in. The opportunities afforded by these new locales and narratives seemed to juice up the filmmaker, to reinvigorate him.

The result is a film that (narrative similarities to *Crimes and Misdemeanors* notwithstanding) is quite unlike any previous Allen work. It is, first of all, atypically and unabashedly erotic. Allen aimed to present "sexuality

You have to learn to push the guilt under the rug and move on, otherwise it overwhelms you.

—Chris Wilton

without showing any real sex," and he succeeded smashingly—from the moment Chris (Jonathan Rhys Meyers) lays eyes on Nola (Scarlett Johannson) as she purrs, "So, who's my next victim," it's not a question of *if* they'll fall into bed but *when*. Their chemistry burbles from that first scene, and the first act burns with the intensity of Chris's erotic longing, manifested in his passive-aggressive back-and-forth with wife Chloe (Emily Mortimer) about doubling to the movies with

Trade ads urged Academy voters to consider *Match Point* for Best Original Screenplay. It would land that nomination—Allen's fourteenth in the category. *Magazine advertisement from the Voyageur Press Collection*

Nola and her fiancé, the disappointment that flashes across his face when she's a no-show, their hesitant and half-inebriated flirting over an afternoon drink, and finally their surrender to passion in the rainy wheat field.

True to his word, Allen forgoes the mechanics of their affair and focuses on its allure. Chris is a heel, an unrepentant social climber who acquires first a rich friend and then, through him, a rich wife and enviable career. His progress seems ruthlessly efficient and entirely calculated, and there is no excuse for his adultery. But it is also difficult not to understand the pull of Nola's oiled-up, tie-blindfolding, blouse-ripping sexuality when it is contrasted with the ritualistic, mechanical precision of his sex life with baby-obsessed Chloe. Yet Nola isn't presented as a mere sexpot; there's a palpable sadness to her demeanor even during the glowing early stages of the affair, an awareness that no good can come of this, and thus her slow unhinging is understandable as well.

Neither character is the plot-driven pawn typical of a murder thriller. They're intelligent, well-defined, fully realized people, which raises the stakes on their decisions and actions. "I was trying to give a little substance to the story so it wasn't just a genre piece," Allen said, by way of explaining not just the three-dimensional characters but the allusions to Dostoevsky and the philosophical realizations of the third act—particularly when Chris is confronted by the ghosts of the women he killed (via an *Another Woman*–style dose of magic realism) in what is presumably his final dark night of the soul before getting on with his now-manageable life, as Judah Rosenthal did in *Crimes*. (For all of the similarities between the two pictures, it's worth noting that Chris's crimes are much more hands-on—there is no mobbed-up brother to handle the job for him—and he suffers sadness, guilt, and regret not only after, but while committing them.)

Woody on Woody

"I loved the fact that I wasn't in it, I loved the fact that it was serious, and when it did come out, it had a good feel for me and good substance and I had a feeling of pride in it."

Allen debuting *Match Point* at Cannes with stars Emily Mortimer, Jonathan Rhys Meyers, and Scarlett Johansson. *AP Photo/ Lionel Cironneau*

Despite Allen's concerns of avoiding something that's "just a genre piece," he handles the genre elements exquisitely. Comparisons to Hitchcock seem a foregone conclusion, from the *Vertigo*-inspired shadowing of Nola through the art museum to the gripping yet elegant double murder sequence to the maddeningly suspenseful moments, both before the crime and after, when Allen lingers on those elements (the tennis bag, the misplaced shell, the tossed ring, the friendly neighbor) that could get his protagonist caught. There are also pronounced echoes of Hitchcock's one-time collaborator Patricia Highsmith, particularly in Chris's Ripleyesque social climbing.

Indeed, in some ways, *Match Point* is almost unrecognizable as a Woody Allen film. He's shooting in a crisp, no-nonsense style of tight scenes and deliberate, purposeful camera moves. And there's far more conventional coverage than we've come to expect by this point in his filmography—it's almost as if, this time, he didn't get tired of the scenes before taking the time to shoot closeups.

Still, many of the classic Allen themes and tones are clearly evident. The script's interest in wealth and social order—a topic that Allen had last addressed, with a great deal more levity, in *Small Time Crooks*—was only boosted by its relocation to class-obsessed Britain, while the intelligence and wit of Allen's dialogue makes the transition surprisingly well; if anything, all those upper-crust accents help soften the occasional formality of his writing. Most importantly, his moral cynicism is intact. As in *Crimes*, bad people— particularly *rich* bad people—do bad things free of punishment; as in *Celebrity*, luck is as important as talent or goodness, perhaps even more so.

Woody speaks of the film in glowing terms, naming it as one of his favorite works, albeit one with which (true to its talk of the vital import of good fortune) he claims he was "very lucky. . . . I don't know if I can ever repeat it or make a film as good." For once, the filmmaker, his critics, and his audience were on the same page. Worldwide, it grossed a healthy $85 million, while film scribes pronounced it a welcome return to form. The message of its success was a heartening one: Even at seventy years old, with nearly forty movies in the can, Woody Allen was still capable of surprising us.

Scarlett Johannson

Allen and Johansson on the set of *Vicky Cristina Barcelona. Lluis Gene/AFP/Getty Images*

"She's great. She just turns it on. She's a wonderful actress."

—Woody Allen

Were it not for Kate Winslet's busy dance card, Woody might not have ended up making three films with Scarlett Johansson. Winslet was originally cast in the role of Nola in *Match Point*—because she's great, and also because Allen assumed he needed to fill the English-financed film with British actors. But when Winslet bowed out at the last minute, Allen discovered he'd fulfilled the contractual obligation and could cast an American. "We sat around and talked and thought Scarlett Johansson would be great, and [casting director] Juliet [Taylor] found she was available. She's just no-nonsense. . . . The first day we did a very hard scene and she did it brilliantly. She's a wonderful actress."

Johansson wasn't just a good actress, nor just a drop-dead sexy one—Allen soon discovered that she was also blessed with a quick wit and a keen interest in "poking him" on set ("Got to make sure he's still awake!" she joked). After her inspired turn as Nola, Woody wrote the lead in his next film, *Scoop*, expressly for her. He wanted to give her the opportunity to be funny in a film, and to give himself the chance to act with her.

Their final collaboration to date, *Vicky Cristina Barcelona*, also feels written for her—surely it's no coincidence that her Cristina, like Nola, is explicitly complimented on her "sensuous" lips. And while both have dismissed the notion that she is his latest muse (Johannson: "I don't think that Woody sits at home with, like, a thing of lo mein and a typewriter thinking, like, 'What is Scarlett doing now and how can her life sort of inspire this tale?' And I know I'm certainly not."), there's no denying that writing with her in mind has increased the eroticism and vibrancy of his European pictures.

Scoop

RELEASE DATE: July 28, 2006

WRITER: Woody Allen

CAST: Allen, Scarlett Johansson, Hugh Jackman, Ian McShane

IN A NUTSHELL: A cub reporter stumbles onto the scoop of a lifetime, thanks to an unexpected visit from a recently deceased journalistic legend.

RECURRING THEMES: Murder; magic ("Your whole life is deception. You're a magician!"); actors and acting; the afterlife as farce

If *Match Point* feels like *Crimes and Misdemeanors* with the lighter half removed, *Scoop* plays like that transplanted comic variation. It followed *Match Point* into theaters by barely half a year, with the British location and much of the same team, including star Scarlett Johansson, intact. "I wanted to do a comedy and enjoy myself and make Scarlett funny and tell some jokes myself," Allen explained, keeping his aims modest. "I indulged myself and what I wound up with at the end is, uh, you know, a light comedy, a dessert." Those are the best terms with which to consider *Scoop*, which met with mixed reviews from critics who were wound up by its predecessor and expecting another picture in its new mold.

If anything, *Scoop* plays like an affectionate curtain call, filled (even more than was customary) by echoes and remembrances of earlier triumphs, but juiced by the new surroundings and Allen's palpable enjoyment of playing off a fine comic sparring partner like Johansson. At long last, Woody is finally playing a magician by trade, a music hall performer named "The Great Splendini" whose stage patter, an endless loop of "with all due respect"s and "with all sincerity"s and "credit to your race"s, is not too far removed from the verbal tics of Danny Rose, who might well have represented an act like Splendini. (An early scene of Joe Strombel's fellow reporters swapping stories and legends recalls that film's wraparound device.) The push-pull investigative dynamic between Sid (Allen) and Sondra (Johansson) mirrors *Manhattan Murder Mystery* ("Why don't you think of this as adding excitement to your life?"), while the eventual discarded-sex-partner motive of *Scoop*'s killer ("there was no other way out") recalls both *Match Point* and *Crimes*.

But such homages are to be expected this deep in a filmography. Primarily, *Scoop* is a thoroughly amusing picture, with more laughs than anything he'd done since the previous decade.

> " You're wrong. I see the glass as half-full— of poison.
> —Sid Waterman "

Scarlett Johansson made her second Allen appearance in *Scoop*, while Woody made his last onscreen appearance for six years. *Poster from the Voyageur Press Collection*

Woody on Woody

"The only thing I have against *Scoop* is a self-indulgent lack of ambition. I don't think that I screwed the movie up. I think the movie's cute—that the jokes are funny, that everyone performs well, that an audience will have some laughs and not want to tar and feather me when they come out of the theater. But it's not ambitious enough."

His instinct to "make Scarlett funny" was a wise one; her stammering, wide-eyed, all-thumbs college newspaper gal is a charming comic dynamo, and the pair zing off each other well, alternating playing each other's foil. He has thankfully surrendered to the inevitability of playing her mentor rather than romantic opposite, and he has fun with the notion—when Sondra creates a cover identity in which he is her father, Sid can't stop referring to her with such rhetorical flourishes as "my child" and "blessed offspring."

There's more quotable dialogue here than in *Small Time Crooks*, *The Curse of the Jade Scorpion*, and *Hollywood Ending* combined, with Allen writing himself delicious gags about religion ("I was born into the Hebrew persuasion, but when I got older, I converted to narcissism"), their surroundings ("This guy is a Lord! They'll take us to the Tower of London and behead us!"), and their suspect ("This guy is not a serial killer, believe me. I'd be surprised if he killed just *one* person"). And it contains Allen's mellowest conception of life after death: a long, slow boat ride, with the *Seventh Seal*–inspired Death at the bow, where the dearly departed can chat and ruminate and perhaps enjoy a card trick.

As its critics noted, *Scoop* broke no new ground for the filmmaker—it's just him having a good time with his latest leading lady in his new locale. But it's light and airy and seemingly effortless, and by this point in his career, Allen had certainly earned that indulgence.

WATCH OUT FOR

Buffy the Vampire Slayer costar Anthony Head as one of the cops taking Peter's statement.

Cassandra's Dream

RELEASE DATE: January 18, 2008

WRITER: Woody Allen

CAST: Ewan McGregor, Colin Farrell, Tom Wilkinson, Hayley Atwell, Sally Hawkins

IN A NUTSHELL: Two brothers, desperate for money, commit a murder for their rich and powerful uncle.

RECURRING THEMES: Murder; class; neurotic actresses ("Don't forget to come backstage and tell me how great I was"); morality ("You always have a choice"); sibling rivalry; California hatred ("Hollywood's where he *belongs*")

W hen I finished *Scoop*," Woody Allen recalled, "I thought to myself, What a nuisance. I'm wasting my time with this little comedy and I could be doing another piece of work like *Match Point*—another meaty thing." The "meaty thing" he landed on was a crime drama with overtones of Greek tragedy, forgoing the parody of *Mighty Aphrodite* for serious reinterpretation, from the title to the themes of familial discord, hubris, and murder.

Cassandra's Dream was set and shot in London, this time with nary an American in sight, and its South London setting makes it the Allen film most preoccupied with issues of class. Ewan McGregor's Ian and Colin Farrell's Terry both describe themselves as "just working lads," but they've got bigger dreams than that; Ian is looking to upgrade from restaurant manager to big-shot investor, vaguely going on about "certain business ventures" he's involved in and showboating around town in sports cars borrowed from his brother's garage. Terry, meanwhile, seeks thrills and wealth via high-stakes gambling. When they go in on a fixer-upper sailboat, it comes to symbolize the life of leisure they both so desperately desire—a life led by Uncle Howard, played by Tom Wilkinson in a performance that personifies quiet, unquestioned wealth and power.

In the continuum of Allen's murder morality plays, *Cassandra's Dream* places greater emphasis than *Crimes and Misdemeanors* and *Match Point* do on the aftermath of such an action. Both *Crimes'* Judah Rosenthal and *Match Point's* Chris Wilton spend long nights wrestling with the demons of guilt and doubt, but their remorse is ultimately short-lived. Terry, on the other hand, simply cannot come to terms with his actions. He drinks heavily, pops pills, loses his job, contemplates suicide, and generally becomes the same sort of "liability" as the man he helped murder.

Relationships between sisters have factored frequently into Allen's storytelling, but *Cassandra's Dream* is his first film to seriously tackle the dynamic between brothers. McGregor and Farrell adroitly play the siblings'

> **66**
> Family is family. Blood is blood. You don't ask questions—you protect your own.
> **—Uncle Howard**
> **99**

similarities and their differences, which become more acute after the murder. In contrasting their actions after the crime, Allen is slyly tinkering with traditional presumptions of masculinity: Tough guy/former jock/grease monkey Terry is overcome with guilt and unable to reshuffle his morality, while intellectual, sensitive Ian reveals himself as the coldly ambitious and ruthlessly heartless one.

Unlike the bright and sunny British films that preceded it, *Cassandra*'s world is often gray and dim, the clouds lifting only in those early, happy moments on the sea. The glidingly elegant camerawork is provided by Vilmos Zsigmond, one of the world's renowned cinematographers (he also shot *Melinda and Melinda*). And for the first time since *Everything You Always Wanted to Know About Sex*, Allen commissioned an original score. Minimalist composer Philip Glass's music saturates the picture with a foreboding sense of dread, and Woody was happy with the collaboration: "He was always enthused over our ideas and very compliant. It's still easier for me to use recordings, but then you don't get to work with a genius."

When *Cassandra's Dream* made the festival rounds in late 2007, critics were oddly cold toward it, so much so that the Weinstein Company bumped the picture from its original awards-season release date into the dumping ground of January. But some critics would come around on it; *The New Yorker*'s Richard Brody picked it as one of the best films of the decade, noting, "Few aging directors so cogently and relentlessly depict the grimly destructive machinery of life, and every time the word 'family' is uttered, the screws tighten just a little more."

Woody on Woody

"*Cassandra's Dream* I thought was a good picture that people have not flocked to in any quantity at all. But I thought it was a completely engrossing movie, brilliantly acted by everybody, and I was very satisfied with it—much more satisfied than with other films of mine that have been much bigger successes."

The low-grossing *Cassandra's Dream*—starring Ewan McGregor and Colin Farrell as conspiring brothers—was met with decidedly mixed reviews, though it has since been reappraised as one of the strongest works of Allen's late period. *AP Photo/CP, Chrystal Films*

• Woody on Death: A Big Subject •

"What is it about death that bothers me so much?
Probably the hours."

—Woody Allen, "Selections from the Allen Notebooks," *Without Feathers*

Woody Allen had his first near-death experience when he was three. It was at the hands of a babysitter, and though it seems he would have been too young to retain such a vivid memory, he still recalls the girl wrapping him in a blanket so tightly that he couldn't breathe, and her quietly assuring him, "I could smother you right now and throw you out in the garbage and no one would ever know the difference." And with that, she nonchalantly let him go. More than seven decades later, Allen shrugged it off: "The world would've been poorer a number of great one-liners." But it was clearly a defining incident for him, a piercing notification that life can end at any moment.

Nearly forty years later, he wrote a scene in *Annie Hall* in which Alvy and Annie go book shopping. Among the volumes he selects for her is Ernest Becker's *The Denial of Death*, which prompts him to announce, "I'm obsessed with death, I think. Big, big subject with me, yeah." The book was no mere prop, arbitrarily chosen. According to biographer John Baxter, the book had a "profound effect" on Allen, who read it as soon as it was published in 1973. "It validated much that he'd already discovered through experience, and provided a philosophical rationalization for half a life spent in just the sort of debilitating flight from fear that it described."

That obsession soon began to appear regularly in Woody's films. He felt that Bergman's *The Seventh Seal* was the "definitive work on the subject," and though *Love and Death*, his first film released after *The Denial of Death*'s publication, features a Death character broadly spoofing Bergman's model, Allen told Richard Schickel

in 2003 that *Love and Death*'s theme is nearly as bleak as Bergman's: "In the end you're screwed by death, that death is ever present, that death is a constant companion in one form or another, either on the battlefield or in attempted suicides or in duels, or because you're rejected in your love life. And love is futile." And thus the fear of death, the awareness of its inescapability despite life's momentary pleasures and distractions, would become the spine running through much of his work.

"As long as you're mired, as we all are, in everyday routine and reality," Allen continued, "we're all going to come to the same nasty end, and have the same grim lives." And so *Interiors*' Renata confesses, "I can't seem to shake this real implication of dying. It's terrifying. The intimacy of it embarrasses me." And *Manhattan*'s Ike looks at the classroom skeleton and despairs, "We're gonna be like him! He was probably one of the beautiful people!" And *Hannah and Her Sisters*' Mickey can't wrap his head around the fact that his father isn't frightened of death ("I'll be unconscious!" his father insists). And so on.

Mickey's ultimate comfort in his march to the grave comes, unsurprisingly, from art. He wanders into a movie theater and is greeted by the Marx Brothers' *Duck Soup*, and the sheer joy of their performance transforms his glum, suicidal outlook into something altogether cheerier: "What if there's no God, and you only go around once and that's it? Well, you know, don't you want to be part of the experience?" In *Manhattan*, Groucho had headed the list of things that make life worth living (along with Marlon Brando, Frank Sinatra, Louis Armstrong, and Cézanne)— so it would seem safe to presume that Allen would gain

Allen with Death in a scene from *Love and Death*. United Artists/Getty Images

some small comfort from the knowledge that his work, like those artists', would earn him some degree of immortality.

Alas, no. "I don't want to achieve immortality through my work. I want to achieve it by not dying," he said in one interview; in another, "Someone once asked me if my dream was to live on in the hearts of my people, and I said I would like to live on in my apartment. And that's really what I would prefer." He's utterly indifferent to the idea of his legacy, "because I'm a firm believer that when you're dead, naming a street after you doesn't help your metabolism. . . . When I'm dead, it wouldn't matter to me for a second if they took all of my films and the negatives of my films—apart from [a] small financial sum for my children—and just dumped them down the sewer."

Some of this attitude is attributable to his noted modesty about the quality of his own work. He presumably doesn't believe that his films place him in the company of Marx, Brando, Sinatra, and the rest, and he seems certain that memories of his works, like those of the personalities on the roof at the conclusion of *Radio Days*, will merely grow dimmer and dimmer with the passing years. But it goes beyond that, to a matter of logistics—even if people are still taking pleasure in *Annie Hall* or *Match Point* in

2053, Woody Allen still won't have a pulse. Or, as Sandy Bates responded to the proclamation that his work would live on: "Yeah, but what good is it if I can't pinch any women or hear any music?"

Woody Allen's preoccupation with death is not a comic affectation or pseudo-intellectual psychobabble. "I think these are the issues that haunt him," Diane Keaton says in *Woody Allen: A Documentary*. "I do believe that's the reason why it's a theme in his movies, because he does think about it a lot." But as he's grown closer to the end of his life, his attitude about that destination has become, well, not less concerned, but certainly more accepting. "The trick is to enjoy life, accepting that it has no meaning whatsoever," says *Vicky Cristina Barcelona*'s Juan Antonio. *Whatever Works*' Boris concurs: "You gotta take what little pleasure you can find in this chamber of horrors." And *Shadows and Fog*'s Felice puts an even finer point on it: "The trick is to have as much wine, as many men, as many laughs as you can before they carry you out in a pine box." Woody's later characters aren't happy about death, but they acknowledge it and act accordingly. Yet as he said in 2010, "My relationship with death remains the same: I'm strongly against it."

Vicky Cristina Barcelona

RELEASE DATE: August 15, 2008

WRITER: Woody Allen

CAST: Rebecca Hall, Javier Bardem, Scarlett Johansson, Penélope Cruz, Patricia Clarkson, Chris Messina

IN A NUTSHELL: Two young American women find their notions of romance challenged during a summer in Barcelona.

RECURRING THEMES: Infidelity; kamikaze women ("You're too damaged." "And you love that"); neurotic actresses; the seductiveness of guitar music

Their faces are fresh, free, and excited. They fill the frame in the opening scene of *Vicky Cristina Barcelona*, after a playful iris-out and a lung-filling look at the sunbaked Spanish exteriors, and a narrator fills us in: "Vicky and Cristina decided to spend their summer vacation in Barcelona." They are a study in opposites: Cristina (Scarlett Johansson) is a free spirit, floating between artistic disciplines and men with equal tentativeness, up for anything because she's sure of nothing. Vicky (Rebecca Hall) is working on her master's thesis and has a whole life waiting for her back in New York: a fiancé, a home, a comfortably preplanned existence. Neither woman is quite prepared for what Juan Antonio does to them.

The characters of Juan Antonio (Javier Bardem) and his estranged love Maria Elena (Penélope Cruz) are important in the Woody Allen canon because they are, in many ways, his first fully formed, focal characters that are not Caucasian. To be sure, we've seen the soulful Latin lover and the fiery, tempestuous Latina before, but the elegant writing and superb playing elevate them from their stock types. Bardem carefully parses out his sexiness, letting it simmer instead of boiling over. There's extensive table setting for Cruz's Maria Elena, awed conversations in hushed tones, before she appears at the fifty-minute mark; that kind of carefully prepared entrance demands that a performer deliver, and boy, does she ever.

Maria Elena is the least stable of Allen's kamikaze women, and the most fascinating: accusatory, smug, chaotic, tender, suicidal, insistent, sexy, and bananas crazy. You understand both how she makes Juan Antonio nuts and how he can't resist her—indeed, how Cristina can't either. The idea of a *ménage a trois* coupling among these three ridiculously attractive people dominated much of the picture's pre-release

> " We are meant for each other and not meant for each other. It is a contradiction.
>
> —Juan Antonio "

Vicky Cristina Barcelona

Javier Bardem and Penélope Cruz's electrifying chemistry would extend off-screen as well. They began dating during *Vicky Cristina Barcelona*'s production and married three years later. *Lobby card from the Voyageur Press Collection*

coverage (as well as its posters), but the development of that relationship is handled far less sensationally than one might imagine. It's organic to the story, which is obsessed with love triangles and never tires of contemplating new ones.

The picture's most intriguing bait-and-switch is that the triangle at its center is not Juan Antonio–Maria Elena–Cristina, but Juan Antonio–Cristina–Vicky. The British actress Hall is wonderful in what amounts to the Woody role, the worried neurotic with the quick wit and charming stammer, but she's far more than merely a *Celebrity*-style stand-in. Her initially unlikely yet highly potent single assignation with Juan Antonio comes to represent the kind of reckless romanticism that she has long presumed is beyond her capacity. But these repressed impulses have a way of kicking back, and with unexpected force.

Through much of its duration, *Vicky Cristina Barcelona* is a light, sexy confection, recalling the gentle, flirtatious, beguiling tone of *A Midsummer Night's Sex Comedy*—and few Allen pictures since. "The basic cosmetics of the film, as you watch it, are not sad," Allen explained, "and so as you watch it, you're seeing a beautiful city and hearing wonderful music, and seeing these beautiful women and this charming guy." But there is, in his words, "a very pessimistic picture" brewing underneath. By the film's conclusion, Juan Antonio and Maria Elena have split yet again, Cristina is still woefully uncertain about what she wants out of life and love, and Vicky has resigned herself to a passionless marriage with a bit of a dolt. The title characters' faces are noticeably more melancholy in the film's closing shots than in its opening, and it is on those conflicted masks that Allen deliberately places his fade-out.

Woody on Woody

"*Vicky Cristina Barcelona* was a pleasant surprise to me. . . . When I cut the film together and put in the music, I was shocked that it seemed to float. I thought, 'Maybe it's just me.' But when we started showing it to people, they really were enthusiastic about it—enormously enthusiastic."

Woody the Tourist:

Allen's European Phase

by Ashley Clark

Between 2005 and 2011, Woody Allen took a step toward emulating his heroes François Truffaut, Federico Fellini, and Ingmar Bergman by embarking on a concerted spell of filmmaking in Europe. This run comprised seven films—*Match Point, Scoop, Cassandra's Dream, Vicky Cristina Barcelona, You Will Meet a Tall Dark Stranger, Midnight in Paris, To Rome with Love*—which took place across a selection of the continent's most cosmopolitan locales: London, Barcelona, Paris, and Rome.

Throughout the period, Allen maintained the prolific productivity for which he has long been famed, churning out films at a rate of roughly one per year, and even interrupting the jaunt for a return to his beloved Manhattan for the 2009 comedy *Whatever Works*. Yet despite the ostensibly radical geographical shift—plus a handful of generic and stylistic oscillations—a closer look suggests that this spell represents more continuum than change in Allen's oeuvre. These films generally broached the familiar themes of love, sex, creativity, and (occasionally) crime among an overwhelmingly white, middle-class selection of people, and they featured a characteristically brisk, unfussy visual style. Most obviously, they are all unabashed city tales: "I would have a

hard time finding stories if I was asked to make a film in a rural setting or in the desert. But not in big cities," Allen told *The Hollywood Reporter* in 2012.

Back in the mid-2000s, Allen's stock with American audiences was low—perhaps at its lowest point to date. After the relative success (more than $17 million at the box office) of the wacky *Small Time Crooks* (2000), a series of Allen's films had failed to set the box office alight or find favor with critics. In response to a particularly disappointing Times Square screening of 2002's *Hollywood Ending*, the *New York Times*, traditionally loyal to Allen, ran a galling front-page story titled "Curse of the Jaded Audience: Woody Allen, in Art and Life," detailing his fall from grace.

So it was in this context that Allen decided to shake things up. The 2005 thriller *Match Point* was Allen's first film to be shot entirely outside of the

The filmmaker with London mayor Ken Livingstone in 2005 following the UK premiere of *Match Point*, the first of four films Allen would shoot in Livingstone's city. *Dave Hogan/Getty Images*

United States, and it proved to be the cinematic embodiment of the old maxim "a change is as good as a rest." A dark, Hitchcockian thriller starring Jonathan Rhys-Meyers and Scarlett Johansson (in her first of three Euro collaborations with the director), it is stripped of Allen's traditional humor, and his most solemn film since 1988's *Another Woman*. With regard to the setting, Allen wasn't looking at London for its geographical specificity. The truth was rather more pragmatic: "When I first wrote it, I was thinking of making it in the United States," he told *Premiere* in 2006. "But then [due to financial reasons] I rewrote it for London, which was easy to do because New York and London are so similar." Allen would come to find that Europeans would finance his films generously, and under his rules, with little interference.

Allen walks down the steps at Barcelona's landmark Park Güell, created by Catalan architect Antoni Gaudí, during shooting of *Vicky Cristina Barcelona*. Cesar Rangel/AFP/Getty Images

Following *Match Point*, Allen made three more films in London: *Scoop* (2006), *Cassandra's Dream* (2007), and *You Will Meet a Talk Dark Stranger* (2010). Of these, *Cassandra's Dream* is the most notable. A lugubrious, twisty morality play about two London brothers (played, with dodgy Cockney accents, by Irishman Colin Farrell and Scotsman Ewan McGregor) inveigled in criminal activity, it's even more solemn than *Match Point*. Unlike the rest of Allen's European films, it does not feature a prominent American actor to function as either a bridge to an American audience or as an Allen proxy. The more upbeat *Scoop* integrated comedy and thriller elements in

a manner redolent of *Manhattan Murder Mystery* (1993 and featured an increasingly rare turn from Allen himself, playing a magician. *You Will Meet a Tall Dark Stranger*, a minor work, found Allen firmly back in lighthearted, comic/romantic mode.

The post–*Match Point* British films performed adequately at the box office in European territories traditionally receptive to Allen: France, Spain, and, to a lesser extent, Germany. Intriguingly, however, the British public and press proved largely resistant to their charms—*Scoop* failed to receive

Allen captured the romance and beauty of both modern-day and 1920s-era Paris in *Midnight in Paris*. *Le Floch/Sipa via AP Images*

UK theatrical distribution, premiering on BBC television in February 2009, while *Cassandra's Dream* took a paltry $239,955. A narrative began to emerge in the British press that Allen's Euro jaunt was at best an extended frippery, at worst further evidence of creative stagnation. In *The Guardian*, Joe Queenan penned a screed entitled "Europe, please stop funding this man," and *The Observer*'s veteran critic Philip French seethed: "Not until *Match Point* . . . did I find [Allen's films] embarrassing or wholly without merit. There was *Scoop* and *Cassandra's Dream*, . . . and I now find myself wishing I were elsewhere when the lights go down."

Perhaps British critics were reacting in part to Allen's failure to harness the country's features in any

significant cinematic way; it's true that the London films all have a particularly utilitarian visual quality and feel as though they could be set anywhere. The same could not be said for Allen's subsequent trips to Barcelona, Paris, and Rome, which would all lovingly glamorize the cities as hubs of passion, creativity, and sexual possibility. *Vicky Cristina Barcelona* (2008) was a sprightly, sensual tale of two young American travelers (Johansson and Rebecca Hall), who wind up enmeshed in a bizarre love quadrangle with a hunky, passionate artist (Javier Bardem) and his hot-tempered ex-wife (an Oscar-winning Penélope Cruz). It is a typically Allen-esque investigation of the intersection of creativity and libido staged within an atypically Allen-esque setting.

Three years later, *Midnight in Paris* would see Allen harking back to the time-bending magical realism of *The Purple Rose of Cairo* (1985) for his most purely whimsical film to date. Owen Wilson shrugs, sighs, and quips as Gil Pender, a troubled screenwriter trying to write a novel and longing for the golden era of Paris in the 1920s. He finds that nostalgia is in the mind of the beholder, and he embarks on a host of psychogenic late-night fugues, meeting the likes of Salvador Dali and Ernest Hemingway in a Paris furnished with Anne Seibel and Hélène Dubreuil's Oscar-nominated art-direction. Gil is the most blatant Woody proxy yet; it's a role that undoubtedly would have been performed by the director were it not for his advanced years. *Midnight in Paris*, very much a love letter to the city of its setting, remains Allen's biggest box office hit on both sides of the Atlantic to date, and it secured him his first Academy Award (for Best Original Screenplay), since he won the same award in 1988 for *Hannah and Her Sisters*.

In 2012 came *To Rome with Love*, a romantic folly that represented a partial return to the vignette structure of 1972's *Everything You Always Wanted To Know About Sex* by way of the omnibus movies popular in Italy in the 1960s. The film garnered a mixed critical response in Italy, but, unsurprisingly, it was the European territory in which the film took the most money. It also inspired an amusing spoof on the Funny or Die website, the fairly self-explanatory "My Wife Doesn't Understand as Much About Jazz as this Beautiful Italian Prostitute." In it, actors playing comically heightened versions of Allen, Jesse Eisenberg, and Wilson lounged on a piazza and discussed their range of hardships ("I'm engaged to a beautiful young woman and she doesn't

know the difference between Count Basie and Jelly Roll Morton!") The satirical sketch captured, with some affection, the whimsical European comfort zone that Allen had willingly slipped into. However, as Allen's next film—the sour, San Francisco-set *Blue Jasmine* (2013)—proved, the fire had not disappeared from his belly.

If one contrasts the state of Allen's filmmaking career before and after this string of European adventures, it seems clear that time away from America contributed to a creative rejuvenation, no doubt linked to the artistic freedoms afforded by sympathetic financiers. Lofty "return to form" claims accompany the late period work of many beloved artists (it's the same whenever, say, David Bowie releases an album), but it would be hard to argue that *Midnight in Paris* and *Blue Jasmine* don't represent a heartening advance on what had gone before.

Moreover, it might be somewhat premature to speak of Allen's Euro period as a self-contained, past entity. At the time of writing, filming has wrapped on *Magic in the Moonlight*, a 1920s period comedy starring Colin Firth and Emma Stone, set on the French Riviera. Given the continent's broadly receptive audiences, and a host of picturesque new territories for the picking (one can easily imagine Allen conjuring a languid romantic comedy on the cobbled streets of Prague or Wroclaw), we may find Allen embarking on something of a permanent vacation, to borrow the title of a film by Jim Jarmusch, another enduring New York filmmaker.

Ashley Clark is a freelance writer, film programmer, and public speaker. His writing has appeared in publications including *Time Out*, *Sight & Sound*, *The Guardian*, *Little White Lies*, *Filmmaker*, *Film4.com*, *Reverse Shot*, *Moving Image Source*, and *Slant Magazine*. He has programmed at venues including BFI Southbank and Clapham Picturehouse. He divides his time between London and New York.

Whatever Works

RELEASE DATE: June 19, 2009

WRITER: Woody Allen

CAST: Larry David, Evan Rachel Wood, Patricia Clarkson, Ed Begley Jr., Michael McKean

IN A NUTSHELL: A misanthropic intellectual takes in a simpleminded southern runaway, whose parents end up following her to New York and changing in unexpected ways.

RECURRING THEMES: Hypochondria ("I said they can't *find* an ulcer, not that I don't *have* one"); infidelity; younger women; rock music hatred ("some eardrum-bursting bilge posing as music"); magic ("I do tricks. . . . D'you have any silk handkerchiefs?"); California hatred ("They paid good money for tickets so some moron in Hollywood could buy a bigger swimming pool"); Groucho idolatry; the value of luck and chance

I t was 2008, and Woody Allen was worried. There was talk of a Screen Actors Guild (SAG) strike over residuals in new media, and if it went through, film and television production would effectively shut down—and Allen wouldn't be able to make his annual film. The solution was to shoot something more quickly than usual, but he was still finishing *Vicky Cristina Barcelona* and couldn't work on a screenplay. And then he remembered *Whatever Works*, initially written as a Zero Mostel vehicle back in the 1970s; when Mostel died in 1977, Allen threw it in the drawer, where it stayed for more than thirty years.

Since the script was likely written after Allen and Mostel acted together in *The Front* (1976), that places its creation immediately before *Annie Hall*, with some retroactively interesting hints of what was to come. Most obviously, it shares *Annie*'s fourth-wall-breaking protagonist, as well as his seeming inability to experience pleasure (even that of a sexual nature, a bridge too far for Alvy Singer). The script also predates *Manhattan*'s dynamic of a cynic spoiled by the carefree affections of an innocent young girl.

But *Whatever Works* isn't solely of interest as a work of cinematic archaeology. It fuses Allen's style with that of *Curb Your Enthusiasm* star Larry David, who had tiny roles in two earlier pictures and had been an admirer from the beginning: "*Take the Money and Run*, I saw when I was in the army. It was playing on the base," David told Robert Weide in *Woody Allen: A Documentary*. "It was the most exhilarating, amazing experience, to just sit there and laugh like that. . . . And I thought wow, I've got a connection to this guy." David's Boris Yelnikoff has a harder edge than most of Allen's protagonists

> " Just so you know, this is not the feel-good movie of the year. So if you're one of those idiots who needs to feel good, go get yourself a foot massage.
> —Boris Yelnikoff "

(Harry Block beats him, but that's about it), and David, who won our hearts playing an unrepentant asshole on television, steps into the role with ease.

Whatever Works has its problems, to be sure. Allen's quickie rewrite of the script mostly involved updating the topical references, but even so, its red state/blue state dichotomy and sneering distaste for flyover country feel dated—not by thirty years, but by five or so. Allen is shooting fish in a barrel here, and the script's presumptions about its southern characters are awfully lazy, a New Yorker's fantasy of the city's inherent, magic ability to unlock a lifetime of dogma in the space of an afternoon.

Some of those scenes could have used a bit more rewriting, is the point, and the film occasionally feels slapped together, both from a writing and directing standpoint (and if he's happy to be working from home for the first time in four years, it hardly shows—he uses New York City simply as a background, like any old filmmaker). But this kind of sloppiness is actually fitting for what Allen seems to be going for: a good, old-fashioned, personality-based comedy. Whether for Mostel or David, *Whatever Works* feels like Allen writing for a bigger-than-life comic persona, crafting something in the mold of those cheapie W. C. Fields and Marx Brothers vehicles at Paramount, and Boris is the kind of utter rogue that Fields or Groucho could have played without skipping a beat (it's surely no accident that the film opens with Groucho crooning "Hello, I Must Be Going"). *Whatever Works* lacks the vibrancy and freshness of the European pictures—but it's very, very funny, and, well, that works.

WATCH OUT FOR
Future "Man of Steel" Henry Cavill and *The Newsroom*'s John Gallagher Jr. as Melodie's handsome suitors; *Daily Show* correspondent Samantha Bee as a chess mother.

Larry David appeared in tiny walk-on roles in *Radio Days* and *New York Stories*, but *Whatever Works* was the first time he played the lead—for Woody or anyone other than himself. *Photo by Jessica Miglio, © Gravier Productions*

You Will Meet A Tall Dark Stranger

RELEASE DATE: September 23, 2010

WRITER: Woody Allen

CAST: Naomi Watts, Josh Brolin, Anthony Hopkins, Antonio Banderas, Gemma Jones, Lucy Punch, Freida Pinto

IN A NUTSHELL: Two London couples try to find happiness by ending their marriages, only to find their problems aren't nearly as simple as they believed.

RECURRING THEMES: Infidelity; frustrated novelists; the seductiveness of guitar music; psychoanalysis ("It's far less expensive than these fancy psychiatrists I've been seeing"); neurotic actresses; prostitution ("The only acting she's ever done is faking an orgasm"); ghostwriting; younger women; the value of luck and chance

Following the cinematic return to his hometown, Woody Allen was back to England for his next picture, a story of infidelity, divorce, and unhappiness that was jaded and cynical even by his standards. "I wouldn't have thought of it when I was young," Allen explained. "It requires years of disillusionment." But what's striking about *You Will Meet a Tall Dark Stranger* (aside from the grammatical horror show that is its title) is how it seems infected by disillusionment for not only life or romance, but filmmaking. An oddly flat and listless affair, it is by far the wobbliest picture of Allen's European phase.

Not that it's a total failure—he has, first off, one of his sharpest ensemble casts, led by the luminous Naomi Watts as Sally, in a performance of real skill and subtle sexiness, most clearly manifested in her playful, potent flirting with boss Greg (Antonio Banderas). The longing, sideways glance she casts at him during their trip to the opera is sheer dynamite; the scene that follows in his car, at the end of that evening of drinking and confessing, is charged with the genuine eroticism of pining. It's an arrestingly sensual scene with no physical contact whatsoever, all played in pauses, looks, and body language.

Likewise, Anthony Hopkins seeks out not just the good lines, but the juicy beats between them. There's a moment late in the picture when the camera holds on his face as he realizes what a grave mistake he's made, and it keeps holding. That expression captures the picture's weary view of romance: Its characters are all dissatisfied in their relationships and eager to change partners, only to discover after the fact what they've not only lost but took for granted for so long. Roy (Josh Brolin) pines for the exotic beauty he glimpses through her window across the way; later, when he moves in to her apartment and she is his for the taking, he glances out that window, sees his ex-wife Sally undressing across the way, and pines for *her*.

Another life. I just have to shed the old one and try again."
—Helena Shepridge

It's not all grim business, these matters of love. There's a cheery romanticism to the flashbacks of Roy and Sally's courtship, and the charge of his flirtation with Dia (Freida Pinto) is undeniable. But such happiness only seems achievable in the early stages of romance, when anything is possible; once lovers settle in, the film seems to argue, our essential unhappiness and wandering eyes will ruin everything.

This is territory Woody has trod before, and there's nothing wrong with that. But he never quite finds the right approach to the material. He doesn't seem sure if it's a comedy or a drama, and as a result, the jokes are halfhearted and the conflicts aren't terribly compelling. The omniscient narrator device is employed again, but it feels this time like a tool for avoiding scenes Allen didn't feel like making, even when he should have—"Sally announced to Roy that she was starting her own gallery and wanted a divorce" sure seems like something that should be in the movie. And while Allen has never shied from open endings, the indeterminate "time's up!" conclusion, and the many threads it leaves dangling, seems less motivated by deliberate ambiguity than by a filmmaker uninterested in his characters and their fates.

A few years later, Allen would make a film that achieved the balance between tragedy and comedy that he aims for, and doesn't quite achieve, here. In the meantime, though, he would travel to France and direct his biggest commercial success in a quarter of a century.

Melinda and Melinda costar Josh Brolin pines for seductive neighbor Freida Pinto in *You Will Meet a Tall Dark Stranger*. *Lobby card from the Voyageur Press Collection*

Midnight in Paris

RELEASE DATE: May 20, 2011

WRITER: Woody Allen

CAST: Owen Wilson, Marion Cotillard, Rachel McAdams, Michael Sheen, Kathy Bates, Adrien Brody

IN A NUTSHELL: A frustrated novelist vacationing in Paris discovers that his midnight walks take him back to the city in its bohemian 1920s heyday.

RECURRING THEMES: Nostalgia; frustrated novelists; past vs. present; magic realism; infidelity; California hatred ("Where I come from, people measure out their time in coke spoons")

Midnight in Paris opens with a device Woody Allen hadn't employed since Another Woman clear back in 1988: the pre-title sequence. In that film, it was used to get the narrative off and running a little more quickly; in Midnight in Paris, it seems, Woody merely can't wait until after his credits are over to let us drink in the beauty of his newest location, in a three-and-a-half-minute montage brimming with affection for the city. He shows us Paris, new and old, in sun and rain and day and night, every image a beauty shot, every frame a postcard. And then he does something he's never done: Instead of playing another old standard over the Windsor-typed credit roll, he gives us dialogue under the titles. From frame one, he's shaking up several of his long-held traditions, which is appropriate to the surprisingly subversive nature of Midnight in Paris—a picture that takes on the idea of nostalgia, which his entire body of work luxuriates in, and shakes it down.

Owen Wilson's Gil is a nostalgist, obsessed with the past, fascinated by its details (none are too small), hungering to walk in the footsteps trod by his idols. While in Paris, he wants to go where his heroes ate and drank and wrote; he entertains notions of living in a Parisian attic apartment, writing a brilliant novel between long, rain-swept walks.

These are qualities typical of a Woody Allen protagonist—and seem to be those of the man himself, based on his classical style, his disdain for pop music, his disinterest in modern technologies. But the dangers of such narrow focus are laid out cleanly in the Versailles visit, when Gil's fiancée (Rachel McAdams) brands him one of the people "who live in the past, people who think their lives would be happier if they lived in an earlier time." Michael Sheen's Paul declares, "Nostalgia is denial. Denial of the painful present." Paul's a smug prick, but he's

> 66
>
> How long have you been dating Picasso? God, did I just say that?
> —Gil Pender
>
> 99

right. Gil entertains "Golden age thinking—the erroneous notion that a different time period is better than the one one's living in."

For Gil, that period is the 1920s, the Jazz Age in which hard-drinking sophisticates like Hemingway, the Fitzgeralds, Cole Porter, and Pablo Picasso dwelled in the bars and drawing rooms of Paris. When Gil gets lost on a Parisian stroll (an iPhone GPS app would disable the entire narrative, but of course someone like Gil would never have one of those), he find himself in his dream era—and that really is the best way to put it, that he "finds himself" there. There is no big "time travel" sequence, no special effects to speak of; he's just *there*, engaging in the kind of casually understated magic we've seen earlier in *Alice* and *The Purple Rose of Cairo*.

It's sort of remarkable that *Midnight in Paris* became Woody's biggest domestic hit since *Hannah and Her Sisters*, since so much of it consists of throwaway jokes for the literary set, lines like "*That* was Djuna Barnes? No wonder she wanted to lead," and in-gags like Hemingway greeting "Alice" at Gertrude Stein's door. The writing is delicate, a bit of a miracle, really; Allen constructs these characters in a way that makes light of their personas (Hemingway's staccato sentences and roaring "WHO WANTS TO FIGHT," for example) without reducing them to caricature.

Woody on Woody

"This film I have great affection for because I have great affection for Paris, and that comes through in this film."

Allen won his third Oscar for Best Original Screenplay for *Midnight in Paris*. Lobby card from the *Voyageur Press Collection*

CONCORDE-FILM

Midnight in Paris
Drehbuch und Regie
Woody Allen

Midnight in Paris was one of Allen's most critically acclaimed films of recent years, and it is also the highest grossing of his long career. *Richard Corkery/NY Daily News via Getty Images*

The central conceit is presumably what audiences attached to, the idea of unexplained magic transporting you to a seemingly perfect past. Allen creates that magic, but the brilliance of *Midnight in Paris* is that he does not stop there. When Gil, who always says that he was "born too late," meets a gorgeous and interesting muse (the luminous Marion Cotillard) in his '20s travels, she feels the same way; she longs for the Belle Époque, which she proclaims the best period of French history. "Really?" he asks. "Better than *now?*" When that same magic transports them to that era, she would rather stay in *her* idealized past than his—even though the people there have an idealized past which *they'd* prefer. It's a never-ending cycle of longingly gazing backwards, oblivious to the pleasures of the present.

This is a tricky theme for Allen to pull off, since he's creating a portrait of Paris in the 1920s that's earnestly romanticized, all warm glow and sophistication, with a legend lurking in every corner booth. Yet it takes going there for Gil to realize that the past can feel perfect because the present is "a little unsatisfying, because *life* is a little unsatisfying." Nostalgia is an escape, in other words, a fantasy, so of course the film brings his fantasy to vivid, lovely life.

What's remarkable about this film, at this moment in Allen's career, is that he's savvy and self-aware enough to acknowledge nostalgia as fantasy, to admit the flaws and traps of dwelling in the past. It's the kind of truth he might not have admitted a decade earlier, but reinvention—and that's certainly what the European phase amounts to—requires coming to terms with the flaws in one's thinking and adjusting accordingly. This is a filmmaker who loves the past, but who has realized that he must live in the present if he wants to have a future.

WATCH OUT FOR

Future Marvel villain Tom Hiddleston and *The Newsroom* ingénue Alison Pill as Scott and Zelda Fitzgerald; former French First Lady Carla Bruni-Sarkozy as the tour guide.

The Surrogates

As Woody got older and aged out of romantic leading-man territory, viewers started to notice certain similarities between characters he was writing for younger actors and the "Woody" roles he wrote for himself. This "became a very fashionable thing to say about characters in my films," Woody later said. "And I just smile and say 'Uh-huh' and move on." But these characters sometimes admitted as much themselves, and it's hard not to watch these performances without thinking of the writer/director behind them.

ACTOR	FILM	WOODY-ISH QUALITIES	WOODY-ESQUE DIALOGUE
Ted Bessell	*Don't Drink the Water* (1969)	Lovable loser; inferiority complex; neurotic	"When I was just a little boy, just a little kid, and I did something wrong, my mother used to hit me with a copy of *Time* magazine—with my father's picture on the cover."
John Cusack	*Bullets Over Broadway*	Writer; intellectual; neurotic; frequent stammering; glasses	"I'm feeling a bit unstable. I think maybe I'll go and check into a sanitarium, and get the help that I need. And we'll talk later, because it's been good! Hasn't it?"
Michael J. Fox	*Don't Drink the Water* (1994)	Lovable loser; inferiority complex; frequent stammering; neurotic	"My father's right, I'm a failure. And your father said it too. And it's not just fathers who've said it: lots of mothers and brothers and sisters have said it. Cousins, uncles. . . ."
Tobey Maguire	*Deconstructing Harry*	Writer; sexually frustrated	"The truth is, I never meet or see a woman where I don't wonder what it would be like in bed with her."
Stanley Tucci	*Deconstructing Harry*	Neurotic; in analysis; drawn to kamikaze women	"You're like a born-again Christian, except you're a Jew!"
Richard Benjamin	*Deconstructing Harry*	Sexually frustrated	(to Woody's Harry Block:) "I'm just you, thinly disguised. You gave me a little bit more maturity and a different name."
Kenneth Branagh	*Celebrity*	All of them, pretty much	"You are the most beautiful cr-creature I've, I've ever seen. I mean, every curve in your body fulfills its promise. If, if, if the universe has any meaning, at all, I'm, I'm looking at it."
Jason Biggs	*Anything Else*	Writer; hopeless romantic; frequent stammering; sexually frustrated; in analysis; drawn to kamikaze women; neurotic	"The doctor had better sex examining her than I've had for six months."
Will Ferrell	*Melinda and Melinda*	Lovable loser; sexually frustrated; frequent stammering	"Yeah, but if you're somebody who's nobody, it's no fun to be around anybody who's everybody."
Scarlett Johansson	*Scoop*	Writer; frequent stammering; glasses	(To the suggestion of "putting our heads together":) "If you put *our* heads together, you'll hear a hollow noise."
Rebecca Hall	*Vicky Cristina Barcelona*	Neurotic; intellectual; sexually frustrated	"Oh, God, look, I wouldn't call our reluctance to leap at your sexual offer being over-analytical. If you would care to join us for some recognized form of social interaction, like a drink, then we'd be fine, but otherwise, I think you should try, you know, offering to some other table."
Larry David	*Whatever Works*	Hypochondriac; intellectual; glasses; neurotic	"I'm not going back on my goddamn medicine! I won't have my mind befuddled by chemicals when I'm the only one who sees the whole picture for exactly what it is! Where's the goddamn vodka?"
Owen Wilson	*Midnight in Paris*	Writer; nostalgic; sexually frustrated; frequent stammering	"I took a, I jumped in the shower, just for a second—you know how I think better in the shower, and I get the positive ions going in there?"
Jesse Eisenberg	*To Rome with Love*	Hopeless romantic; frequent stammering; drawn to kamikaze women	"It's incredible that the Coliseum is still standing after thousands of years. Y'know, Sally and I have to re-tile the bathroom every six months."

To Rome with Love

RELEASE DATE: June 22, 2012

WRITER: Woody Allen

CAST: Allen, Alec Baldwin, Judy Davis, Penélope Cruz, Roberto Benigni, Jesse Eisenberg, Ellen Page, Greta Gerwig

IN A NUTSHELL: Four comic vignettes with only one thing in common: their setting in the city of Rome, Italy.

RECURRING THEMES: Infidelity; celebrity; nostalgia; show business; neurotic actresses ("Tell any actress that she could play Miss Julie, and you can have her way with her"); kamikaze women; psychoanalysis ("Don't psychoanalyze me, Phyllis. Many have tried, all have failed"); prostitution; past vs. present; magic realism

As Woody Allen himself discovered with *Oedipus Wrecks*, the trouble with anthology films is that they're only as strong as their weakest link, and the stories are inevitably compared to one another. His work in *New York Stories* was stacked against Scorsese and Coppola; in *To Rome with Love*, he had only himself to compete with, but that doesn't mean the results are any less scattershot. Of the four short stories in his Roman romp, two are throwaways, one has a bit more meat (and laughs), and one is plain terrific. But the fillers tend to crowd out the successes in the viewer's memory.

The best of the bunch concerns John (Alec Baldwin), a successful architect returning to Rome and enjoying a nostalgic glow for his last visit there, thirty years previous. "I'm not a good sightseer," he warns his companions. "I prefer just to walk the little streets"—much like *Midnight in Paris*'s Gil Pender. And like Pender, that walk allows him to stumble into a bit of casual magic: He encounters a younger architect named "Jack" (Jesse Eisenberg) who takes him to his apartment ("This might've been my exact street," John notes, as they approach). There, Jack introduces his girlfriend Sally (Greta Gerwig), who says her best friend, a neurotic actress and maneater named Monica (Ellen Page), is coming for a visit. For John, the alarm bells go off: "I see it so clearly now—but I'm older."

And thus, whenever we return to Jack and Monica, John is there but he isn't; an observer, commenting and advising Jack (a la Bogie in *Play It Again, Sam*, or Baldwin himself in *Alice*), but not a participant. His walk, which covers months of Jack's life but only an afternoon of his own, is a reflective return to a disastrous relationship in his past. As with *Midnight*, the film has a quietly powerful theme about nostalgia, this time for one's own past: We can

> 66
> Beautiful, funny, smart, sexual, and also neurotic—it's like filling an inside straight!
> —John
> 99

Allen directs Alec Baldwin, Jesse Eisenberg, Greta Gerwig, and Ellen Page. *AP Photo/Sony Pictures Classics, Philippe Antonello*

relive it, and question our decisions, but we cannot change them. And that's for the best, since they ultimately make us who we are. It's a lovely vignette (aside from the miscasting of Page and Gerwig, who clearly should've switched roles), and one that could well have been its own feature.

The picture's second-best story is that of Leopoldo (Roberto Benigni), an average family man and office drone who awakes one day to find himself inexplicably famous, a swarm of paparazzi constantly at his heels, reporters asking him mundane questions about his day and his breakfast—stripping away the artifice of promotion and artistry from fame, and laying bare its essential ridiculousness. The silliness of celebrity is a topic Allen has covered before, most memorably in *Stardust Memories* and (of course) *Celebrity*; what's new here is a phenomenon that became an epidemic in the years since the latter picture, that of the Hiltons, Kardashians, and their ilk, famous, as Leopoldo is told, "for being famous." The story nicely reflects Allen's own mixed views on celebrity; the character hates the attention and is thrilled when it ends, but he misses it desperately soon thereafter.

The other two segments have the feel of *New Yorker* pieces that have yet to be fleshed out. Neither story—a newlywed who must convince a prostitute to masquerade as his wife, and an American director who finds a remarkable opera singer who can only perform in the shower—ever quite manages to transcend its one-joke premise, with the former collapsing into spit takes and pratfalls, and the latter sinking into endless opera sequences. But both stories have their pleasures, and the latter gives us Allen's first onscreen appearance since *Scoop*, opposite the wonderful Judy Davis, the two of them working a *Small Time Crooks*–esque love/hate dynamic. Yet those performances don't quite manage to lift the drag their segments place on this rather overlong and decidedly minor work.

173

The Process: How Woody Makes a Movie

"Show business is dog eat dog. It's worse than dog eat dog.
It's dog doesn't return dog's phone calls."
—Cliff (Woody Allen), *Crimes and Misdemeanors*

Talking with the New York *Daily News* in 1974, Woody Allen made this pronouncement: "Moviemaking has become a high-pressure business with a low survival rate. I'm for turning out a comedy every year. Some of the other comedians could do it, too. I wish we could just keep turning them out." In the forty years since that statement, Allen has missed that goal only twice (in 1976 and 1981), and while not all of the films have been comedies, they have all been uniquely his: He wrote them, directed them, often starred in them, and supervised their editing and promotion. It's an output unrivaled among his American contemporaries, but true to form, Allen dismisses the achievement. "To do one film a year is not a big accomplishment," he said in 1999. "A few months to write, a couple months' pre-production, a couple months' shooting—all in all, making a movie takes about nine months, and it's not even a concentrated nine months. Then I have three months of nothing."

His productivity is enabled by a few factors: his endless well (or, in his case, bottomless drawer) of ideas, his love for the work, his desire to keep busy. But most importantly, after forty-five years of filmmaking, he also has the process down cold, the production of his pictures on a virtual assembly line. He has a core company of producers, crew members, actors, and technicians at his disposal. It's something akin to the old studio system—the key difference being his active participation in every step of the process. "To me the movie is a handmade product," he explained in 2005. "It would be unthinkable

for me not to be in on every inch of the movie—and this is not out of any sort of ego or sense of having to control; I just can't imagine it any other way."

Writing

A new Allen script begins with an idea, which is tossed in a drawer. His "ideas drawer" is next to his bed, filled with scraps of paper, envelopes, napkins—anything that's nearby when he thinks of something that might make for a good film, or play, or prose piece. An idea can come from anywhere: "For instance, when I wrote *Broadway Danny Rose*, it was a character I knew Mia wanted to play. And that helped me to find the story. In *Radio Days* it was those songs I wanted to use in some way. In *Another Woman* it was those sounds coming through the wall. It's always different."

Choosing what comes next is equally instinctual. "Sometimes it's a natural chain of events: I finish a film and I immediately have a new idea, or I pull one out of my drawer. But other times, I really tell myself, in reaction to the previous film: 'My God, I've spent one year of my life on a very serious film, or on the other hand a very zany film, it's time for a change.'"

Once he's decided what's next, the writing begins. He does so initially in longhand, writing in pencil (as Renata does in *Interiors*) while lying on his four-poster bed. There is no music or outside noise. He stops only occasionally, to think and walk through his apartment. If he's really blocked, he'll take a hot shower. He uses short character

Woody at work on the fabled Olympia typewriter. *Brian Hamill/ Getty Images*

Preproduction and Casting

When the script is ready to shoot, its first stop is in the hands of co-producer/unit production manager Helen Robin, who works up a budget and a shooting schedule. Because of his clockwork calendar, Allen's production team typically already has financing lined up (recently, with the European films, the funding may be contingent on shooting in the country of origin, which will have influenced the script), and the two-month preproduction process begins. And Allen and his casting team—led by Juliet Taylor, who has been with him since *Annie Hall*— start looking at actors.

"Once in a while someone will call me up," Allen said, "like Jodie Foster, and say, 'I'd love to do something in one of your movies,'" and he'll find something for them. But more often than not, Taylor will bring Allen suggestions, with the buzziest up-and-coming stars among them. Over the years, being summoned by Woody has become a rite of passage for the young actor on the rise; it's all about the cachet, the symbolism of the thing. It's certainly not about the money, which is frequently union scale. "And afterwards," Woody explained, "they go back to their career as stars."

His audition process is notorious for its brevity. Allen dislikes it immensely ("The whole thing is awkward. They have nothing to say, I have nothing to say, they're being . . . *looked at*."), and actors coming in are warned that it will be very brief and they should not be offended. He (or Taylor) will explain the timeframe of the shoot, why they're there ("I just wanted to see you. Just to take a look at you physically so I don't have to do this from photographs. We'll let you know."), and thank them for their time. The whole thing usually lasts about thirty seconds.

Sometimes he doesn't even do that. "I got a call from my agent saying that Woody had a script he'd like me to read," recalled Cate Blanchett, of being cast in *Blue Jasmine*. "So he and I spoke for about three and a half minutes, and he said, 'Can I send it to you?' and I said,

names, because when he types up the script, "I don't want to type too much." The themes, when they reveal themselves, are "instinctive"; "You feel, when writing the script, when it should surface again. When one feels it's correct for it to surface, you let it happen." He starts early and gets seven hours of sleep a night, making sure to leave one hour a day for practicing his clarinet.

Dramas take him about three months, but comedies typically only take a month (*Scoop*, for example, was the third of three scripts written in a twelve-week period, after two others that didn't work out for various reasons). Once he's done writing the script in longhand, he takes it to the old Olympia portable typewriter and types it up, rewriting as he goes. "Writing is the great life," he says in *Woody Allen: A Documentary*, "because you wake up in the morning, and you write in your room. When you're in the room, everything is great, because you don't have to deliver. . . . But when you have to take it out and do it, then reality sets in. And all your schemes about making a masterpiece are reduced to, 'I'll prostitute myself anyway I have to, to survive this catastrophe.'"

'Love to read it,' and he said, 'Well, call me when you're finished,' and I read it straight away. I mean, that's a script that you do read straight away . . . and then we spoke for another forty-five seconds when we agreed to do the film together, and then I saw him at the camera test in San Francisco."

Audition or no, actors are then sent a letter and a script—often just of their scenes. The scripts are hand-delivered, for immediate reading and return. Louis C.K. recalled his casting in the same film: "I got a letter that said someone who works for Woody is coming to your house tomorrow with an envelope, and a young woman came to my house, gave me an envelope, and said, 'I have to take this back with me, so you can have it for 40 minutes.'" The notes are either handwritten or typed, often with an altogether unnecessary introduction ("You

may remember me," went Josh Brolin's note for *You Will Meet a Tall Dark Stranger*. "You did a movie called *Melinda and Melinda*. I was the director"), an offer of a role, and encouragement to rephrase the dialogue at will (which few ever do). Once the cast and crew are locked, they charge on to the shoot.

Shooting

"I don't have any great anecdotes that have happened to me in a film," Allen said in 1999. "I come in the morning, talk sports with my camera crew, have lunch, shoot. There are no tantrums by any of the actors, no tantrums by me. It's a very ordinary kind of thing." This is not an understatement—by all accounts, a Woody Allen set is a quiet, relaxed, yet businesslike environment.

He says he has "no idea of what I'm going to be filming" when he arrives on set each morning. "I like it to be spontaneous at the time." He is handed the day's pages, "and I see what it is I'm in for." He'll walk the set with the cinematographer and make a rough plan for how the scene will be photographed—more often than not, in a single shot that will follow and frame (most of) the action. The set is lit, which can take several hours for such an elaborate setup. "Then, and only then, I call the actors in." He'll give them general blocking, nothing too specific, trusting their instincts. "And at three o'clock in the afternoon, or four o'clock or something, the actors will do it. And they'll do it a couple of times—I don't shoot a lot of takes—and it's over."

Often the first take is the one that makes the film. "What is important," he has said, "is to avoid a kind of perfection. It's not bad that sometimes their lines overlap, that there are mistakes: it creates an air of freedom." That freshness and spontaneity is also why he never

Allen cast Cate Blanchett in *Blue Jasmine* over two phone calls, each less than five minutes long. *Alo Ceballos/FilmMagic/Getty Images*

Allen and his crew on the set of *Annie Hall. Brian Hamill/Getty Images*

rehearses with his actors: "I like the first virginal attempts to be their ideas without inhibition or guidance from me."

That hands-off approach has made him somewhat legendary in the acting community. Some dislike it; after working with him on *Manhattan*, Meryl Streep said, "I don't think Woody Allen even remembers me," while Sam Shepard said, after working with Allen on the aborted first version of *September*, that he was "piss-poor" as an actor's director, with "no respect for actors," insisting, "Allen knows even less than Altman, which is nothing."

"I've worked with tremendous people," Allen says with a shrug, "and I don't direct them a lot. I try to speak to them as infrequently as possible, you know." But he defends his method. "I don't see the point in hiring a great actor . . . and then hovering over them and bothering them. They have a good instinct for what they do. They read the part. If they have any questions, they ask me. Very often they don't ask me anything. They understand what it is. They do it, and they do it very well." (When they don't, and when Allen finds he can't make it work, he'll quietly replace them. Michael Keaton met with that fate on *The Purple Rose of Cairo*, as did Emily Lloyd in *Husbands and Wives*.) Whatever your feelings about his approach, the results speak for themselves: He has directed actors to six Academy Awards and nine more nominations.

Allen takes a similarly laid-back approach to his own direction. "I'm not a workaholic—that's a big myth about me," he told Richard Schickel. "When I make a film, if I don't have it too great, but could make one more shot, and it's six o'clock at night, and I've got to be at Madison Square Garden for the Knicks at seven, I blow the shot off and go to the Knicks game, all the time. I mean films are not a religion with me."

Woody in the editing room, whipping *Annie Hall* into shape. *Brian Hamill/Getty Images*

Post-Production

"I always feel, with a film, you're writing it at every moment," Woody told Stig Björkman. "I change the script while we're working on the set, and I change it in editing the film. I have no problem with that at all. I'm happy to take a scene which is supposed to be scene number 20 and stick it first. Film is a constantly evolving thing." To be as connected as possible to that evolution, Woody and editor Alisa Lepselter, who has edited every one of his films since 1999's *Sweet and Lowdown*, don't start working until the shoot is complete. "Most directors have the editor doing a rough cut as they're shooting," according to Lepselter. "Woody has a lot more freedom to work at his own pace, and he wants to be in the cutting room with me from day one when he's done shooting. He comes in and we review all the material, and start cutting from the beginning, from scene one, sequentially, which is also very helpful, because you understand what the tone is as you're going along."

They don't do a "kitchen sink" rough cut of all the material. He likes to start at the beginning and edit precisely as they go, sculpting the film as closely as possible to its final form. "I could almost show my first cut to an audience," Woody said in 1980—but not always. Seeing the initial shoot and edit as a "rough draft," he'll often reshoot scenes, sometimes entire subplots. "I've never had a film that I didn't do extensive reshooting on," he said in 1986. "Most of them are made in the reshooting." That's changed a bit in recent years, presumably due to the complexities of his international shoots. But he remains ruthless in the cutting room. "When a scene died, Woody never looked back," wrote his first regular editor, Ralph Rosenblum. "His sense of ownership as a writer is nonexistent. He was ruthless in what he would throw out."

Post-production is also when Allen introduces one of the most familiar elements of his films: jazz and pop standards from the first half of the twentieth century. "I put in the music that I like to listen to because it's my movie," he jokes. He keeps all his records on a shelf in the editing room. "I just pick up the world's great music and melodies, and I can choose whatever I want. And I need no finesse. I can turn it up when I want to. I can turn it off when I want to. So I started doing that, and I never stopped."

Release

"I conceive the film," Woody said in 1986, "I sit home and write it—and when I conceive it, it's brilliant. Everything is *true* Chekhov or Shakespeare: it's *great*! And then you start work, and the truck with fresh compromises drives up every day." On certain films, "I knew when I was making them that nobody was going to go and see them." Yet he doesn't make his films out of spite, or to purposefully buck trends. "I always hope the public will enjoy the movie," he told Eric Lax, "but I must never fall into the trap of doing anything but exactly what I want in an effort to be liked. Better to be disliked but good. Better to try to grow and fail humiliatingly than play it safe or, worse, curry favor."

So he stopped paying attention to reviews years ago—and in fact seems deeply suspicious of the pop success of films like *Manhattan* and *Annie Hall*, a film that, remember, opens with his retelling of the Groucho Marx quote about not wanting to belong to any club that would have someone like him for a member. He places no stock in awards ("dust gatherers"). He does not revisit his films on DVD, and if he flips past one on television, he keeps flipping. And when he completes one film, with nary a day off, he starts on the next one. "I've been working on the quantity theory," he said recently. "I feel if I keep making films, and just keeping making them, every once in a while, I'll get lucky and one'll come out. And that's exactly what happens."

Allen and his cast, unveiling *Midnight in Paris* at Cannes. *Vittorio Zunino Celotto/Getty Images*

Blue Jasmine

RELEASE DATE: July 26, 2013

WRITER: Woody Allen

CAST: Alec Baldwin, Cate Blanchett, Bobby Cannavale, Louis C.K., Andrew Dice Clay, Sally Hawkins, Peter Sarsgaard, Michael Stuhlbarg

IN A NUTSHELL: A New York society wife retreats to her sister's modest San Francisco home after her rich husband is unmasked as a philandering con man.

RECURRING THEMES: Sibling rivalry; infidelity; class ("Y'know, having wealth is nothing to be ashamed of"); past vs. present; eavesdropping; estranged children; suicide; the role of luck and chance; younger women ("Are you out of your mind? She's a teenager, for Christ's sake!")

Woody Allen returns (briefly) to New York and soaks in the beauty of San Francisco—shooting his forty-fifth film in the same city he shot his first, *Take the Money and Run.* That geographic circularity keenly pinpoints his tremendous growth as a filmmaker, from purveyor of roughhouse slapstick to sophisticated and tricky psychological comedy/drama.

As the best of his hybrids do, *Jasmine* begins as a much funnier story than it will become. Its title character (Cate Blanchett) seems at first a slightly obnoxious over-sharer, spilling her life's secrets to an older woman who turns out (in a nice comic reveal) to be merely her airplane seatmate. But Jasmine will talk even when no one is there. After the arrest and death of her Bernie Madoff–inspired husband (Alec Baldwin), she has a nervous breakdown, and though she's going to San Francisco to stay with her lower-class sister (Sally Hawkins) and "start a new life out here," she cannot escape her past.

Her memories become a simultaneous story, intercutting her upscale life in New York with her current, floundering existence, and the film becomes an internal narrative, following Jasmine's mind down the rabbit holes that keep troublesomely appearing. That stream-of-consciousness structure, and the way scenes are keyed off of transitional cue words and phrases, recalls (slightly) *Annie Hall.* And just as the present triggers the past, the past pushes itself into the present—and the dialectic between the two is, ultimately, what *Blue Jasmine* is really about (much as it was in the Baldwin/Eisenberg sections of *To Rome with Love*).

Ultimately, as usual, the past wrecks the present. Jasmine's previous life in New York (which plays, for once, the villain in the grand scheme of Allen's storytelling) is exposed, at a particularly inopportune moment, by her former brother-in-law ("Some people," he explains, "they don't put things behind so easily"). That

> There's only so many traumas a person can withstand before they take to the streets and start screaming."
>
> —Jasmine

Allen originally read Louis C.K. for the role of Augie, which C.K. knew he wasn't right for. Once fellow standup comedian Andrew Dice Clay was cast, Allen offered Louis C.K. the secondary role of Al. *AP Photo/Sony Pictures Classics*

encounter prompts Jasmine to visit her estranged, adult son, just as Val did at the conclusion of *Hollywood Ending*. It is worth remembering, too, that Allen has an estranged adult son of his own, formerly Satchel Farrow, now Ronan—though Mia Farrow made headlines shortly after *Jasmine*'s release by hinting that Ronan's father wasn't Allen at all, but first husband Frank Sinatra. Ronan's witty Twitter response to the controversy ("Listen, we're all *possibly* Frank Sinatra's son") did more to prove his connection to Woody than any DNA test could have. In *Hollywood Ending*, Val and his son reconcile. In *Blue Jasmine*, the young man refuses her olive branch: "I've become a different person," he says, which is something like taking on a different name. "Just get out of my life so I can move on."

Ultimately, it is *his* rejection, not that of her new fiancé (Peter Sarsgaard), that drives Jasmine over the edge. Throughout the film, she keeps telling lies in the hope that she'll eventually believe them herself. By the end of the picture, she's alienated everyone, and there's no one left to listen; she sits on a park bench talking to no one, and the woman next to her gathers her things and quietly moves away. And after a few more moments, so do we.

The complexity and theatricality of Jasmine's character, and the film's uncommonly critical view of the male of the species (every man in the film is either a cheater, a loser, or both), aren't all that set *Blue Jasmine* apart from what came before. After all, Allen spent much of the last two decades (with occasional exceptions) devoted to making pictures that were very clearly either comic or dramatic in nature. But here, Allen not only navigates between those tones as confidently as he toggles between time frames, but he also finds fertile soil somewhere in between, leaving the viewer consistently surprised but never unsteady. The result is a film not quite like any of his other work—a considerable achievement for an artist who's already done so much.

Closing: The Escape Artist

Woody Allen's genius and prolificness are no mere illusion. He has been a tireless filmmaker for more than forty-five years.
Brian Hamill/Getty Images

In 2015, Woody Allen will turn eighty years old. By that age, most filmmakers have retired, or at the very least slowed their pace. Woody will do no such thing. It seems safe to presume that, as he has every year since 1969, he will make a film, with complete autonomy, answering only to his own well-tested instincts. He will, when the mood strikes him, write something for *The New Yorker*. Every Monday, he will go to play with his jazz band. He will work every day, for his is a life of order and routine—or, as Pauline Kael noted, "Free and messy people don't play the clarinet."

What drives him? What compels him to keep working at such a tireless pace, long past the point where his place in the canon of cinema is secure? Filmmaker Robert Weide, who in 2012 made the definitive documentary film about him, put it this way: "I think there's a practical side to it and a psychological element. The practical part is he just likes to keep busy, and even though moviemaking can be a drag, I think there's a part of it that he enjoys. Now, the psychological component is that he's truly a dark, morose guy, and if he's not occupied, his mind *will* wander into areas that he'd rather it didn't."

"I think I've burned over a low flame of depression my whole lifetime," Allen confessed to Eric Lax. He once confessed to Roger Ebert that "hardly a day passes when he doesn't seriously consider suicide—not out of despair, but simply as a choice." And thus, for him, moviemaking is about more than simply a creative

>
>
> It's true. Everybody loves his illusions.
>
> **—Roustabout**
>
> Loves them? They need them like they need the air.
>
> **—Magician (*Shadows and Fog*)**

act; as he told collaborator Douglas McGrath, "The only value of a film is the diversion of doing it. I'm so involved in figuring out the second act, I don't have time to think about life's terrible anxieties." Or, put another way (as he did to Richard Schickel): "It's like a patient in an institution who they give basket weaving to, or finger painting, because it makes him feel better."

That's a mighty grim way to approach a group of films that have provided such a surplus of laughter and joy to so many people. But if you look more closely at the work, those themes are present, and not even all that deeply buried. In the closing moments of *September*, after Lane (Mia Farrow) has had her heart broken and her very existence is at its bleakest, her friend Stephanie (Dianne Wiest) consoles her: "Tomorrow will come and you'll find some distractions. You'll get rid of this place, you'll move back to the city, you'll work, you'll fall in love, and maybe it'll work out, and maybe it won't, but you'll find a million petty little things to keep you going, and distractions to keep you from focusing on—" And Lane interrupts: "On the truth."

Allen was seventy-six years old when he started filming *Blue Jasmine*, his forty-sixth film as writer/director. *Alo Ceballos/ FilmMagic/Getty Images*

Another of Farrow's characters comes even closer to Allen's worldview. He has said, on multiple occasions, that the protagonist with whom he has the most in common is not Alvy Singer or Ike Davis or Harry Block—none of the characters he played (nor those, like Lee Simon or Jerry Falk, who were played *like* him). He identifies with poor Cecilia, the movie-loving housewife at the center of *The Purple Rose of Cairo*.

"I lived in Brooklyn," he recalled to Stig Björkman, "and on those hot, hazy summer days when it was humid and you couldn't move and nobody had anything to do, there were thousands of movie houses around, and you could walk in for 25 cents. Suddenly it was cool and air-conditioned and dark, and there was candy and popcorn. You could sit down and there would be two features. And you would see pirates and you would be on the sea. And then you would be in a penthouse in Manhattan with beautiful people. . . . One of the pleasures of going into a movie house is to avoid the harsh realities of life."

Cecilia goes the Jewel Theater to escape the Depression, her dull job, her loveless marriage to a worthless louse who cheats on her. And Woody Allen,

The filmmaker, circa 1971.
*John Minihan/Evening
Standard/Getty Images*

as obsessive about making movies as Cecilia is about going to them, creates the films that will play in the Jewel and the multiplexes that replaced it, finding in his ability to create fantasy worlds an escape valve from the real one. "You create a world you would like to live in," he said. "You like the people you create. You like what they wear, where they live, how they talk, and it gives you a chance for some months to live in that world. And those people move to beautiful music, and you're in that world."

And within those works, Woody's characters seek similar escapes. Via casual magic that Allen passes from his fingertips to their own, they flee into the past (*Midnight in Paris*), into the spirit world (*A Midsummer Night's Sex Comedy*), into their own memories (*To Rome with Love*) and fantasies (*Alice*). They fall under a hypnotist's spell and confess their deepest desires (*The Curse of the Jade Scorpion*); they step into a magician's box and traverse space and time (*Oedipus Wrecks, Scoop, Shadows and Fog*).

But the greatest magic occurs in the movie theater. In *Hannah and Her Sisters*, the sheer joy of the Marx Brothers on screen turns sunny the dark thoughts of a suicidal man. In *Radio Days*, the majesty of Radio City Music Hall is presented as a lush, perfect, awe-inspiring heaven on earth. In *Purple Rose*, film is so magical that a character not only can step out of the frame and into the "real" world but can traverse the divide again to bring someone into the movies with him. And when Cecilia returns to that cathedral alone, abandoned by both the man she thought loved her and the man she was too good for, the movies are still there for her, a sparkling black-and-white portal out of her brutally drab existence.

"I've escaped into a life in the cinema on the other side of the camera rather than the audience side of it," Allen confessed. "Ironic that I make escapist films, but it's not the audience that escapes—it's me." Yet it's not entirely a matter of escapism; what he's done is far trickier than that. Rather than block out entirely the fears that preoccupy him—of death, of life being meaningless, of not mattering, of not being loved, of being cheated on—he turns those fears into works of art. Or, as Judy Davis's Lucy pointedly jabs in *Deconstructing Harry*, "Your latest magnum opus emerges from this sewer of an apartment where you take everyone's suffering and turn it into gold, into literary gold. You take everyone's misery—you even cause them misery—and mix your fucking alchemy and turn it into gold, like some sort of black magician."

The joy that flickers and then settles on Cecilia's face at the conclusion of *The Purple Rose of Cairo* speaks to the transformative power of that escape, which the cinema provides for her. But by all accounts, Woody Allen himself does not experience that joy. He won't take time off when he completes a project to rest, relax, or luxuriate (not even a single day, it is said). He moves on, immediately, to the next one: "My philosophy has always been that if I just keep working, just focus on my work, everything else will fall into place."

So perhaps the film whose final frames are most appropriate as the closing image to this volume is not *The Purple Rose of Cairo*, but *Stardust Memories*. The picture concludes with the ending of a film-within-a-film, the result of great soul-searching and soul-baring by director Sandy Bates (Allen). When it's over, the assembled parties wander out. They argue over interpretations ("What do you think the Rolls-Royce represented?" "I think that, uh, represented his car"). His leading ladies compare notes about his poor kissing technique. Complaints are overheard ("From this he makes a living? I like a melodrama, a musical comedy with a plot").

After the theater has emptied, Sandy returns—he has left his sunglasses on his seat. As he puts them on and starts to leave, he turns once more to look at the blank screen. Unlike *Purple Rose*, which ends with a lingering closeup of Cecilia's face gazing at the screen, or *Play It Again, Sam*, which opens with one, the camera is positioned behind Sandy. We do not see how he looks at the screen, and can thus only know that he looks at it for some period, regarding it, it seems, as a fact. His latest work has unspooled upon it, and now it is done. And then there will be another, and another after that. He leaves. The image fades to black. The credits roll.

Bibliography

Adler, Bill, and Jeffrey Feinman. *Woody Allen: Clown Prince of American Humor.* New York: Pinnacle Books, 1975.

Allen, Woody. *Four Films of Woody Allen.* New York: Random House, 1982.

———. *Side Effects.* New York: Random House, 1980.

———. *Standup Comic* (CD). Los Angeles: Rhino Records, 1999.

———. *Without Feathers.* New York: Random House, 1975.

Altman, Mark. *Woody Allen Encyclopedia.* Las Vegas: Pioneer Books, 1990.

Bailey, Peter J. *The Reluctant Film Art of Woody Allen.* Lexington: The University Press of Kentucky, 2001.

Barnhizer, David (director). *The Dick Cavett Show: Comic Legends.* Los Angeles: Shout Factory, 2006.

Baxter, John. *Woody Allen: A Biography.* London: HarperCollins, 1998.

Biskind, Peter. "Reconstructing Woody." *Vanity Fair,* December 2005. http://www.vanityfair.com/culture/features/2005/12/woodyallen200512

Björkman, Stig. *Woody Allen on Woody Allen.* New York: Grove Press, 1993.

Blanchett, Cate. *Blue Jasmine* Press Conference, July 22, 2013, New York.

Brody, Richard. "Best of the Decade." *The New Yorker* Blog, November 30, 2009. http://www.newyorker.com/online/blogs/movies/2009/11/best-films-of-the-decade.html

Box Office Mojo, http://www.boxofficemojo.com/

Cadwallardr, Carole. "Woody Allen: 'My Wife Hasn't Seen Most of My Films . . . and She Thinks My Clarinet Playing is Torture.'" *The Guardian,* March 12, 2011. http://www.theguardian.com/film/2011/mar/13/woody-allen-interview-carole-cadwalladr

Canby, Vincent. "Husbands and Wives." *The New York Times,* September 18, 1992. http://www.nytimes.com/movie/review?res=9E0CEEDA143EF93BA2575AC0A964958260

Champlin, Charles. *Woody Allen at Work: The Photographs of Brian Hamill.* New York: Harry N. Abrams, Inc., 1995.

C.K., Louie. *Blue Jasmine* Press Conference, July 22, 2013, New York.

Colombani, Florence. *Masters of Cinema: Woody Allen.* Paris: Cahiers du cinema Sarl, 2007.

Conard, Mark T., and Aeon J. Skoble (editors). *Woody Allen and Philosophy: You Mean My Whole Fallacy Is Wrong?* Chicago: Open Court, 2011.

De Navacelle, Thierry. *Woody Allen on Locations.* New York: William Morrow and Company, 1987.

Ebert, Roger. "Another Woman." *The Chicago Sun-Times,* November 18, 1988. http://www.rogerebert.com/reviews/another-woman-1988

———. "Anything Else." *The Chicago Sun-Times,* September 19, 2003. http://www.rogerebert.com/reviews/anything-else-2003

———. "Manhattan." *The Chicago Sun-Times,* January 1, 1979. http://www.rogerebert.com/reviews/manhattan-1979

———. *Roger Ebert's Video Companion: 1991 Edition.* Kansas City: Andrews and McMeel Publishing, 1990.

Foundas, Scott. "Woody Allen's European Vacation." *L.A. Weekly,* August 13, 2008. http://www.laweekly.com/2008-08-14/film-tv/woody-allen-39-s-european-vacation-vicky-cristina-barcelona/

Fox, Michael J. *Lucky Man: A Memoir.* New York: Hyperion, 2003.

Gross, Terry. "Woody Allen on Life, Films, and 'Whatever Works.'" *NPR Fresh Air*, June 15, 2009. http://www.npr.org/templates/transcript/transcript.php?storyId=105400872

Gussow, Mel. "Woody Allen Fights Anhedonia." *New York Times*, April 20, 1977. http://www.nytimes.com/packages/html/movies/bestpictures/annie-ar.html

Hirsch, Foster. *Love, Sex, Death, and the Meaning of Life: The Films of Woody Allen*. Cambridge: Da Capo Press, 2001.

Horovitz, Louis J. (director). *The Concert for New York City* (DVD). Los Angeles: Sony, 2002.

Itzkoff, Dave. "Woody Allen on Faith, Fortune Tellers, and New York." *New York Times*, September 14, 2010. http://www.nytimes.com/2010/09/15/movies/15woody.html

Jameson, A. D. "The Longest Average Shot Lengths in Modern Hollywood." *Press Play*, June 26, 2013. http://blogs.indiewire.com/pressplay/the-longest-average-shot-lengths-in-modern-hollywood

Kael, Pauline. *Taking It All In*. New York: Holt, Rinehart, and Winston, 1984.

Kakutani, Michiko. "Mia Farrow and Her Director on Their Film Collaboration." *New York Times*, January 22, 1984. http://www.nytimes.com/books/97/02/23/reviews/farrow-allen.html

Kapsis, Robert E., and Kathie Coblentz. *Woody Allen: Interviews*. Jackson: University Press of Mississippi, 2006.

Lax, Eric. *Conversations with Woody Allen*. New York: Alfred A. Knopf, 2007.

———. *Woody Allen: A Biography*. Cambridge: Da Capo Press, 1991.

Meade, Marion. *The Unruly Life of Woody Allen: An Unauthorized Biography*. London: Pan McMillan, 1999.

Nichols, Mary P. *Reconstructing Woody: Art, Love, and Life in the Films of Woody Allen*. Lanham, Md.: Rowan & Littlefield Publishers, 1998.

Palmer, Myles. *Woody Allen*. New York: Proteus Publishing, 1980.

Schickel, Richard. *Woody Allen: A Life in Film*. Chicago: Ivan R. Dee, 2003.

Silet, Charles L. P. (editor). *The Films of Woody Allen: Critical Essays*. Lanham, Md.: Scarecrow Press, 2006.

Steigbigel, Matthew. "Editor Alisa Lepselter Talks *Blue Jasmine*, Her 15th Woody Allen Collab." *The Credits*, July 25, 2013. http://www.thecredits.org/2013/07/editor-alisa-lepselter-talks-blue-jasmine-her-15th-woody-allen-collab/

Sunshine, Linda (editor). *The Illustrated Woody Allen Reader*. New York: Alfred A. Knopf, 1993.

Tobias, Scott. "Woody Allen: The *AV Club* Interview." *The AV Club*, August 13, 2008. http://www.avclub.com/article woody-allen-14292

Weide, Robert. Author Interview, November 21, 2013.

———. *Woody Allen: A Documentary* (DVD). Los Angeles: Docurama/New Video, 2012.

Weintraub, Steven. "Scarlett Johannson Interview." *Collider*, August 14, 2008. http://collider.com/entertainment/interviews/article.asp/aid/8865/tcid/1

Index

People

Aaron, Caroline, 73
Alda, Alan, 73, 77, 83, 85, 100, 114
Allen, Woody. *See also* Allan
    Stewart Konisberg.
    "bad luck" philosophy featured in
      his films, 86–89
    character and persona on stage
      and in films, 121–125
    childhood, 8–9
    early films, 10–16
    deleted scenes from his films,
      76–77
    films he's appeared in other than
      his own, 108–110
    films that influenced his work,
      18–19
    films that imitate his style, 111
    first job writing jokes, 9
    his movie-making process, 174–
      179
    his signature style when making
      films, 142–144
    love of music and using that in
      film, 8, 46, 53–54, 70–71,
      114–117, 128–133
    making dramas vs. comedies, 80
    Oscar wins, 34, 69, 143, 163, 169
    reusing ideas, material from "the
      black reels," 117
    scandal surrounding breakup
      with Mia Farrow, 94–96, 100,
      102
    setting his films in European
      locales, 148, 152, 158–163
    shooting in black and white, 42–
      43, 50, 53, 61, 93, 126, 133
    showing his love of New York
      City on film, 42, 47–49
    taking a "mockumentarian"
      approach, 54–59
    working at Taminent, 10, 13
Argo, Victor, 73

Aronson, Letty, 103, 136
Baldwin, Alec, 73, 90, 172–173, 180
Banderas, Antonio, 166
Bardem, Javier, 158–159, 162
Benigni, Roberto, 173
Benjamin, Richard, 171
Bergman, Ingmar, 18–19, 28–29, 38,
    54, 68–69, 79, 86, 89, 104, 111,
    131, 144, 156, 160
Bergmann, Martin, 83
Berkley, Elizabeth, 137
Berrymore, Drew, 115–116
Bialik, Mayim, 107
Biggs, Jason, 37, 140–141, 171
Blanchett, Cate, 175–176, 180
Bosco, Philip, 73
Branagh, Kenneth, 91, 126, 171
Brickman, Marshall, 26–27, 30, 34,
    43, 100, 117
Brolin, Josh, 166–167, 176
Brooks, Mel, 9
Caesar, Sid, 10, 13
Caine, Michael, 65–66, 69
Chaplin, Charlie, 14, 16, 26, 124, 139
Cherry, Nettie, 8
Clark, Ashley, 160–163
Clay, Andrew Dice, 181
Cloquet, Ghislain, 29
Conroy, Francis, 73
Cruz, Penélope, 158–159, 162
Cusack, John, 91, 103–104, 171
Danner, Blythe, 73
David, Larry, 35, 71, 73, 82, 164
Davis, Judy, 72–73, 94, 127, 173, 185
Dennis, Sandy, 79
Detmer, David, 86–89
DeVito, Danny, 37
Di Palma, Carlo, 68, 93, 106, 144
DiCaprio, Leonardo, 126–127
Doumanian, Jean, 102, 106, 109, 136
Dunham, Lena, 35
Dunst, Kirsten, 82
Durning, Charles, 74, 77

Eisenberg, Jesse, 163, 171–173, 180
Ejiofor, Ellis, 147
Elliot, Denholm, 74, 77
Ephron, Nora, 96, 98
Farrell, Colin, 154, 161
Farrow, Mia, 55, 57–58, 60–62, 65–
    68, 71–72, 74–75, 77–78, 83,
    89–91, 93–96, 98, 100, 102, 124,
    181, 183
    child custody battle with Allen,
      112, 116
    scandal surrounding breakup
      with Allen, 43, 65, 94–96, 103
Feldman, Charles, 11, 25
Ferrell, Will, 147
Firth, Colin, 163
Forte, Nick Apollo, 36, 61
Fox, Michael J., 106–107, 171
Garner, Jennifer, 120
Gerwig, Greta, 172–173
Giamatti, Paul, 120
Gleason, Jackie, 25
Glinter, Ezra, 35–37
Goldblum, Jeff, 33
Green, Seth, 70
Greenhut, Robert, 95, 116
Griffith, Kristin, 39
Griffith, Melanie, 126
Gubbels, Jason, 130–133
Hannah, Daryl, 77
Hawkins, Sally, 180
Hawn, Goldie, 115
Hemingway, Mariel, 44, 120
Hershey, Barbara, 66–68
Hope, Bob, 14, 16, 18, 21, 25, 29, 92,
    109, 121–122
Hunt, Helen, 136
Hurt, Mary Beth, 39, 40
Hurt, William, 90
Huston, Angelica, 100
Janney, Allison, 127
Joffe, Charles H., 10–11, 25, 61
Johannson, Scarlett, 149–152, 158, 161

Kane, Carol, 32, 35
Kavner, Julie, 72, 107
Keaton, Buster, 14, 26–27, 72, 139
Keaton, Diane, 23, 27–28, 30, 33–34,
    39, 41–42, 44, 65, 76, 99–101,
    117, 123, 125, 132, 143, 157
Konisberg, Allan Stewart (a.k.a.
    Woody Allen), 8–9
Konisberg, Martin, 8
Landau, Martin, 36, 77, 84
Lasser, Louise, 16–17, 39, 73, 76, 124
Leoni, Téa, 138–139
Lepselter, Alisa, 178
Lewis, Juliette, 95
Lippin, Renée, 72
Loquasto, Santo, 93, 116, 136
Louis C.K., 176, 181
Louis-Dreyfus, Julia, 68
Mantegna, Joe, 53, 59, 90
Margolin, Janet, 15
Martin, Steve, 77
Marx, Groucho and brothers, 16, 18,
    21, 28–29, 107, 115, 120–121,
    129, 133, 156–157, 165, 179, 184
May, Elaine, 135
McGrath, Douglas, 103, 105, 107,
    110, 127, 183
McGregor, Ewan, 154–155, 161
McGuire, Tobey, 171
Melamed, Fred, 73
Messing, Debra, 127, 138
Metzman, Irving, 73
Meyers, Jonathan Rhys, 132, 149–
    150, 161
Midler, Bette, 109
Mitchell, Radha, 147
Mizrahi, Isaac, 73, 135
Morse, Susan E., 56, 116, 127
Mortimer, Emily, 149–150
Morton, Samantha, 129
Murphy, Rosemary, 73
Nelkin, Stacey, 44, 103
Norton, Edward, 116

Nykvist, Sven, 79, 126, 144
Orbach, Jerry, 84
Orth, Zak, 73
O'Sullivan, Maureen, 66, 74, 77, 95
Page, Ellen, 172–173
Palminteri, Chazz, 104
Pine, Larry, 73
Pinto, Freida, 167
Pollack, Sydney, 94, 97
Previn, Soon-Yi, 43, 66, 94, 102–103,
    109, 112, 125
Rampling, Charlotte, 44, 51, 132
Randall, Tony, 20–21
Rappaport, Michael, 135
Reiner, Rob, 98, 103
Reinhardt, Django, 128, 133
Reynolds, Burt, 21
Ricci, Christina, 141
Roberts, Julia, 115
Roberts, Tony, 23, 32, 34, 52, 72, 77,
    106–107
Rollins, Jack, 10–11, 25, 61
Rothman, John, 72
Rose, Mickey, 14, 16, 30, 34, 100
Rosenblum, Ralph, 30–33, 178
Ross, Herbert, 22, 142
Rowlands, Gena, 78–79
Shawn, Wallace, 73
Shepard, Sam, 74, 77, 177
Shumacher, Joel, 40
Simon, Danny, 9
Simon, Paul, 34
Sinatra, Frank, 60
Sirico, Tony, 73
Sorvino, Mira, 112–113
Stallone, Sylvester, 17, 110
Steenburgen, Mary, 54
Stiers, David Ogden, 73
Stone, Emma, 163
Stone, Sharon, 52, 110
Streep, Meryl, 46, 177
Stritch, Elaine, 74–75
Taylor, Juliet, 68, 112, 116, 151, 175

Theron, Charlize, 126, 137
Tilly, Jennifer, 105
Tomlin, Lily, 93
Tucci, Stanley, 171
Ullman, Tracey, 134–135
Walken, Christopher, 32–33, 74, 77,
    110
Warden, Jack, 73–74, 105
Waters, John, 129
Waterson, Sam, 73–75, 84
Watts, Naomi, 166
Wilder, Gene, 21
Wilkinson, Tom, 154
Weaver, Sigourney, 33
Wiest, Diane, 67, 69, 72–74, 105,
    130, 183
Willis, Gordon, 32–33, 39, 42, 50, 52,
    54, 56, 61, 68, 133, 142–145
Wilson, Owen, 168, 171
Young, Sean, 77
Zsigmond, Vilmos, 155

Movie Characters

Andrew and Ariel (*Midsummer Night's
    Sex Comedy*), 54–55
Antonio, Juan and Maria Elena,
    157–159
Ash, Linda, 112–113
Bates, Sandy, 50–52, 124, 132, 157,
    185
Baxter, Tom, 62–64, 98
Block, Harry, 104, 118–120, 124, 165,
    183
Dandridge, Bob and Steffi, 114–115
Davis, Isaac (Ike), 42–46, 98, 133,
    156, 183
Canova, Lou, 36, 61
Cecilia (*Purple Rose of Cairo*), 62–64,
    89, 98, 183–185
Chase, Amanda, 98, 140–141
Cheech (*Bullets Over Broadway*), 104–
    105, 107, 128

Cristina and Vicky (*Vicky Cristina Barcelona*), 158–159
Elliot and Hannah (*Hannah and Her Sisters*), 66–69, 77
Falk, Jerry, 37, 98, 140–141, 183
Felix, Allan, 22
Fletcher, Dr. Eudora Nesbitt, 57–59, 98
Gabe and Judy Roth, 94–96, 100
Grushenko, Boris, 28, 157
Hall, Annie, 30–34, 44, 77, 79, 98, 117, 141, 143
Hattie (*Sweet and Lowdown*), 129
Hollander, Walter, 106–107
Ian and Terry (*Cassandra's Dream*), 155
Jack and Sally (*Husbands and Wives*), 94, 96–97
Jasmine (*Blue Jasmine*), 181
Joe (*Alice*), 90–91
Joey (*Interiors*), 38, 40, 68
John (*To Rome with Love*), 172
Kleinman (*Shadows and Fog*), 92–93
Magee, Axel, 106–107
Mary (*Manhattan*), 42, 46, 98
Mellish, Fielding, 16, 35, 76
Monroe, Miles, 26, 76
Lee and Holly (*Hannah and Her Sisters*), 66–68, 77, 130
Lipton, Larry and Carol, 100
Pender, Gil, 117, 163, 168–170, 172
Post, Marion, 78–79
Pransky, Sondra, 152
Rain (*Husbands and Wives*), 95, 97
Ray and Frenchy (*Small Time Crooks*), 134–135
Ray, Emmet, 104, 128, 133
Reed, Halley, 83
Rice, Nola, 149–151
Rose, Danny, 60–61, 98, 134, 152
Rosenthal, Ben, 83–84
Rosenthal, Judah, 36, 84–85, 149, 154

Roy and Sally (*You Will Meet a Tall Dark Stranger*), 167
Sachs, Mickey, 18, 66, 68, 77, 98, 130, 156
Schlosser, Luna, 27, 76
Shayne, David, 102–105, 129, 165
Simon, Lee, 126–127, 183
Sinclair, Helen, 102, 105
Singer, Alvy, 30–36, 45, 76–77, 79, 98, 117, 130, 141, 143, 183
Starkwell, Virgil, 14
Stern, Cliff, 83, 85
Tate, Alice, 90
Vitale, Tina, 60–61, 98
Waterman, Sid, 152
Waxman, Val, 138–139
Weinrib, Lennie, 112–113
Wilton, Chris, 132, 148, 150, 154
Yelnikoff, Boris, 86, 164
Zelig, Leonard, 57–59, 98

Movies, TV Shows, and Plays
Alice, 90–91, 98, 143, 169, 172, 184
Annie Hall, 14, 26, 28, 30–34, 38–39, 41–43, 45, 51, 70, 79–81, 116–117, 123, 125, 130, 132, 135, 140, 142, 148, 156–157, 164, 177–178
as a romantic comedy, 98–100
deleted scenes from, 76
Jewish themes in, 35–36
romanticizing New York, 47
showcasing Allen's individual style, 143–144
Another Woman, 19, 78–81, 85, 92, 168, 174, 179–180
Antz, 109–110, 134
Anything Else, 37, 98, 124, 140–141, 171
Bananas, 14, 16–19, 29, 35, 47, 63, 76, 128, 130, 142
Blue Jasmine, 19, 39, 81, 163, 175–176, 180–181, 183

Broadway Danny Rose, 36–37, 53, 60–61, 65, 98, 130, 174
Bullets Over Broadway, 18, 102–106, 110, 127–129, 135, 143, 171
Casino Royale, 25, 108
Cassandra's Dream, 39, 81, 98, 130, 154–155, 160–162
Celebrity, 19, 53, 59, 98, 126–127, 135, 137, 150, 159, 171
Company Man, 110
Crimes and Misdemeanors, 36, 55, 77, 81, 83–85, 92, 97–98, 130, 132, 141, 146–150, 152, 154, 174
Curse of the Jade Scorpion, The, 53, 136–139, 153, 184
Deconstructing Harry, 19, 67, 104, 110, 117–120, 125–126, 145, 171, 185
Don't Drink the Water (play), 11, 23, 105–106
Don't Drink the Water (film, 1969), 25, 106, 171
Don't Drink the Water (film, 1994), 106–107, 171
Everyone Says I Love You, 78, 98, 114–117, 132, 148
Everything You Always Wanted to Know about Sex (*But Were Afraid to Ask*), 20–21, 76, 84, 142, 155, 163
Fading Gigolo, 110
Front, The, 108
Hannah and Her Sisters, 18, 39, 47, 55, 65–69, 77, 81, 92, 116, 130, 156, 163, 184
Hollywood Ending, 132, 138–139, 153, 181
Husbands and Wives, 19, 39, 59, 67, 94–95, 98, 100, 102, 107, 124–125, 127, 145, 177
Imposters, The, 110
Interiors, 19, 38–42, 54, 68, 80–81, 123–124, 156, 174
King Lear, 108

L.A. Story, 77, 111

Love and Death, 19, 28–29, 38, 61, 63, 92, 98–99, 130, 156–157

Magic in Moonlight, 163

Manhattan, 19, 26, 35, 41–46, 50, 53–54, 69, 81, 97–99, 101, 103, 108, 116–117, 120, 123, 125, 130, 133, 156, 177, 179

Manhattan Murder Mystery, 28, 100–101, 103, 107, 117–118, 126, 152, 161

Match Point, 81, 86, 88, 98, 124, 131, 148–152, 154, 157, 160–162

Melinda and Melinda, 81, 98, 146–147, 155, 167, 176

Midnight in Paris, 98, 117, 160, 162–163, 168–172, 179, 184

Midsummer Night's Sex Comedy, A, 54–56, 84, 99, 159, 184

Mighty Aphrodite, 112–113, 116, 131, 154

NBC Comedy Hour, The, 9

New York Stories: Oedipus Wrecks, 82, 99, 117, 165, 172, 184

Picking Up the Pieces, 110

Play It Again, Sam, 22–24, 27, 90, 123, 142, 172, 185

Purple Rose of Cairo, The 53, 62–64, 81, 88–89, 98–99, 117, 163, 169, 177, 183, 185

Radio Days, 19, 36, 39, 53, 55, 65, 70–71, 77, 84, 117, 123, 132–133, 157, 165, 174, 184

Scenes from a Mall, 109

Scoop, 19, 98, 151–154, 160–162, 173, 175, 184

September, 19, 74–75, 77, 81, 147, 177, 183

Shadows and Fog, 53, 92–93, 104, 117, 157, 182

Sleeper, 14, 18–19, 26–27, 41, 76, 81, 132, 142

Small Time Crooks, 98, 131, 134–137, 150, 153, 160, 173

Stardust Memories, 19, 44, 50–52, 55–57, 63, 77, 99, 116–117, 119, 123–124, 132, 173, 185

Sweet and Lowdown, 53, 59, 98, 104, 128–129, 132–133, 178

Sunshine Boys, The, 109

Take the Money and Run, 14–15, 29, 35, 56, 59, 106, 123, 128, 134, 164, 180

To Rome with Love, 160, 171–173, 180, 184

Vicky Cristina Barcelona, 81, 151, 157, 160–162, 164

Whatever Works, 86, 132, 157, 160, 164–165

What's New Pussycat?, 10–12, 24–25, 103, 106

What's Up, Tiger Lily?, 12–13, 103, 123, 130

When Harry Met Sally, 96, 98, 111

Wild Man Blues, 109, 129, 132

You Will Meet a Tall Dark Stranger, 145, 160–161, 166–167, 176

Zelig, 35, 54–59, 98, 99, 123, 132

Recurring Themes in Woody Allen Movies

actors and acting, 62, 70, 102, 112, 146, 148, 152

anti-authoritarianism, 16, 26, 30, 50

art vs. life, 50, 56, 62, 66, 70, 83, 94, 100, 102, 118

California hatred, 30, 138, 154, 164, 168

celebrity, 16, 50, 56, 60, 70, 126, 134, 172–173

class, 62, 102, 134, 148, 154, 180

God (or lack thereof), 28, 50, 83–84

Groucho idolatry, 14, 42, 50, 66, 112, 114, 164

hypochondria, 22–23, 66, 138, 164

infidelity, 28, 30, 38, 42, 54, 60, 62, 66, 70, 74, 78, 83, 90, 92, 94, 100, 102, 112, 114, 118, 126, 128, 136, 138, 140, 146, 148, 158, 164, 166, 168, 172, 180

Judaism, Jewish mothers, and the rabbi as a punchline, 12, 20, 30, 35–37, 50, 56–57, 66, 70, 83, 92–93, 106, 112, 118, 140

kamikaze women, 50, 82–83, 94, 126, 136, 140, 146, 148, 158, 172

magic and magic realism, 22–23, 50, 54, 60, 62, 74, 79, 82, 90, 92, 106, 136, 146, 148–149, 152, 163–164, 168, 172

murder, 74, 83, 100, 146, 148, 152, 154

obsession with death, 28, 30, 38, 42, 50, 54, 66, 86, 114, 118, 156–157

organized crime, 60, 70, 102, 114, 128

past vs. present, 30, 50, 78, 90, 134, 140, 168, 180

prostitution, 12, 62, 92, 94, 112, 118, 126, 128, 166, 172

psychoanalysis, 16, 38, 42, 56, 78, 140, 146, 166, 172

sexless relationships, 20, 28, 30, 140, 146, 148

younger women, 42–43, 94, 166, 180

Movie Studios and Companies

DreamWorks, 134, 141

Miramax Films, 105–106, 116

Orion Pictures, 16, 64, 93, 102

Sweetland Films, 102–103, 116, 148

United Artists, 16, 38, 45, 52, 128

Acknowledgments

Before we'd even put our last book to bed, I was eager to get another project going with Voyageur Press, and my editor, Josh Leventhal, waded through weeks of subpar pitches before seizing on this nutty idea of a book about forty-plus movies instead of just one. His tireless enthusiasm, marvelous ideas, firm editorial hand (Josh, I'll tell you what I told my last editor: sorry about all the semicolons), and love for the subject not only made this volume possible but infinitely better.

Every piece in this book was first read by Rebekah Dryden, who is not only a great editor but a wonderful wife, terrific mother, and all-around dreamboat. Sweetie, as Alvy told Annie, love is too weak a word, and I lurve you. As before, Mike Hull read the entire text before it went out of my hands, and provided invaluable new eyes and tremendous insight. My ever-supporting Flavorwire editor, Judy Berman, also gave some helpful suggestions on key essays, and I thank my *Annie Hall* viewing party pals (Jillian Steinhauer, Marni Chan, Amy Hughey, Mac Welch, Brenda Welch, and Liam Welch) for helping form a lot of the key ideas about that movie and the work in general.

Of course, many thanks to Ezra Glinter, David Detmer, Jason Gubbels, and Ashley Clark for their brilliant guest essays. Big thanks to Sarah Fonder for assists with transcription, the biggest drag in a project like this. And particular gratitude is due to Eric Lax, Richard Schickel, Stig Björkman, and Robert Weide, whose in-depth work on Woody provided so much guidance.

And most of all, thanks to Woody Allen, who keeps writing, keeps working, and keeps amazing. I'm sure he'll never read this book, and that's maybe for the best, since he'd probably disagree with just about everything in it.

About the author

Jason Bailey is the author of *Pulp Fiction: The Complete Story of Quentin Tarantino's Masterpiece*, also available from Voyageur Press. A graduate of the Cultural Reporting and Criticism program at New York University's Arthur L. Carter Journalism Institute, he is film editor for the pop culture blog Flavorwire, and his writing has appeared in *The Atlantic*, *Slate*, *Salon*, and *The Village Voice*. He lives with his wife, Rebekah, and his daughter, Lucy, in New York, where he sees too many movies and tweets too much (@jasondashbailey).